Presented to:

Butler Area Public Library

In Memory of
George Kelly, Sr.

Donor
Janice and Harold Larrick

Behind the Cyberspace Veil

Behind the Cyberspace Veil

THE HIDDEN EVOLUTION OF THE AIR FORCE OFFICER CORPS

Brian J. Collins

Praeger Security International
Westport, Connecticut • London

Library of Congress Cataloging-in-Publication Data

Collins, Brian J.
    Behind the cyberspace veil : the hidden evolution of the Air Force officer corps /
Brian J. Collins.
        p. cm.
    Includes bibliographical references and index.
    ISBN 978-0-313-34965-2 (alk. paper)
    1. United States. Air Force—Officers.   2. United States. Air Force—Personnel
management. 3. Air pilots, Military—United States.   4. Command and control
systems—United States—History.   I. Title.   II. Title: Hidden evolution of the
Air Force officer corps.
    UG793.C65   2008
    358.4'13320973—dc22   2007048778

British Library Cataloguing in Publication Data is available.

Library of Congress Catalog Card Number: 2007048778
ISBN-13: 978–0-313–34965–2

First published in 2008

Praeger Security International, 88 Post Road West, Westport, CT 06881
An imprint of Greenwood Publishing Group, Inc.
www.praeger.com

Printed in the United States of America

The paper used in this book complies with the
Permanent Paper Standard issued by the National
Information Standards Organization (Z39.48–1984).

10 9 8 7 6 5 4 3 2 1

The views expressed in this work are those of the author and do not necessarily
reflect the official policy or position of the United States Air Force, the National
Defense University, the National War College, the Department of Defense, or the
U.S. Government.

This book is dedicated to the men and women who serve, have served, or will serve in the United States Air Force.

Contents

Illustrations

Acknowledgments

I have discovered that a book is no small endeavor. Its success rests not on my persistence but on the assistance of countless people. Starting from the inner circle and moving out, I would like to thank my unofficial readers, Nancy, Erin, and Sean. I suspect that they may be the only people that have actually read each and every page of the earlier manuscripts. Erin deserves special credit as my research assistant, locating and reading all those general officer biographies and learning who almost crashed while taking his wife up for a spin, who hung out with the headhunter tribe while waiting to be rescued, who devoted himself to his tulip garden, who had a preference for gray suits and scotch, and a horde of other minutiae.

Moving out a bit, I would like to thank Dr. Andy Bennett and Dr. George Shambaugh of Georgetown University as well as Harvey Rishikof of the National War College for their mentorship through the wickets of my PhD program. Their guidance was important in my researching and creating the material that forms the core of this book.

I would also like to thank the librarians and staff at the National Defense University Library and the Georgetown University Library, and especially Yvonne Kinkaid at the Library of the U.S. Air Force Historical Studies Office.

There have been a lot of other people along the way, from grade school through the university level, that have tried to fix my writing. However, I will not embarrass them here for fear that they will realize that they ultimately failed in their endeavors.

The list of friends, colleagues, students, soldiers, sailors, marines, coasties, and airmen, from the United States and from other countries, who have stimulated my thinking and tried to help me understand things in a variety of ways over the years would be equally long and perhaps equally embarrassing.

Finally, I thank Margie for her help along the way. This book, and many more important things in my life, would not have come to fruition without her support.

Abbreviations

AAA	Antiaircraft Artillery
ABCCC	Airborne Battlefield Command and Control Center
ABM	Air Battle Manager
ACC	Air Combat Command
ACTS	Air Corps Tactical School
ADC	Air Defense Command, later Aerospace Defense Command
AF	Air Force
AFA	Air Force Academy
AFB	Air Force Base
AFR	Air Force Reserve
AFROTC	Air Force Reserve Officer Training Corps
AFSC	Air Force Specialty Code
AGM	Air-to-Ground Missile
AIM	Air Intercept Missile
ALCM	Air-Launched Cruise Missile
AMRAAM	Advanced Medium-Range Air-to-Air Missile
ANG	Air National Guard
ARM	Anti-(Radar) Radiation Missile
ASOC	Air Support Operations Center
ATACMS	Army Tactical Missile System

AWACS	Airborne Warning and Control System as in the E-3 AWACS aircraft
BPZ	Below-Primary (Promotion) Zone
CAOC	Combined Air Operations Center
C2	Command and Control
C4ISR	Command, Control, Communications, Computers, Intelligence, Surveillance, and Reconnaissance
CEP	Circle Error Probable. The radius of a circle in which 50% of the fired/dropped ordnance can be expected to fall.
CINCS	Commanders-in-Chief
CRC	Control and Reporting Center
CRP	Control and Reporting Post
DASC	Direct Air Support Center
DEW	Distant Early Warning
EWO	Electronic Warfare Officer/Operator
FAC	Forward Air Controller. In the Air Force, it typically refers to an officer, usually a pilot, who acts as a man on the scene coordinator between Army or Marine units on the ground and aircraft providing close air support for the ground troops. The FAC may be on the ground or airborne, and he specifically directs the supporting aircraft as they attack the targets the he assigns them. However, there are also enlisted positions that do some of the work under a ground FACs' supervision, and in Special Forces Units enlisted members perform FAC duties. Consequently, I often use "FAC" in the broader sense of all these positions that directly assign targets, mark targets with lasers, and control aircraft performing close air support. This would include soldiers, sailors, marines, and airmen serving as a *Joint Terminal Attack Controller* (JTAC).
FEAF	Far East Air Forces
FWS	Fighter Weapons School
GLCM	Ground-Launched Cruise Missile
GO	General Officer
GPS	Global Positioning System
HAF	Headquarters Air Force
HARM	High-speed Anti-(Radar) Radiation Missile
ICBM	Intercontinental Ballistic Missile
IFF	Identification Friend or Foe
INS	Inertial Navigation System
IPZ	In-Primary (Promotion) Zone

JDAM	Joint Direct Attack Munition. Family of INS or GPS guided munitions.
JFACC	Joint Force Air Component Commander
JOC	Joint Operations Center
JSTARS	Joint Surveillance Target Attack Radar System, as in the E-8 JSTARS aircraft
JTAC	Joint Terminal Attack Controller
MATS	Military Air Transport Service
MRBM	Medium-Range Ballistic Missile
NORAD	North American Air (Later Aerospace) Defense Command
OTS	Officer Training School
PACAF	Pacific Air Forces
PGM	Precision Guided Munition
PME	Professional Military Education
RAF	Royal Air Force
RIF	Reduction in Force
ROE	Rules of Engagement
ROTC	Reserve Officers Training Corps
RSO	Reserve Supplement Officer
SAC	Strategic Air Command
SAGE	Semi-Automatic Ground Environment System
SALT	Strategic Arms Limitation Treaty
SAM	Surface-to-Air Missile
SIOP	Single Integrated Operational Plan
SLBM	Submarine-launched Ballistic Missile
START	Strategic Arms Reduction Treaty
TAC	Tactical Air Command
TACC	Tactical Air Control Center
TADC	Tactical Air Direction Center
TLAM	Navy Tomahawk Land Attack Missile
TOA	Total Obligational Authority
UAV	Unmanned Aerial Vehicle
UCAV	Unmanned Combat Air Vehicle
UNT	Undergraduate Navigator Training
UPT	Undergraduate Pilot Training
USAF	United States Air Force

USAFA	United States Air Force Academy
USAFE	United States Air Forces in Europe
WSO	Weapons System Officer/Operator

Introduction

"And what do you do?"

"I'm an Air Force officer."

"Ah, so you're in the Air Force, are you? Are you a pilot?"

It seems a natural progression. The other variant is:

"And what do you do?"

"I'm an Air Force officer."

"Ah, so you're in the Air Force, are you? What do you fly?"

In either case, it seems clear that the expectation is that people in the Air Force should be pilots and fly airplanes.

"After all, it is the *Air Force*, isn't it? Yes, there are probably a few people who might be mechanics or something, but aren't there navigators and bombardiers and radiomen and such who also fly? Surely most officers in the Air Force must be some kind of aviator."

"Well, actually not. In fact, if you're talking about occupational groupings within the Air Force, there are more officers in the medical and C4ISR fields together than pilots and navigators in today's Air Force."

"C4 . . . What?"

"C4ISR. Command, control, communications, computers, intelligence, surveillance, and reconnaissance. You know. All the people and stuff that plan and control the missions so that you can see that missile cruise through the second window from the right on the front side of the building and go boom on TV."

"Oh yeah. So that's C4I . . . whatever?"

"You might also know it as *cyberspace*. The Air Force added that to its Mission Statement in 2005. We now fly and fight in the air, in space, and in cyberspace, at least kind of. We don't really fight in space, at least not yet, and cyberspace is complicated because it depends on what you mean by *cyberspace.*"

"Ah, excuse me; I think that I see someone I need to say 'hi' to."

A very plausible conversation. Society does have a general expectation that the Air Force is all about flying, and yes, if one of the services is involved in space, it is more likely to be the Air Force than the other ones. But this cyberspace thing?

The Air Force is in a paradigm shift. Whereas pilots used to constitute about half of the Air Force officer corps, pilots now account for only about one-fifth of the officer corps. When the Air Force became independent from the Army in 1947, pilots accounted for 90% of the Air Force general officers; today roughly 60% are pilots (see figure 1). These declines have been relatively steady over the independent Air Force's history, and they have been carried out under the leadership of almost exclusively pilot senior general officers. However, very few people in or out of the Air Force appear to be aware of the dramatic shifts occurring within the officer corps. The *cyberspace veil* is largely a veil of ignorance.

If you are not sure whether I have stumbled onto something interesting yet, it might be more provocative if I "flip" the statistics around. About 80% of the members of the contemporary Air Force officer corps are not pilots. If this is shocking, it is because the initial Air Force officer corps did an extraordinarily

Figure 1
Pilots as a Percentage of General Officers (GOs) versus Pilots as a Percentage of Total Officers

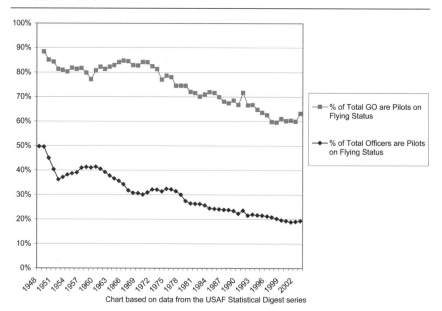

Chart based on data from the USAF Statistical Digest series

good job of selling its flying expertise in its quest for public recognition of its status as a unique profession. If not, read another page or two and see if you get hooked. From the perspective of being all about flying, maybe it is a good thing that 60% of the general officers are still pilots. Somebody in charge should know what is going on with all those airplanes. But then what should the Air Force do when C4ISR becomes more important—have more C4ISR generals?

After I stumbled on this story, it took a while to come up with the best way to tell it. For example, I could conceivably try to place the narrative within the framework of bureaucratic politics, organizational culture, or business models. From a bureaucratic politics perspective, the question is why a group (pilots) that was obviously the dominant group and possessed a near monopoly on political power within the organization lost its position.[1] From an organizational culture perspective, the question is what factors caused the disconnect between the organizational culture, which was so dominated by the pilot in mythos and in practice, and the actual declining percentage of pilots. Furthermore, what is the effect of the decreasing percentages of pilots on the organizational culture? From a business perspective, however, the basic question changes. If the percentage of total Air Force officers who are pilots has already dropped so precipitously because they are no longer needed in such numbers and because the Air Force is moving aggressively into new non-pilot markets, why are there still so many pilot general officers? This might also spin off into the tangential issue of what made the pilot general officers so accepting of new technologies that take the company into new markets that appear to run counter to their own experiences.

Although all these were interesting questions, especially from the business perspective, and they could serve as frameworks for worthwhile examinations of the Air Force officer corps, all of them seemed to me to be a bit off the mark. To my mind, perhaps because I am an insider, the distinguishing characteristic of the Air Force officer corps is that it identifies itself as a profession. Studies of the military based on bureaucratic politics perspectives meet with minimal acceptance by Air Force and military officers. The officer corps does not see itself or its members as bureaucrats engaged in daily struggles to gain a bit more political power or a few more resources here, while defending against Army or Navy encroachments there. Although some higher-level Air Force staff jobs certainly deal with Congress, the Department of Defense bureaucracy, and contentious issues of inter-service rivalry, the focus of Air Force officership is war—preparing for war, conducting war, and making life and death decisions under battle conditions. The Air Force officer corps is a profession, not a bureaucracy. It is a calling. Officers do not join the Air Force for personal gain or to amass political power, and their tenures in senior leadership positions are too short to enable them to wield any power that they might gain. Instead, many would say that the Air Force officer corps is part of the traditional profession of arms, whose members have taken on the obligation of defending the nation.

That being said, the Air Force officer corps considers itself to be a different and special breed within the military profession. Its culture is that of airmen and airpower, a culture beyond the capacities of mere ordinary earth-bound mortals to understand or to participate in. This dichotomy is not based in a sense of bureaucratic politics but in a conviction that the Air Force officer corps' visionary sense of its particular expertise is the best way to win wars and defend the nation. The Air Force officer corps has difficulty articulating this point of view because it is trapped to an extent in its conception of the military profession as a single, static, multi-service entity. This study dispenses with that formulation. Instead, it treats the Air Force officer corps as an independent profession. Since the officer corps is the military and professional leadership within the Air Force organization, the focus is on the Air Force officer corps and its internal evolution against the backdrop of the dynamic competition between professions.

This perspective shifts the focus away from the "Air Force," the big bureaucratic mixture of civilian, military, active duty, and reserve forces under the Secretary of the Air Force's purview, to the relatively small Air Force officer corps. Civilians and enlisted airmen are traditionally excluded, since the expertise in the art of war making and the responsibility for the effects of specific military actions are generally believed to reside in the officer level.[2] The officer corps is the keeper of the expertise and also the largely independent decider of who becomes an officer, who stays, and who is promoted within the officer ranks. Consequently, the officer corps as seen through the prism of profession is the focus of this book.

A profession develops new fields of expertise in order to maintain its relevancy in the face of the changing character and nature of warfare, and the officer corps' composition changes as its expertise changes. The primary motivations for these changes are the responsibilities inherent in the profession's contract with society. The general public perceives itself to have a stake in the officer corps' composition, and it is more than an abstract or passing interest.[3] Major adjustments in professional expertise require society's acceptance in the form of an award of jurisdiction over a specific competency to one or more professions.

The combination of responsibility and jurisdictional competition resulted in pilot general officers making choices that over time have led to an Air Force in which the locus of decision making is evolving out of the cockpit and into the C4ISR system. Pilots and flying, once the hallmarks of the Air Force, are still present but have become much less important. However, pilots remain overrepresented in the general officer ranks, largely because of the strategies that the officer corps employed in its struggle to establish itself as a new profession, independent of the Army and the other military services. In fact, the effects of these strategies have masked the dramatic changes in the Air Force officer corps' expertise, composition, and jurisdiction. On one track, the Air Force officer corps reassures society that the profession is continuing to meet its obligation to defend the nation in an effective and efficient manner. On another track, the officer corps is looking for society to grant it monopolistic jurisdiction over C4ISR and visionary forms of warfare.[4] C4ISR is important because it is the backbone of all Air Force operations today—nothing can be done without it—and visionary forms of warfare are important because they may replace manned flying operations tomorrow. Ergo, the recent addition of cyberspace to the Air Force Mission Statement.

On a broader scale, the concept of a profession offers an explanation for why an organization's leadership might implement a strategy that not only opposes a prominent strand of the organization's culture but over the long haul portends the demise of that core group. After all, pilot general officers have been shepherding the transformation of the Air Force officer corps away from piloting to C4ISR or cyberspace. These pilot general officers have long recognized the growing importance of C4ISR to the Air Force and have begun to increase the percentages of both general officers and Air Force officers at large with C4ISR experience. However, they have not led the transformation in a public way and have concurrently continued to champion the flying image of the Air Force officer corps. The *veil of cyberspace* is not so much about secrecy concerning technology as it is about secrecy concerning the transformation of the officer corps' composition and the officer corps' expertise.

As technology reduces the required workforce and shifts the locus of decision making authority to higher, more centralized levels, it becomes clear that the old way of doing business is fast coming to a close and that new career paths may be needed for the new decision makers. Piloting and traditional concepts of Air Force command may no longer be the best preparation for senior Air Force leaders. Whereas many appear to believe that publicly acknowledging this would shake the Air Force officer corps to its very core, this is a reflection of a concept of profession that is stagnant. If on the other hand, one takes professions as competing and changing entities, the Air Force officer corps' shift from piloting to cyberspace could be quite natural. In fact, this juncture provides a place to view and analyze competing archetypes within the profession, their roles in defining who makes up the profession and what work the profession does, as well as the impact of the demands of professional jurisdiction and professional social responsibility.

CHAPTER 1

Descriptive Model of the Contemporary Military Professions

It is important to have a working model of profession for the officer corps, because both society and the officer corps depend on it for the legitimacy of violence. Modern states monopolize organized violence and delegate this function to restricted groups. Since these groups perform a special, vital function and must remain obedient to the state, using bureaucratic politics or business models to explain or normalize their behavior runs the risk of indicating that bureaucratic or business grounds might be sufficient justification to alter this subordination to the state and/or society. The professional perspective, on the other hand, reinforces the contractual nature between the military and society.

I begin with the traditional works on concepts of profession within the military, Samuel Huntington's *The Soldier and the State* and Morris Janowitz's *The Professional Soldier,* to establish the foundation of military officership as a profession. A lot has changed in the course of the fifty years since Huntington and Janowitz published their books. The officer corps and the large standing army are not viewed as threats to American society, and in fact, the military is frequently listed as one of the most trustworthy institutions in the country. Although this is no doubt the product of the officer corps' and society's acceptance of Huntington's argument, his model remains trapped in time. It does not allow for adaptation of the officer corps as the world changes. In addition, Huntington's model does not account for service differences and inter-service rivalry, since it treats the services as a monolith. It also does not explain the

A version of chapter 1 was previously published in *Joint Forces Quarterly.* See Brian J. Collins, "The Officer Corps and Profession: Time for a New Model," *Joint Forces Quarterly* 45 (2nd Quarter, 2007): 104–110.

birth of the Air Force or why the Air Force added the concept of fighting in cyberspace to its Mission Statement in December 2005.

Consequently, I borrow from Andrew Abbott's *The System of Professions* to introduce the concept that professions are dynamic, competitive, and evolving in a world of changing jurisdictions. *Jurisdiction* is societal or governmental recognition that a particular profession has competence to perform a particular type of work. The resulting descriptive model of profession provides a new perspective for studying the evolution, or transformation, within the individual service officer corps, inter-service competition, and changing concepts of war and combatants.

EXPERTISE, CORPORATENESS, AND RESPONSIBILITY

Samuel Huntington's *The Soldier and the State* is the foundation for discussions on the issue of profession and the post–World War II U.S. military. Huntington's book was first published in 1957, ten years into the history of the independent U.S. Air Force. It would not be a stretch to say that all officers are familiar with Huntington's definition of a profession, involving expertise, responsibility, and corporateness, and that the military's expertise is the management of violence. The division of profession into three points appears almost tailor-made to match traditional military briefing techniques used in places like the service academies and in the various levels of professional military education. No American military officer would disagree with Huntington's statement that "the modern officer corps is a professional body, and the modern military officer is a professional man."[1] The officer corps has long considered itself a profession, but Huntington's *The Soldier and the State* provided a logical argument to buttress the claim, academic recognition of the claim, and a basis for the indoctrination of successive generations of military officers.

Huntington's definition of expertise requires professional knowledge "in a significant field of human endeavor." In addition, that knowledge is "intellectual in nature."[2] Huntington further discusses the importance of the connection between the academic and practical aspects of a profession and the use of tools such as professional journals and conferences and the rotation of professionals between practical and teaching experiences, to entwine and ground the professional in both aspects as well as the past, present, and future of the profession. Education and experience are the foundations of a profession's expertise. Huntington further divides education into two levels. The first is a broad, liberal arts–style education that provides the requisite foundation upon which the second, the specifically profession-oriented education, is built. The second level not only imparts the specific knowledge necessary to do the profession's work but also knowledge of the history of the profession and its place and function in society.

These requirements, however, are somewhat problematic for the Air Force officer corps, since it is not quite clear exactly where piloting aircraft and other Air Force specialties fall in Huntington's definition. For example, flying may not be a significant field of human endeavor. We do not credit driving a bicycle, car, or boat with this status in contemporary society, although there were times when each of these was seen as a somewhat exotic skill. Flying an airplane also does not seem to require a liberal arts education or an understanding of the occupation's roots. In fact, the Aviation Cadet Program, whose graduates provided the Air Service, Air Corps, and Air Force with pilot officers for roughly forty years, was based on the idea that a college degree was not a prerequisite for becoming a pilot or an officer.

When Huntington published *The Soldier and the State* in 1957, over half of the Air Force's officers did not have a bachelor's degree. With general officers serving for up to 35 years, there were still general officers serving in the 1990s who had initially joined the Air Force without a bachelor's degree. In addition, there has been a clear preference historically for degrees in math, engineering, and sciences, not liberal arts. Consequently, the Air Force officer corps seems to stand in opposition to some of Huntington's basics on profession. However, since Huntington was trying to get his arms around officers in all services, he skirted the issue of where specific career fields fit into the scope of profession through the use of abstraction. He declared that the military officer's expertise was best summed up by Harold Lasswell's phrase: "The management of violence."[3] From this perspective, the expertise that the Air Force officer corps proffers is not the technical skill of flying or piloting but the more embracing concept of airpower.

Responsibility means that the professional, by employing his or her expertise, is performing an essential role in both the basic existence and the general functioning of society. Furthermore, Huntington implies that there is a social contract of sorts involved here. Society has granted the profession the right to monopolize its area of expertise, and in return, the professional will perform the monopolized function when needed by society. Consequently, this obligation overrides the professional's interest in payment for his or her services as the primary motivation. This, of course, is not to imply that the professional does not expect to be compensated for the provision of his or her service. The profession, as such, must then regulate the behavior of its members between themselves and with society at large, so that society feels that the profession meets its obligations and thereby can continue its monopoly concession.[4] This then ties into corporateness, since the profession must be organized to establish and enforce standards as demanded by the obligations of social responsibility. The profession must also regulate membership and set standards of competency and experience.

Huntington admits that no profession matches the ideal, and that the military falls shorter of the ideal than the more traditional professions of law and medicine. Nevertheless, he includes officership in the professions, partly because "officership is strongest and most effective when it most closely approaches the professional ideal."[5] In other words, it is best for the military to be striving toward the professional ideal than for the officer corps to be denied professional status by society and academia and to be cast adrift to search on its own for some sort of unifying sense of purpose. That would have been dangerous, even in a democratic society, as America was coming to terms with the concept of maintaining a large standing army in peacetime.

Huntington's three points provide a good structural basis for the descriptive model of officership as a profession. *Expertise* is the profession's peculiar knowledge and skill. It is what the profession knows, teaches, and thinks that it can do. *Responsibility* captures both a sense of higher calling in the rather nebulous ideal of defending the nation by forfeiting one's life if necessary and an agreement of sorts to actually provide that service if called upon. It is why the profession does what it does. *Corporateness* concerns who makes up the profession and how the members and the profession as a whole are regulated. Finally, although Huntington treats each point in isolation and in the seemingly static early Cold War situation, there must be significant interplay between the three concepts. Modifying one surely affects the others.

For example, society might say that it wants the military not just to manage violence abroad but also to be a disaster relief profession. This would entail a renegotiation of the existing contract of social responsibility, a broadening of military expertise, and potentially a modification of the military's personnel and procedures to accommodate the new area of expertise. Consequently, Figure 1.1 transforms the simple, static, three-bullet Huntington briefing slide into a more complex picture. Expertise, corporateness, and responsibility are all parts of the same thing—the profession—and the demands of each interact with the others within the profession. The arrows symbolize this interaction. We now take this adaptation of Huntington forward to see what insights a study of Janowitz might add.

TENSION: VISIONARY VERSUS HEROIC WARRIORS

In *The Professional Soldier: A Social and Political Portrait*, Morris Janowitz analyzes social and political changes in the U.S. Army's and the Department of the Navy's highest-ranking career officers over roughly the first half of the twentieth century. He also includes Air Force officers as a group of interest, but a large part of the Air Force's history is still entwined with the Army during the period of his study. Janowitz uses the concept of profession as a tool to analyze changes in the U.S. military officer corps. He does not provide a three-bullet definition of profession, and in fact treats it more as a way to simply categorize officers as a specific group of interest. Janowitz focuses on the changing social makeup of the officer corps, specifically its evolution from a homogenous, somewhat aloof, and pseudoaristocratic social group to a diverse group that is more representative of American society. In fact, the Air Force leads the other services in terms of the transition to this new officer corps.

Janowitz is primarily concerned about what he sees as clear implications for civil-military relations in this evolution, and he makes several points that

Figure 1.1
Huntington as the Basis of the Descriptive Model

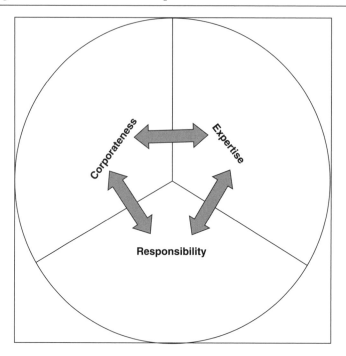

are relevant to the model. First, Janowitz presents two officer archetypes, the heroic old school and the civilianized military manager, which exemplify the divide that he sees growing in the officer corps. In addition, he works through several supporting hypotheses with examples that often illustrate large differences between the individual services' officer corps. In the end, it is clear that Janowitz's overarching premise is that the change in the social and political makeup of military officers is changing the nature of the profession. The profession is not static but in flux.

Janowitz tangentially touches on officership as a profession, with a variety of examples, without getting bogged down in specific definitions. In Huntington's terms, Janowitz is interested primarily in corporateness and responsibility. Janowitz does not completely neglect to mention expertise, though. For example, he labels honor, public service, and career commitment as "the traditional dogmas of the military profession," then he distills the essence of the professional soldier to a person who *always fights*.[6] A professional officer does not turn down combat assignments or opportunities for combat.

This is a rather limited description, since it does not avail itself of traditional concepts associated with the military expertise, like leadership or management of men or a specific expertise that requires special study and training. In addition, only an officer in a position to experience combat could conceivably turn down combat assignments. Consequently, Janowitz implies that only a select portion of the officer corps, those in combat arms, are the core of the profession. In fact, he specifically deals with this issue in one of his supporting hypotheses. In the Air Force case, this core of the profession would only be a small portion of the Air Force officer corps, principally the pilots of fighter, attack, and bomber aircraft.

The essence of Janowitz's argument is manifest in his characterization of officers as being one of three (actually two) types: (1) the heroic leader, who embodies "traditionalism and glory"; (2) the military manager, who is "concerned with the scientific and rational conduct of war"; and (3) the military technologist, or technical specialist.[7] However, Janowitz also wrote that "The military technologist is not a scientist, or for that matter an engineer; basically he is a military manager, with a fund of technical knowledge and a quality for dramatizing the need for technological progress."[8] This means that Janowitz actually has only two archetypes—the heroic leader and the military manager.

Furthermore, Janowitz admits that many officers are actually composites, exhibiting characteristics of each archetype at times. To Janowitz, "the heroic leader is a perpetuation of the warrior type, the mounted officer who embodies the martial spirit and the theme of personal valor."[9] The heroic leader is the military professional who always fights. On the other side, "the military manager reflects the scientific and pragmatic dimensions of war-making; he is the professional with effective links to civilian society."[10] The military manager is looking for efficiencies in war and is open to technology, but the heroic leader does not embrace technology and prefers traditions and cavalry charges. These officer types also embody the overall point of Janowitz's book: that is, the post–World War II U.S. military officer corps is caught in a struggle between two conceptions: (1) the military as the traditional profession; and (2) a civilianization of the officer corps. Janowitz sees the struggle manifested in changes in leadership styles (authoritarian versus manager), officer corps composition (small and "aristocratic" versus large and diverse), officer skills (combat versus technical and administrative), officer corps tolerance for innovation (limited versus embracing), and thinking skills (limited versus critical).

Janowitz admits that his distinction between civilianized managers and heroic leaders is harder to make in the Air Force case than in the other services, since the new technology of the airplane can arguably be placed in both categories. On the one hand, at least in the first half of the twentieth century, only a heroic type would dare take wing in a flimsy flying machine, facing death by accident as much as by enemy action. On the other hand, embracing the airplane as a technological innovation that brings new efficiencies to industrial-age warfare is clearly managerial by Janowitz's description. Janowitz casts his lot and lumps the flying of airplanes under heroic leadership. He then asserts that the Air Force has the highest concentrations of heroic leaders in the general officer ranks. Furthermore, without explanation, he states that this heroic style is most apparent in bombers, which also have the highest prestige in the Air Force at the time. Janowitz associates Air Force military managers more with tactical air forces and air transport, both of which are heavily involved in joint operations.[11]

Janowitz's main emphasis in 1960 was that the military manager was in the ascendancy, and the heroic leader was fast disappearing. The Air Force bomber pilot was a last bastion of the heroic leader, but he, too, was no doubt destined to transition to civilian-style management techniques. My model borrows Janowitz's idea of the competition between the two types, but modifies them slightly. Today, the case can be made that the archetypical heroic leader lives on in the form of the combat pilot. For example, the combat pilot still counts coups, although in an updated sort of way.[12] Modern Air Force general officer biographies, whether destined for internal Air Force consumption or presented when the general is a candidate for a board position in an insurance company, invariably contain a sentence along these lines: "General X is a command fighter pilot with more than 3,100 flight hours," or "He flew more than 100 combat missions in Southeast Asia." Such statements clearly say, "I've risked my life YY times in combat," or "I've spent 3,100 hours of my life defying death while piloting aircraft." They are counting coups, and exemplify the old warrior traditions—a professional officer always fights.

However, the Air Force heroic warrior archetype is not particularly authoritarian, aristocratic, or against technology. He is, however, tradition bound in the sense that he would stand by the axiom, "The job of the Air Force is to fly and fight, and don't you forget it!" He has a sense of responsibility to the nation, but this ethos is flavored by his perceptions of the Air Force officer corps' expertise and sense of corporateness. To him, the Air Force officer's expertise is the delivery of weapons from manned aircraft. This formulation already shows a separation from the Air Force's initial basis of independence, strategic bombing, and an acceptance of technological innovation on the part of the heroic warrior. In addition, he naturally sees the composition of the Air Force officer corps as paralleling the expertise. He expects pilots to predominate in both quantity and quality in terms of manning senior, key, and combat-critical positions.

Janowitz contrasted the heroic warrior with the military manager. However, the present study uses the terms *visionary* and *warrior* instead of *manager* for a variety of reasons. First of all, within the military profession, *manager* has negative connotations. Whereas officers *lead* people, a storekeeper *manages* his inventory, the organizational man *manages* various undifferentiated projects, and a bureaucrat *manages* a robotic bureaucracy. Second, because the Air Force simultaneously uses two different but overlapping systems for organization and leadership/management, the terms *leader*, *manager*, *command*, and *command and control* can quickly become hopelessly confused. Finally, in the Air Force, *vision*, as evidenced by both pilots and other officers, is the counter to the heroic traditionalist, although both were critical to the Air Force's independence.

By the time the Air Force became independent in 1947, its primary justification—independent, massed, and heroic strategic bombing raids—was already a piece of history, or at best a practice whose days were plainly numbered in the face of atomic bombs, long-range ballistic missiles, radar, and other technologies and innovations. As Janowitz noted:

Despite the ascendance of air power, the typical Air Force colonel or general had the least consistent self-image. Air Force traditions are not powerful enough to offset the realization that, in the not too distant future, heroic fighters and military managers will be outnumbered by military engineers. Air Force officers were fully aware, but reluctant to admit, that more of a "leadership" role would reside in the Army and in the Navy.[13]

Janowitz's prophecy has not come true. Military engineers do not exist as a separate archetype in the Air Force. They are subsumed within the prevailing heroic warrior and visionary warrior archetypes. The focus of the officer corps remains war, not airplanes and technology, and the contentious issues are how that war should be conducted and by what types of people. Consequently, the Air Force officer corps was not shunted off into a technical track that could only support military courses of action determined by more broadly minded Army and naval officers.

It is important to note that the archetypes are just that. They are representations of particular characteristics and points of view, used as tools to clarify different positions in the analysis of the changing nature of the Air Force officer corps.[14] Pilots are probably more likely to take on the mantle of the heroic warrior archetype, but this is not meant to be exclusive of other career fields, nor is it meant to be all-inclusive of every pilot. Pilots, as well as officers in other career fields, also fall under the visionary warrior rubric. In reality, many officers probably exhibit characteristics of both archetypes in different situations or under different conditions. For this study, however, the heroic and visionary archetypes struggle to define just who is in the Air Force officership profession (corporateness) and what work (expertise) exactly encompasses the profession's self-concept; this forms the basis of claims for jurisdictional competence.

Consequently, the descriptive model now looks like figure 1.2. The newly added outer ring depicts the archetypes of *heroic warrior* and *visionary warrior*, broken out into each of Huntington's pillars. The arrows in the outer ring indicate the tension between the heroic warrior and visionary warrior archetypes in the areas of expertise and corporateness. Expertise tends to be dominated by the visionary archetype, as illustrated by the long-standing involvement with a variety of missile types, the growing influence of command and control systems in the profession, the recent introduction of unmanned combat aircraft, and the addition of cyberspace to the mission statement. Technology has a large impact on expertise. The concept of corporateness is most heavily dominated by the heroic archetype, since things from uniforms

Figure 1.2
Janowitz-Type Modifications Added to the Descriptive Model

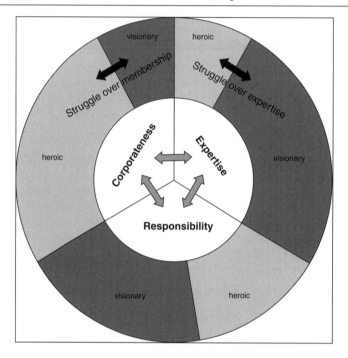

and pilot wings to education, promotions, and discussions as to whether non-pilots are really members of the profession or are fit to command fall in this bailiwick. Responsibility is depicted as being equal between the archetypes, since both feel the obligation in similar terms; there is no struggle over the pillar of responsibility.

COMPETITION BETWEEN PROFESSIONS

Andrew Abbott, in *The System of Professions*, changes the focus of the study of professions from the analysis of organizational structures of existing professions to an analysis of the work that the professions actually do. This shift in focus leads to different perspectives on how professions are created, exist, evolve, and sometimes decline. Through the examination of professions' work, it quickly becomes evident that many professions are actually doing very similar work. In fact, they are often competing with each other in a particular line of work. In Abbott's terms, they are competing for jurisdiction.

Abbott's classic example is the case of the treatment of mental illness. At various times, jailers, ministers, medical doctors, psychiatrists, psychologists, sociologists, case workers, and others have sought or been given jurisdiction over the mentally ill. If one uses the more standard structural approaches, along the lines of Huntington for example, to studying professions, then some of the occupational groups immediately drop out because they are not considered *professional*. Jailers, in particular, lack an expertise in dealing with the mentally ill, they are not particularly well educated, they do not have a particular sense of corporateness, and society does not view them as carrying a particular burden of social responsibility. Finally, and in many ways the most important factor in studying professions in general, there is the fact that society does not think of jailers as professionals. Society does not accord them professional status. Psychologists possess in-depth, specialized training for dealing with mental illness, they do have a sense of corporateness, and they are accorded responsibility along the lines of a medical doctor. Therein lies the problem, though, since they are not medical doctors. They are not psychiatrists, who as medical doctors are seen as members of a traditional profession. They are somewhere between jailers and psychiatrists, though obviously closer to psychiatrists. They could be considered psychiatrists' helpers, but psychologists argue that they are the equals of psychiatrists. Psychologists have different training, different knowledge, and different skills, but they claim an expertise that overlaps with psychiatry.

Definitions and prisms become important because they help form jurisdictional boxes. It is fairly easy to recognize a person's behavior as being somehow different. But once people move on to the next step and try to categorize the difference, they become trapped in words. Diagnoses and treatments tend to be paired in people's minds, and this forms part of the basis of a profession's claim to jurisdiction over particular cases. People with the devil in them are best treated by men of god. People who are just plain crazy are bound for permanent stays in jail or the asylum. People lacking a bit of self-discipline will get straightened out by a hitch in the Army. Artists, being creative, are supposed to be a bit different, and people with a mental illness are best treated by medical professionals, and so forth.

Society does not come up with the labels, then create professions to handle them. As knowledge, technology, and culture change, professions develop to fill emerging voids or established professions move to cover the emerging voids. Voids may also develop when a profession moves to cover a new jurisdiction and either leaves its old jurisdiction or is no longer in a position to control it.[15] Professions may also create the perception that there is a void. There is obviously a strong similarity to business marketing concepts here. In any case, professions play a role in the labeling process, which in turn affects which profession gets to handle the problem. This is a key part of Abbott's concept of jurisdiction:

But to perform skilled acts and justify them cognitively is not yet to hold jurisdiction. In claiming jurisdiction, a profession asks society to recognize its cognitive structure through exclusive rights; jurisdiction has not only a culture, but also a social structure. These claimed rights may include absolute monopoly of practices and of public payments, rights of self-discipline and of unconstrained employment, control of professional training, of recruitment, and of licensing, to mention only a few. . . . The claims also depend on the profession's own desires; not all professions aim for domination of practice in all their jurisdictions.[16]

This simple example indicates that the competition can become quite complex, because definitions of the work itself, the jurisdiction, and who or what actually forms the profession itself are in flux. In addition, professions may arrive at compromises and share jurisdiction, as between psychiatrists and psychologists.

Although Abbott does not delve at any length into the military as a profession, his work provides a catalyst for further exploration of the military profession. Although he sometimes treats the military in toto as a profession, he does imply at points that each service is an individual profession.[17] Abbott opens the possibility of acknowledging that the equipment, training, and doctrine differ greatly from service to service, which results in different perspectives on war and how to wage it. Each service has its own sense of corporateness with its own uniforms, traditions, promotions, education system, bases, and so on.[18] Although there is a joint Department of Defense umbrella over all the services, it does make sense to use Abbott's work on competition between professions to explore differences between the services. After all, they are in competition for funding, recruits, status, and perspectives on how best to defend the nation. The services have specific competencies or missions, which are essentially jurisdictions that they try to monopolize. Consequently, the model treats the Air Force officer corps as a profession in its own right.

Abbott uses "the very loose definition that professions are exclusive occupational groups applying somewhat abstract knowledge to particular cases."[19] The term *abstract knowledge* mirrors Huntington's concept of professional knowledge. The skill required of a professional is more than a simple physical ability or a routinized process. It involves thinking and applying professional knowledge to new situations. A surgeon requires some hand-eye coordination, but what makes medicine a profession is the ability to use medical knowledge and skills in reaching a diagnosis and treating the patient, and modifying the diagnosis or treatment if needed. As the use of computer-assisted lasers and robotics increases, the doctor's knowledge and skill are still recognized as what merits professional status. Therefore, in Huntington's terms, Abbott includes corporateness and expertise in his definition, but he completely excludes ideas of social responsibility. He ignores responsibility because as he makes the work his emphasis, occupations such as those of the auto mechanic and the medical doctor turn out to be quite similar at a certain level of abstraction in terms of diagnosing, inferring, and treating a problem.

Most people would reject the comparison's implication that mechanics are members of a profession with the same status as medical doctors. They would quickly run through a structure similar to Huntington's and point out that mechanics lack a broad-based education, have a minimal sense of corporateness, and bear no social responsibility. The counters are that a doctor's broad-based education does not contribute to most diagnoses, and that medical corporateness has been used to create the illusion of social responsibility in the doctor's case. The doctor has professional status partly because traditional professions are associated with higher socio-economic levels in society. As Abbott and many others who study professions point out, there is a darker version of profession. That is, it can be argued that (1) professions actually define social needs that match their services; (2) the leadership of a professional organization can dominate the membership instead of relying on a collegial organizational style; and (3) professions essentially create economic monopolies over specific services that tend to be beyond state or market controls.[20]

On the other hand, part of the perception of what makes an occupation a profession rests on the ability of the profession to abstract its knowledge systems to levels beyond routine cases or skills tied to specific tasks, technologies, or organizational structures. The ability to abstract tasks and knowledge to such levels and to apply it to new situations or define old problems in new ways may well have some basis in a person's education, training, or experience. As Abbott writes, abstraction enables a profession to survive and compete.[21] Society will not grant professional status to an occupation that does not involve some use of abstract and esoteric knowledge and thinking. If the task is so simple that anyone can do it, it is not the task of a profession. To Abbott, a profession requires the skills of diagnosis, inference, and treatment in its work. *Diagnosis* and *treatment* basically concern the input and output of information, but *inference* is the skill that makes an occupational group a profession. Inference "relates professional knowledge, client characteristics and chance in ways that are often obscure."[22] In addition, non-abstract knowledge runs the risk of becoming useless in the face of new technology or restructuring. Such is the case with the Air Force and airplanes. Flying airplanes is not a particularly abstract task in and of itself, and missiles and unmanned aircraft reduce the importance of pilots. Abstraction is also critical because it is the basis for finding, creating, or taking over jurisdiction.

Abbott also points out that the concept of professions can become twisted in the workplace. If a professional is incompetent, or there is too much professional work in an organization, the organizational imperative may require a non-professional to pick up the slack. *Workplace assimilation* occurs when nonprofessionals pick up an abridged version of the profession's knowledge system through on-the-job experience or training. The military offers numerous examples of workplace assimilation, especially with the overlap of senior non-commissioned officers and junior officers. In fact, the case can be made that non-commissioned officers are part of the profession.[23]

Finally, Abbott points out that professions often set high barriers to entry, requiring extensive education and exams, for example. This tends to keep the profession small in terms of numbers of members, but higher in terms of quality standards. In addition, it keeps the profession monopolistic. However, such professions run into problems if demand for the professional work rises and cannot be met. If a profession cannot meet the demand, it may lose its jurisdiction. In such a profession, however, the only ways to increase output are to lower the entry standards or let subordinate professions grow to take up the slack. However, Abbott cautions that this has only been successful in the medical arena. In most other cases, the profession does not adapt or cannot quickly modify its requirements, so other professions or formerly subordinate professions jump into the void and win jurisdiction.[24]

The Army Air Corps' heavy reliance on the Aviation Cadet Program is arguably a successful case of lowering entry standards to increase output, and the Air Force's eventual independence from the Army could be portrayed as a case of a subordinate profession growing to take up the slack. In addition, the historically increasing percentages of non-pilot Air Force officers and general officers can be portrayed as the changing of Air Force officer corps' entry standards in order to meet increased demand for its professional work.

As a final note, it is important to emphasize that jurisdiction is not the same as expertise. Expertise is the knowledge base and skills that the profession considers the basis for what work it can perform. Jurisdiction is the realm that society, as in the public at large or the government through regulation, accords a profession. A profession can have a monopoly jurisdiction or share its jurisdiction by any number of means. For example, the Air Force officer corps considers itself to have an expertise in the conduct of war from manned aircraft. However, it does not have exclusive jurisdiction in this field, since the officer corps of the Navy, Marine Corps, and Army each possess the same expertise to varying degrees. Each has some jurisdiction in this line of work, both in the public's mind and in a series of inter-service agreements. In the case of the various military officer corps, expertise tends to be what the members of the profession think they can or could do, whereas jurisdiction tends to be what they are allowed to do.

In the end, Abbott's concept unveils jurisdictional struggles between professions and is a very useful addition to the model. The completed descriptive model is shown in figure 1.3. The large arrow indicates the struggle between the Air Force officer corps and outside groups for jurisdiction in areas where the officer corps believes it has or wants to have expertise or jurisdiction. In areas where the officer corps believes it has expertise but no jurisdiction, it is seeking jurisdiction or attempting to create public awareness that a new jurisdiction has been created that the Air Force officer corps should fill. If the officer corps already has jurisdiction in an area, it must defend that claim against competitors. For the sake of simplicity, the diagram does not show the outside groups, but they would be represented as other spheres in a three-dimensional space. Like soap bubbles, as the professions compete, the personnel and missions at the peripheries may become entwined, and the dominant profession may totally absorb the other profession. Conversely, as was the case with the Air Force officer corps, a bubble might develop within an existing profession's bubble, and then pop off, forming its own bubble. It is also possible for the bubbles to remain intact and share a jurisdiction, or

Figure 1.3
Completed Descriptive Model, Incorporating Abbott

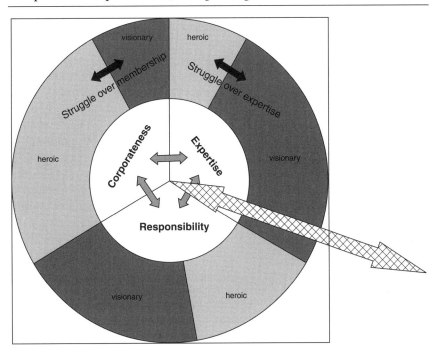

for a new profession's bubble to seemingly pop out of nowhere, that is, to come from a non-profession, with the personnel and expertise to fill a new jurisdiction.

THE MODEL AND THE AIR FORCE

This model of profession explains the breadth of the Air Force as well as the transformation of the Air Force officer corps, its expertise, and potentially its jurisdiction. As new technologies emerged and world events unfolded, the Air Force's missions and the officer corps' expertise began to change. The concept of airpower began to change from an airplane-centric view as it absorbed tertiary supporting areas. New technologies for aircraft and weapons meant that fewer aircraft were needed to accomplish more tasks. Aircraft and weapons technology also began to shift the locus of decision making out of the cockpit. As quality began to substitute for quantity, it became more important to have centralized control over the smaller numbers of aircraft. In addition, targeting and planning required more intelligence support. Furthermore, the growth of command and control systems led to the need to counter enemy command and control.

Things like the use of space for communications, navigation, and reconnaissance, as well as electronic warfare, information, and cyber warfare, which were initially developed to manage, lead, assist, or protect aircraft performing airpower missions, began to eclipse aircraft in importance. The term *airpower* was being contorted in all sorts of ways, and no longer fit. The Air Force officer corps is still very much about flying and airpower, but that is no longer its primary focus. Over time, it has developed command, control, communications, computers, intelligence, and surveillance and reconnaissance (C4ISR) in order to support and to manage the organization's application of violence, while simultaneously opening the door to further visionary forms of warfare such as cyber and information warfare as well as effects-based operations. C4ISR and visionary forms of warfare were born out of airpower, but they break out of the currently medium-defined box of jurisdictions. C4ISR and visionary forms of warfare go beyond airpower and incorporate space, the electronic ether, counter-command and control, and cyber and information warfare.

CHAPTER 2

Historical Perspective: The Emerging Air Force Jurisdiction for Command and Control

The early proponents of airpower were quick to call for its independence, but they meant independence from direct subordination to ground units and the piecemeal doling out of aircraft to various ground unit commanders. The independent air force was not about each pilot or squadron doing its own thing. In fact, it was quite the contrary. The driving idea behind the independent air force movement was the promise that centralized control over aircraft would be able to quickly mass air forces at critical points and times in battle, as was done, for example, to support ground forces in the attacks on the German St. Mihiel salient in the waning days of World War I. Whether in the pursuit of strategic bombing objectives, air superiority, tactical support to ground forces, or defense of one's own airspace, centralized control over all air assets would permit the commander to mass aerial firepower and selectively apply it where desired or needed. The initiative would always rest with the commander, who centrally controlled all of his side's air assets.

Consequently, a major fundament of an independent air force was its ability to centralize command over its assets at meaningful levels. However, this concept was not based on the idea that all the independent air force's assets in a theater would be parked at one airfield, presenting a massive target for enemy forces. Instead, the concept called for aircraft to be parked at a variety of airfields but still to be centrally commanded. If large numbers of friendly aircraft were attacking in the center, but enemy bombers attacked in the south, fighters from the north had to be able to come and assist in the south. The concept was straightforward and it was dependent on communications technology for its implementation. More important, it also required a different way of thinking about command than the standard military hierarchical pyramid. In practice it was dramatically different from an army's and perhaps even a navy's task force experience. For example, General Creighton Abrams, Army Chief of Staff in the mid-1970s and a former COMUSMACV (Commander U.S. Military Advisory Command Vietnam) described the U.S. Air Force's command and control system in Vietnam in awed tones:

I'm talking about sheer power in terms of tonnage, bombs on target, and that sort of thing, and rockets, because high performance fixed-wing aircraft carry a much greater payload. And you can focus that very quickly. . . . I don't mean from the first brigade to the second brigade. I'm talking about going anywhere, instead of putting it in MR-4, you go to MR-1 [U.S. military designations used for geographic areas in Vietnam. The distance between MR-4 and MR-1 is roughly 150 to 225 miles]. You switch the whole faucet, and you do it in about 45 minutes. *The whole control system and base system that supports that, there is nothing in the Army like it. There is nothing anywhere in the world like it.*[1]

This chapter looks at how the Air Force's unrivaled command and control system came to be. It includes a historical review of the evolution of this system, beginning with a high-level view of command and control in World War II and Korea, providing a more detailed look at the Cold War SAGE/F-106 strategic air defense environment, and concluding with the command and control of tactical fighter operations. This review highlights the impact of technology as well as the differences between the heroic and visionary warrior archetypes. In addition, it also reveals some differences in command between the Air Force officer corps and those of the other services. Finally, as with the development of weapons technology, the ever-increasing intrusion of the command and control system into flying operations, at a minimum, raises the issue of whether flying skills can over the long run continue to dominate discussions of command, leadership, and expertise.

OVERVIEW OF C4ISR EVOLUTION, WORLD WAR I THROUGH KOREA

As aircraft as well as command and control system technologies evolved, conceptions of command and control became specialized, matching the missions performed. Strategic bombing, for example, was designed to fly deep into the enemy's heartland, far beyond practical communication or radar range.[2] Planning and procedures became critical means of control. Strategic air defense, on the other hand, could be flown entirely under radio and radar coverage, allowing the deepest penetration of ground-based decision making and control over aerial operations. Tactical missions fell in the middle. Missions might be flown under friendly radar and radio coverage, and close air support missions required close coordination with the ground units being supported. In any event, tactical aircraft required some degree of control and coordination, if for nothing else than to prevent friendly ground forces from firing at friendly fighters flying air defense over the top of them or at friendly aircraft returning from missions.

In World War I, the chain of command over pilots and aircraft was essentially the same for both administrative and operational duties. Command and control over the aircraft was accomplished via the overall plan as translated into air tasking orders provided to the flying units, established procedures, and any other details passed to the pilots before they took off. Without radios, the airplanes were on their own once they took off. Pilots were limited to hand and aircraft signals, and air commanders on the ground at all levels were isolated in an information void until the aircraft returned. Pilots would report their results after landing, and if they had to land at another base, they might be able to update their status from there. The plan and the tasking orders were the concerns of air headquarters, but the missions themselves were left to the pilots. This was "centralized control, but decentralized execution."[3]

Plans and procedures provide a degree of control over subordinates, but a real-time communications system provided a big boost in the control of air forces. By World War II, radio signals were being used for navigational aids and communications. Radios were standard equipment in airplanes, although frequency selection was limited. Headquarters would develop the plan and send out air tasking orders with details for targets, timings, and so forth. Depending on the mission, squadrons and even groups, wings, or higher levels of command might fly together in formations under the command of the unit's senior officer. The radios allowed some degree of coordination and the ability to carry out minor modifications in the air. The plan and ensuing orders delineated the participating units and their respective targets and/or missions, as well as the overall timings and routes.

The big bombing raids were massive undertakings, and there was no tolerance for individual pilot independence. There was centralized command but no decentralized execution in mass bomber raids. Over enemy territory, the bombers tried to stay in tight formations for self-protection and to achieve closer bomb patterns. Pathfinders or else the unit's lead aircraft would get the formation to the target and call the bomb drop. A regular bomber pilot's room for decision making was limited to deciding whether to abort the mission if the aircraft encountered technical problems or was shot up.

Commanders of escort fighters had some flexibility in determining how to best escort their charges and when and how to go after enemy fighters, and once an attack started, pilots had leeway in how to fight their particular part of the mêlée. Although commanders led their units in battle, the opportunities to manage an organization doing violence were minimal. The fighter-bombers worked under the concept of centralized command and decentralized execution, but they were not flying in large-unit-sized groups.

Airborne radios permitted commanders on the ground to follow some operations and have a sense of what was going on. The commander on the ground's access to information was limited by the aircraft radios' power, frequency, range, and altitude. A commander on the ground might even issue directives or at least concur in changes such as switching to secondary targets because of weather over the primary targets. Aircraft in a flight or raid could communicate with each other and perhaps with commanders on the ground. Commanders on the ground could also get more immediate feedback on the success of the mission.

This was the standard for World War II missions, which were generally flown beyond friendly radar coverage and often radio (in the case of fighters) contact with commanders on the ground. Headquarters was still responsible for central planning and the development and distribution of air tasking orders assigning missions. The pilots, squadron commanders, and higher-level operational commanders aboard aircraft were primarily responsible for completing the missions, but there was now some room for information sharing and the potential for commander intervention from the ground. Strategic bombing missions have not evolved dramatically from this point.

Radar was the next ingredient added to the command and control system. Radar made its debut in aerial warfare during the Battle of Britain in World War II. During the war, both sides improved their radar technology, learned to conduct electronic intelligence gathering, and developed rudimentary countermeasures. However, ground-based radars are limited in coverage by the curvature of the earth. The further away a target is from the ground-based radar, the higher it must be in order to be seen. In addition, the radar's power, sensitivity, and sweep-rate affect its range. Since radars were not typically placed right at the border or the forward edge of the battle area and airborne surveillance radars were not a reality until after the Korean War, radar coverage was typically limited, with the best coverage over one's own territory. Therefore, ground-based radars were primarily seen as a key part of air defense, with limited practical application for offensive missions. Planes could fly faster and higher than previously, but the pilot's or crewmembers' eyes still provided the most situational awareness. Bomb sighting was predominantly done visually, and the effective range of the onboard guns was within visual range.

On the air defense side, however, the combination of radio, radar, and signals exploitation technologies led to a new development—the ability for people on the ground to actually control aircraft in flight and direct them in accomplishing their mission. The command and control system jumped beyond control via planning and procedures. The British and the German air forces gained the most experience with strategic air defense systems in the war. In essence, radar, ground observer reports, intercepted communications, and common sense were blended together to provide a picture of an impending raid, its direction, likely targets, altitude, size, and so on. As the raid approached, the ground-based radars would continue to track it, providing real-time updates on the raid's heading and altitude (altitude information was not as accurate as heading information) as well as information to calculate or to make informed guesses as to its speed, size, and targets. The air defense center would scramble the appropriate number of fighter units available near the anticipated bomber raid's flight path, provide warnings to potential targets, alert antiaircraft artillery units, and deconflict their fire from the fighter-interceptors.

Once airborne, the fighters would be directed by an intercept controller on the ground to fly a prescribed path at a prescribed altitude that was calculated to bring the fighters to a position from which they could see and attack the incoming bombers. Once the fighter leader saw the bombers, he would take over the intercept, engage the bombers with his unit, and return to base. The fighters and intercept controller were on the same frequency; the intercept controller heard details of the fight and received reports as the planes returned to base.

Although the intelligence from Ultra decryptions, radio intercepts, and ground observer reports could have been correlated and plotted in the absence of radar, the information would not have been as accurate or up-to-date. Knowing that the Germans planned a raid to bomb the dockyards in London at 10:00 PM and intercepting radio chatter as the planes formed up across the Channel would not be enough to tell exactly where the bomber raid was at any given time. Furthermore, the planes might experience a slight delay or be a bit early over the target, and clouds might force them to a higher or lower altitude than planned. In addition, they might make a navigational error or fall prey to British tricks and simply bomb the wrong place. Ground observers were not particularly accurate and there was an inherent delay in gathering and consolidating their reports.

Consequently, without radar, the defensive fighters could not wait at their airfields, saving gasoline, to be scrambled when the bombers were in intercept range and the bombers' course and altitude were relatively clear. If there had been no radar, the Royal Air Force (RAF) would have had to rotate squadrons through combat air patrols over the dockyards along the Thames, hoping to have the maximum number of fighters with relatively full fuel tanks airborne in the area and at the right altitude when the bombers arrived. The fighters would have had to patrol, searching every direction and potential altitude in the dark until they discovered the bombers, hopefully before they began bombing. Radar, however, gave steady and accurate updates on the raid's location. The radar updates, combined with the other intelligence, made it possible to accurately track the bombers' locations. In addition, the RAF's Identification Friend or Foe (IFF) feature distinguished British aircraft from enemy aircraft.

Radar systems improved during the course of the war; by its end, night fighters with airborne intercept radars were in use. The air defense system illustrated several important results of technology for potential air force officer expertise. First of all, it was not only possible but necessary for an intercept controller on the ground to direct the fighters to the target. Flying around aimlessly looking for bombers was a waste of fuel and had a low probability of success. If one did not know exactly where the bombers were, where they were going, and at what altitude, they were hard to find. In addition, even if the bombers were seen, they might be at an altitude and distance that precluded attack. The public below had a keen interest in seeing that the fighters intercepted and engaged the bombers. Civilian lives depended on it; so it became a sort of public review of the air force officer corps' jurisdiction. Was the air force officer corps upholding its end of the contract and effectively defending the country? In the RAF's case, the fighters and the then-largely secret ground-based air defense system earned their nation's eternal gratitude.

A second major change, at least in the solo-flying night fighters, was that there was no real difference during flying operations as to whether the pilot was a unit commander or rank-and-file pilot. To the intercept controller, a night fighter was just a night fighter, regardless of who was piloting it. Command on the ground had obvious ramifications in terms of unit manning, equipment, training, and morale, but it was immaterial in the air. There was a split: on the ground, the flying unit's commander had responsibilities that stopped when one or more of his aircraft took off. Once airborne, a voice on the radio belonging to someone that the pilot had probably never met was in charge, directing the pilot's actions. Furthermore, this voice did not necessarily belong to an officer or a pilot. This is not to say that the pilot's role was now devoid of responsibility and decision making. At some point, the pilot still took over the intercept, determined his tactics, and engaged the enemy aircraft.

However, a big piece of Huntington's management of a human organization conducting violence moved from the cockpit to the intercept controller on the ground. And although that intercept controller was in a chain of command that passed through sector amalgamations to some point at which it joined the same commander somewhere high up in the fighter pilot's chain of command, the intercept controller was not simply a member of the commander's staff, giving advice or making plans. The intercept controller was essentially commanding, or at least in tactical control over, the aircraft assigned to him. The intercept controller was the bottom link in the command and control chain and simultaneously, for a brief period of time, the top link in the tactical operations chain. However, when the pilot landed, he reverted to his squadron chain of command for administrative, training, morale, and discipline purposes. The air defense model is noteworthy not only because of the differentiation between the administrative command on the ground and the command and control in combat functions, but also because different types of personnel with different training were used for each position.

In addition, as is often the case in flying operations, functional positions, not ranks, are important. The intercept controller could be a lieutenant, perhaps even a sergeant, and the aircraft under control could be a single night fighter flown by a lieutenant or lieutenant colonel, or a fighter wing led by the wing commander. In either case, the intercept controller was still responsible for directing the aircraft into a position where the fighter aircraft could take over the intercept and engage the enemy aircraft.[4]

STRATEGIC AIR DEFENSE: SAGE AND THE F-106

In the early days of the independent U.S. Air Force, the heroic warrior archetype may have been able to downplay the RAF's experience in the Battle of Britain as a peculiarly British event. After all, the Germans could not stop the strategic bombing campaign against them, at least not after drop tanks made it possible for the escort fighters to cover bombers for the duration of their ingress and egress. In the Pacific, the strategic bombing campaign was also a success, partly because it did not start until the Navy's submarine campaign effectively cut Japan off from its sources of gasoline and other natural resources. With those minor caveats, the pre-war theories of independent airpower were proven. The U.S. Air Force gained independence, and gleaming bombers carrying atomic bombs would be unstoppable. Or would they? The Soviet Union's development of a B-29 look-alike and the atomic bomb gave cause for public reflection—Air Force bombers may be unstoppable, but Soviet bombers had better be stoppable. Heroic warriors or not, the Air Force officer corps had both a public and legal jurisdiction for the air defense of the United States.

The Air Force began a massive buildup of air defenses to meet its responsibility. For example, in 1948, Strategic Air Command (SAC) had 340 fighters to escort its bombers. At the same time Tactical Air Command (TAC) had 331 fighters, and Air Defense Command (ADC) had a paltry 166 fighters. By 1956, SAC still had 375 fighters in 15 squadrons and TAC had 582 fighters in 35 squadrons, but ADC's fighter strength rose to 1,937 fighters in 68 squadrons. Of course, fighters were only a small part of the equation. The Air Force also introduced another weapon that was anathema to the heroic warrior—the surface-to-air missile (SAM). Adding insult to injury was the short-lived designation of Air Force SAMs as unmanned fighters, which they essentially were. The Bomarc had a range of several hundred miles. Of course, as with the unmanned bombers, the designation unmanned fighter also carried the association that this expertise lay within the Air Force officer corps' jurisdiction. The Air Force possessed 110 Bomarc SAMs in 1960. The number of Air Force Bomarcs peaked in 1963 at 368, but they remained in operational service through 1972. Command and control was the key to the strategic air defense system. The number of officers who were intercept controllers (also known as weapons controllers/directors and later as air battle managers) rose from 231 in 1950 to 3,921 in 1963. The United States and Canada joined together in the North American Air Defense Command (NORAD), which for the first time placed both Canadian and U.S. military units under a joint commander in peacetime. NORAD began operations in 1957, the same year the Distant Early Warning (DEW) Line began operations.[5]

The culmination of the tremendous investment in continental air defense in the 1950s was the technological marvel of its day—the SAGE air defense system with its primary weapons, the F-106 fighter-interceptor and the Bomarc unmanned interceptor (SAM). Although in some ways irrelevant before it was completely deployed, because of Sputnik and its foreshadowing of the Soviet intercontinental ballistic missile (ICBM), the SAGE and the F-106 system continued to be the backbone of U.S. continental air defense into the 1980s. Developed in the early age of computers, the contemporary descriptions of SAGE stated:

The advent of the high-speed long-range all-weather bomber and missiles of various stages has made it mandatory that our present ground environment be revitalized. Men, alone, do not have the capability to comprehend a complex, constantly shifting air situation and make the required decisions in the few seconds that modern high-speed aircraft and missiles allow. The successful development of the high-speed digital computer provided a machine that can perform complex mathematical problems in seconds that would ordinarily take months to solve. Scientists—quick to realize the benefits to be derived from this computer—envisioned its use in Air Defense. Thus, the Semi-Automatic Ground Environment System, commonly referred to as SAGE, was born.[6]

Although many functions were performed automatically, the system was only "semi-automatic," because men were still needed to make decisions. The decisions requiring the man in the loop primarily involved whether to and how to intercept inbound aircraft. Specifically, the surveillance and identification section of the SAGE center had to decide whether an inbound aircraft met the identification criteria for categorization as friendly, in which case no interception was required. If the inbound aircraft could not be adequately identified with available information, it would be classified as unknown, which might require its interception and visual identification. Finally, if an inbound aircraft met the criteria for classification as hostile, it would be intercepted, engaged, and destroyed. If an intercept was required, the intercept controller and his superiors would then be able to look over the readiness statuses of various fighter and SAM units, determine which was optimal for the particular mission, and order the fighter scrambled or the missile prepared for the engagement. In addition, the man was also in the loop to monitor the computer and to modify or override computer-generated information as needed. SAGE was "ground environment" because there was conceptually a partner "airborne element," which eventually was embodied by the E-3 Airborne Warning and Control System (AWACS) aircraft, whose software largely duplicated the SAGE system's algorithms and capabilities.

The F-106, as well as the SAGE system itself, was on the cutting edge of technology and experienced many technical problems and delays in becoming fully operational. The F-106 was designed to be an all-weather supersonic fighter-interceptor. It first flew in 1956, and the Air Force began accepting deliveries in 1959. In 1959, the F-106 set a speed record at 1,525 miles per hour. Its speed, maneuverability and range were important assets, but its critical feature was its electronic package:

The Delta Dart [F-106] is equipped with the Hughes MA-1 electronic guidance and fire control system which is designed to operate with the SAGE air defense system. Using this system F-106s may be guided by the SAGE computer to within range of the intercept target where the pilot can select and automatically or manually fire the weapons on board. Weapons can be fired only with the active participation of the pilot.

The MA-1 system can control the F-106 from soon after takeoff, through climb and cruise, to attack position. The aircraft's radar is used by the pilot to detect the target, lock onto it and signal when to fire the selected ordnance to achieve the greatest kill probability. . . . This system also could guide the aircraft back to its home base or alternate base, but the pilot actually lands the plane. On an intercept mission the pilot may either monitor the electronic guidance and fire control system, or he may use its data for his own decisions while he manually flies the aircraft. If the SAGE system becomes inoperative or is destroyed, the F-106 can operate by using the MA-1 airborne computer.[7]

The SAGE/F-106 system required the onboard pilot to take off, land, and flip switches to arm his missile and to let the on-board computer take over the firing of the missiles when the F-106 was in the launch envelope. The combination of the data-linked SAGE and the MA-1 computers could do everything else. The intercept controller on the ground could use his computer to scramble a battle-ready F-106 and order the F-106 computer via data-link to intercept a particular target, order the intercept for visual identification or destruction of the target, set all speeds, altitudes, and headings of the F-106, select whether the intercept was to be made head-on, from the side, or from the stern, and after the intercept, order the F-106 to another intercept, to a point in space, or to return to home base or an alternate landing base. The heroic warrior in the F-106 was a few toggles away from drone status.

However, the F-106 was not a failed unmanned combat air vehicle (UCAV) of the 1950s. The F-106 was never intended to be a super SAM—that was the Bomarc's job, and its operational range was several hundred miles. The available technology and the expected scenario played major parts in the development of the SAGE/F-106 system. The worst-case scenario called for hordes of Soviet bombers to come over the North Pole with additional aircraft that could jam radars and communications. By the time that SAGE and the F-106 were operational, the Soviets were also capable of clearing out some of the SAGE system with intercontinental ballistic missiles (ICBMs) or long-range air-to-surface missiles.

Consequently, the system was designed to have several layers of redundancies. If the NORAD command center was destroyed or out of communication, sector commanders would take over full responsibility for their sectors. If a sector command center went down, its neighboring sector command centers or its subordinate centers could take over its area of responsibility. In fact, the SAGE system was designed to be able to quickly dump its data to another facility to continue operations. If an intercept control center was destroyed, down for maintenance, or out of the communications loop, adjacent centers could take up the load. As each senior node disappeared, responsibility would continually shift downwards or sideways. Consequently, since intercept controllers would be expected to handle ever more interceptors over larger areas, automated data-linked commands would make this easier. Data-linked commands would also be less vulnerable to jamming. Fighter-interceptor radars were very limited in coverage, so they needed precise guidance to find and intercept the bombers. If all the ground intercept control sites or data-link and voice radio sites were destroyed, manned fighters and SAM operators would be the last line of defense, each doing the best it could without any external direction. The AWACS aircraft were originally developed to fill in radar, communication, and intercept controller gaps, and to take over ever-larger areas of responsibility as ground sites went down.

In addition, day-to-day peacetime operations required the capability to send an aircraft up to visually inspect an inbound aircraft or strange situation. An aircraft might be labeled unknown as a result of any of a number of technical problems with the flight plan system or the aircraft itself that might cause it to deviate from its flight plan or assigned identification code. Unmanned interceptors did not provide a capability, at that time at least, to transmit video footage of the aircraft, then loiter while waiting for a decision to shoot down the aircraft or to go home. In addition, the ground-based radars might miss a small aircraft flying between the fighters and the inbound target; so the pilot provided a safety check in seeing and avoiding other aircraft in the area during an actual intercept. Finally, the F-106 (and F-101) could be equipped with an atomic air-to-air rocket, the AIR-2A Genie, which would of course be fired into the hordes of Soviet bombers *over Canadian or US territory*. The pilot and intercept controller together provided a final check on the employment of such a politically charged weapon.[8]

In the end, there was a certain amount of distrust of all the electronic magic and concern as to whether it would all work correctly. Consequently, the heroic warrior in the cockpit fulfilled a final man in the loop sanity check. His eyes were the ultimate arbiters. If there was any question as to who or what a particular aircraft was, it was simple enough to scramble a flight and have them go and take a look. The crew's visual identification overrode all the electrons, inferences, flight plan correlations, and other methods of identification.[9] This man in the loop role is still very much in evidence today in the post 9/11 world. In most cases, the command and control system still prefers to have a person's eyes view a deviant aircraft before making the decision on whether to down that aircraft. This quasi-peacetime scenario remains a major justification for retaining the heroic warrior pilot in the cockpit.

The AWACS and the SAGE system's replacement continued to possess data-link capabilities between command and control centers as well as from a command and control center to fighter-interceptors. However, the Bomarc SAM was phased out without a replacement in the 1970s, and Air Force did not replace the F-106 with another aircraft designed specifically for the interceptor role. The threat that prompted the development of the SAGE/BOMARC/F-106 combined system, that is, massive Soviet bomber raids with nuclear weapons, had long since lost its importance in comparison to the threat of a massive Soviet nuclear ICBM and submarine-launched ballistic missile (SLBM) strike.[10] As the F-106 was gradually phased out in the late 1970s and early 1980s, tactical Air Force fighters were moved into the strategic air defense mission, but they were not wired for the directive, one-way command and control center to fighter-interceptor data-link.[11] F-4s, F-15s and F-16s could not be "flown" by intercept controllers using data-link, but their pilots were still under the voice control of intercept controllers. The fighter radars could not "see" as far as the networked ground-based air defense radars or the airborne AWACS surveillance radar. The fighters still required assistance locating targets and were not left to their own devices to find and intercept targets unless there was no command and control system present.

At the same time, however, the use of modern F-16 and F-15 aircraft in the interceptor role also meant that the aircraft were less reliant on close control from air battle managers. The newer fighters could acquire the targets with their onboard radars at extremely long ranges in comparison to the F-106 or even the F-4. They also had better look-down capabilities and could detect targets that the ground-based air defense or AWACS radar might not. This meant that the modern fighters could take over the intercepts while still well beyond visual range from the targets, or run intercepts on targets that the command and control system did not see. In addition, the F-15s could interrogate the aircraft being intercepted for IFF responses, potentially eliminating the need for visual identification.

These factors changed the relationship between the air battle manager and the pilot. The air battle manager was still the last link in the command and control system. However, the control became looser, with a broader application to tactical air warfare in general than the very tight control required to position the older strategic air defense fighter-interceptors into their extremely small weapons envelopes. The command and control system still provided early warning of an attack, detected aircraft entering U.S./Canadian airspace, and determined when intercepts were required for identification. Fighters, theoretically coming up from ground scrambles, still needed initial vectors and point outs to find their targets. In addition, they needed to know what type of intercept to run and what the aircraft was likely to be. Fighters were not on constant patrol in the air defense identification zones along the periphery of the U.S./Canadian borders. Even with the improved fighter radars, a defense based on this concept would be ineffective and very costly. On the other hand, there was obviously something calming to the public about manned fighters flying combat air patrols over select cities in the aftermath of 9/11. In order to meet its societal responsibility and to maintain its jurisdiction over strategic air defense, the Air Force quickly scrambled fighters and AWACS aircraft to assume patrol stations under NORAD command—aircraft that could be seen, visibly protecting the nation.[12]

At the height of its glory, the strategic air defense system provided the capability for people on the ground to control not only fighter-interceptors but SAMs and antiaircraft artillery as well in a cohesive system. The command and control system had the deep-look radar picture and the means to identify and categorize incoming aircraft, thereby preventing fratricide of friendly aircraft returning from missions in a wartime situation. In addition, by being able at least to categorize aircraft into friendly, unknown, or hostile, the intercept controllers could better manage the battle and also select the best tactics for each situation. Friendly aircraft did not require interception. Hostile aircraft could be engaged beyond visual range, and only unknowns required visual identification. A fighter without this knowledge would have to close to visual range on all targets. Intercept controllers literally had the big picture as well as the communications to most efficiently direct the entire air defense system in real time. Fighter-interceptors could be kept on ground alert, saving gas, and be scrambled when required. Pilot opportunities for decision making or taking "initiative" became more constrained, but not just in the strategic air defense mission.

COMMAND AND CONTROL OF TACTICAL AIR OPERATIONS

There were parallels in the development of command and control of tactical flying operations, which included air-to-ground as well as offensive and defensive air-to-air missions. Strategic air defense protects the United States and Canada from air attack, whereas tactical air defense missions protect friendly ground troops and maritime forces, allies, and air bases in the theater of combat operations. In both North Africa and Europe in World War II, tactical air forces were paired with ground forces units. Each of these Tactical Air Commands ran its own Joint Operations Center (JOC). The JOC was not *joint*, but an air command center with representatives from the ground units. The JOC developed the plans and sent out the air tasking orders with the missions, the weapons loads, the targets, and the level of effort to be given to various missions. Although the tactical air commands preferred to fly interdiction missions against enemy personnel and materiel beyond the friendly ground forces' area of operations, the JOC was also the focal point for close air support missions, that is, using aircraft to support troops in contact with the enemy. The JOC also contained a section that was the highest-level control facility in the tactical air control system, which in turn oversaw the actual radar and control sites.[13] This part of the system controlled the aircraft executing the daily air tasking orders and JOC-directed changes. Each of the Tactical Air Commands was responsible for all offensive and defensive air operations within its assigned area. Since radar and radio coverage was limited, in most cases, ground control over offensive air missions was not practical in World War II.

In the beginning, the Korean air war was fought in largely the same way. In the offensive air-to-air arena, fighters would escort bombers or fly patrols, trolling for enemy fighters. If enemy fighters rose to the challenge, they had to be acquired visually as the Migs rolled in to attack the American fighters. This was not the optimum way to conduct air battles, since it ceded the initiative to the Migs, which were under ground-based intercept control and vectored into attack positions. However, in a visionary move to extend the command and control system's radar and radio coverage along the Yalu, that is, to support offensive, not defensive, air operations, the Air Force put a Tactical Air Direction Center (TADC) on Cho-Do Island in June 1952. The TADC provided radar and radio coverage over the Mig bases on the Chinese side of the Yalu River. Intercept controllers could then warn the F-86s when Migs were approaching and direct the F-86s into position to attack the Migs. General Momyer reports that the U.S. air-to-air kill rate went up dramatically after the TADC on Cho-Do went into operation.[14] Consequently, the command and control system, and specifically intercept controllers, could now direct fighters flying *offensive* counter-air missions at altitude over enemy territory. There was also a warning capability inherent in this setup. Aircraft flying missions over North Korea could potentially be warned when the Migs were up and if they were headed their way, although the standard procedure was to have fighters up in a screen between the Yalu Mig bases and any friendly bombers or other aircraft conducting missions.

The overall tendency has been to use technology to expand the command and control system over ever more aircraft missions and phases of flight. For example, one of the first Air Force units deployed to Vietnam was a Control and Reporting Post (CRP), that is, a mobile ground-based radar surveillance and control system, manned by U.S. personnel, to Tan Son Nhut Air Base in January 1962.[15] By December 1962, the CRP at Tan Son Nhut was upgraded to a larger and more capable Control and Reporting Center (CRC). A subordinate CRP was established in the highlands in South Vietnam at Pleiku, and linked to a second CRC, which was established at Danang. "By the end of the year [1962], aircraft for the first time could be radar controlled in all areas of South Vietnam. This radar system remained throughout the war and was later enlarged by the establishment of two additional CRPs."[16] By the end of the war, the Air Force had positioned several radars in Thailand as well as in South Vietnam in order to expand the radar coverage, not just for air defense and warning but to maximize the radar, radio, and control umbrella over fighter-bombers, attack aircraft, and their escorting air-to-air fighters. At the highest level, tactical air operations were planned, directed, and controlled by two Tactical Air Control Centers (TACC). One had responsibility for operations in South Vietnam, the other for operations over North Vietnam and adjacent areas, with a backup, subordinate TACC in Thailand. The Air Force also brought over the EC-121, the AWACS forerunner, originally designed to supplement the SAGE system in NORAD. The EC-121 had a large-area surveillance radar as well as a height-finder radar, a communications suite, intercept controllers, and a partial command and control center capability. The EC-121 supplemented the ground-based radars, but was limited in its ability to filter out ground-clutter. Navy ships in the Gulf of Tonkin were also part of the command and control network. Consequently, the United States had an extensive command and control network with coverage over parts of North as well as South Vietnam, Laos, and Cambodia, at least at higher altitudes.

In addition, at night and during bad weather, Air Force AN-MSQ-77 Radar Bomb Directing Central (MSQ) radar control sites controlled fighter and bomber strikes in South Vietnam, Laos, Cambodia, and parts of North Vietnam. The controller would direct the aircraft's heading, altitude, speed, and bomb release, without the fighters or bombers ever seeing the targets visually or with radar. This became the primary method for B-52 bombing after

1965 in South Vietnam because of its accuracy. The B-52s flying at high altitude could not see most targets with their radar, and ground-radar-controlled bombing was more accurate than using offset aim points. Under the Combat Skyspot controllers, B-52s bombed within one-sixth of a mile of the base perimeter at Khe Sanh during the North Vietnamese siege in 1968.[17] This situation is somewhat reminiscent of the air defense situation. Once again, the aircraft fly in drone-like fashion, following the commands of a controller on the ground, attacking a target that the crew did not necessarily ever see.

Radio-relay aircraft and the Airborne Battlefield Command and Control Center (ABCCC) aircraft let commanders on the ground stay informed about raids flown beyond the ground-based radar and radio coverage. General Momyer consistently makes the case that extending the coverage, which led to a higher degree of control over aircraft, was an important and very beneficial achievement:

The necessity for having positive control of the forces operating over enemy territory was demonstrated many times. With jet aircraft operating at such high speeds and with missiles permitting a greater variety of firing opportunities, control of the battle is more critical, complex, and demanding than ever.[18]

However, in his book, General Momyer takes an interesting turn after this statement. Immediately after stressing the need for "positive control," he turns from the visionary to the heroic warrior perspective and states: "Through pilot skill, improvisation, and training, the air battle over the skies of North Vietnam was fought and won."[19]

In the long term, however, the Air Force profession came to the conclusion that the command and control system was indeed important. The Vietnam experience resulted in a big change in emphasis on the future role of AWACS. AWACS was originally designed to supplement or take over SAGE sectors in strategic air defense missions. As the Air Force analyzed operations in Southeast Asia, however, the AWACS requirements shifted to include the role of providing the big picture radar and radio control over aircraft flying in tactical combat operations. AWACS, which became operational in 1977, provides radar coverage from the earth's surface to high altitudes out to the radar horizon. Such a system greatly expands the area under "positive control" and would have filled most of the holes and gaps in radar and radio coverage during the war in Southeast Asia.

The Vietnam War brought other changes as well. The most obvious was the heavy use of the surface-to-air missiles (SAMs) by North Vietnam. The SAMs meant that the North Vietnamese did not have to contest the control of its airspace with fighters and antiaircraft artillery (AAA) as in World War II and Korea. SAMs were more accurate and could reach aircraft at higher altitudes than AAA. Consequently, SAMs denied the Air Force relative sanctuary at altitudes above accurate AAA fire. In addition, flying low enough to evade the SAMs meant a significantly increased risk of being hit by AAA.

Even under conditions of air superiority, fighters could no longer simply fly to a target alone, bomb it, and go home. The Air Force needed some sort of defense against the SAMs. Defenses against SAMS, however, required both accurate and timely information on the SAM sites.

The solution to these problems included a combination of measures. First, signals intelligence aircraft flew frequent sorties to identify SAM locations and modes of operation. If a SAM site became active, and for example went into a tracking radar mode, the intelligence aircraft could pass this information to the command and control system for broadcast to friendly aircraft, or the intelligence aircraft could potentially broadcast such information directly to aircraft at large. Second, electronic warfare aircraft and bombers could jam specific frequencies and/or lay chaff to disrupt the tracking of friendly aircraft on strike missions. In addition, electronic warfare pods were developed for tactical aircraft to carry in order to jam specific radar frequencies. Carrying such pods became mandatory during the Vietnam War, and different tactics were developed to maximize the use of the pods for protection. Finally, the concept of Wild Weasels was developed. The Wild Weasels were aircraft modified to scan specific frequencies and attack enemy radars with anti-radiation (anti-radar) missiles.

The Air Force developed raid packaging, that is, combining several small groups of different types of aircraft from different squadrons and even different bases, to counter the variety of threats aligned against friendly aircraft. The raid package was built around air-to-ground fighters, whose bombing mission forms the whole point of the raid. The raid package might also contain, for example, some air-to-air fighters to protect the raid package from enemy fighters, electronic warfare aircraft that physically attack radars and surface-to-air missile sites, and reconnaissance aircraft. In addition, the raid package commander is designated.[20]

These systems increased the importance of the command and control system, since more coordination and information was required. In the non-nuclear scenario, the command and control system, through the air tasking order, builds a plan much like the nuclear Single Integrated Operational Plan (SIOP) for preplanned attacks on specific targets, setting targets, routes, timings, and so on. As in the SIOP, this has become very complex, and for the same reason. Missions are interlocking, with aircraft and missiles from different services and operating locations each playing their part. If electronic reconnaissance aircraft or Wild Weasels were scheduled to support a strike mission but did not arrive on time, the mission might be canceled or diverted to other targets. Furthermore, if the raid package was delayed, jamming and chaff-laying needed to be delayed as well, since doing either would telegraph the raid, and the chaff might blow away before the package arrived. Finally, it was important to know the exact locations of SAM sites and their characteristics, so that they could be effectively detected and jammed or attacked with the correct munitions.

In addition, the Airborne Battlefield Command and Control Center (ABCCC) was used to command, control, and coordinate interdiction and close air support missions. The ABCCC was a capsule carried in specific

C-130Es modified to support the ABCCC. The ABCCC had no radar, but was well stocked with radios and kept a running tabulation of missions and changes to the air tasking order. The ABCCC was responsible for deciding which targets to give to which fighters as they came up on the ABCCC frequency for guidance. In addition, the ABCCC typically had the authority to divert aircraft from one mission to another if fleeting, high-priority targets were discovered. During interdiction missions over Laos, for example, "if 7th Air Force intelligence developed a target of opportunity or if reconnaissance produced a 'perishable' target, the information was immediately passed to the ABCCC for execution."[21] If the ABCCC did not have aircraft on hand to attack that target, 7th Air Force could divert other aircraft from other missions to the ABCCC for that purpose. For close air support missions, the ABCCC could also maintain communications with the Air Support Operations Center (ASOC), in which Air Force and ground forces representatives planned and coordinated the close air support missions.

Forward Air Controllers (FACs), flying in slow, propeller-driven aircraft, were used effectively in Korea to control the fighters attacking targets in support of, and in close proximity to, friendly ground units. In Korea, the Air Force used the T-6 aircraft for FACs. The FAC was tasked by the Air Force command and control system and maintained contact with the ground unit he was supporting, coordinating the overall situation, specific targets, and the forward positions of friendly forces.

In Vietnam, the concept was similar, but FACs also became responsible for directing some interdiction missions as well. In addition, the command and control system was further extended down to the FAC, with the addition of the ABCCC. In Vietnam, FACs flew the O-1 or O-2, and later the OV-10. The Air Force also used "fast FACs" flying in jet fighters over high-risk areas. The FAC would be tasked to control fighters flying interdiction missions or to support an Army battalion. The air tasking order would task FACs with on-station times as well as target areas and contact information for the ABCCC. As the FAC flew inbound, the ABCCC would assign the FAC to a sub-area, where he might remain for several hours. Since FACs typically flew low and slow, they could better survey the target area. They would typically work the same general area in successive missions; so that over time they became familiar with its terrain and potential targets, and could report back to the ABCCC enemy progress in repairing bridges, for example. In close air support missions the FAC, from his airborne vantage point, might also discover new targets in the area, unknown to the ground unit he was working with. The FAC could report these to both the ground unit and the ABCCC, which could pass that information back to headquarters and also decide on the priority of attacking the new targets.

Fast-flying fighters tasked for close air support were given either planned target area times or designated ground-alert periods, during which they waited for targets to be discovered. After takeoff, the fighters would be cycled through the command and control system to the ABCCC, who would assign them to a particular FAC. The FAC would paint them a verbal picture of the area, situation, and target, and perhaps shoot smoke rockets for the fighters to use as cues as he directed them onto the target in a high-speed run. The FAC would make a damage assessment and might direct the same or another aircraft to attack the same target or move on to a new target. In any case, the fighter pilot's decision-making realm was severely constrained. The FAC selected the target, determined the target run direction, helped the fighter to acquire the target, and determined whether the target was adequately destroyed. The FAC also reported the results to ABCCC. In near drone-like precision, the fighter pilot did his best to hit the target—even though he probably never saw it! As General Momyer writes:

The greatest percentage of targets in South Vietnam were not visible to the fighter pilot because of terrain, jungle cover, or speed of the aircraft; usually it was a combination of all three. In most instances, the fighter pilots never actually saw the specific target because it was hidden in the dense vegetation of the jungle. These men had to rely almost entirely on the eyes of the FAC to get their ordnance on target. At all times, the FAC was the final air authority on whether or not the strike would continue. He was, in fact, the local air commander for the conduct of air operations, and his authority was recognized by the ground force commander and flight leader alike.[22]

The FACs became particularly important in Southeast Asia, because there was no delineated battlefield. In World War II and Korea, for example, it was possible for the Air Force and other services to agree on a *bomb line* or *fire support coordination line*, an imaginary line beyond which no friendly troops were operating. This procedural method of command and control allowed pilots to freely attack any military forces they discovered beyond the bomb line. Of course, bridges, for example, might not be open game if the ground forces planned to use them in the course of their advance. Nevertheless, this is the area that tactical air forces most prefer to operate in, since they can attack practically anything of military significance. Inside the bomb line, however, friendly ground forces are likely to be operating, so attacks must be coordinated, through the command and control system, with ground unit commanders, to minimize fratricide and to maximize the effect that the commander of the ground forces seeks.

In Korea, the FAC became an important asset because the targets tended to be small, scattered across the front lines, and close to friendly forces. The rugged terrain in Korea and parts of Southeast Asia also limited the usefulness of ground-based FACs, leading to an emphasis on airborne FACs. The vantage from an aircraft was much more effective in detecting targets and changes in this environment. These factors were further amplified in the Vietnam War because of the lack of a front in the traditional sense. In addition, because there was considerable concern over the political ramifications of high numbers of civilian casualties, it became important to have somebody visually acquire and confirm targets.[23] Furthermore, the Air Force's transition to an all jet combat force after the Korean War meant that it was more difficult for faster-flying pilots to visually acquire targets. Therefore, the FAC role expanded beyond the traditional close air support mission, and although the Air Force dabbled with the concept of fast FACs in jets, it still meant that the FAC, not the fighter pilot or the ground unit commander, was in charge of close air support air strikes.

The trends evident by the end of the Vietnam War continue by and large into the present, although many names and acronyms have changed from Vietnam, through Desert Storm, Allied Force, and the current operations in Afghanistan and Iraq. The command and control system has continued to relieve the decision-making responsibilities of the pilot in the cockpit. This is especially true in the realm of what was once called tactical or conventional warfare. The joint service agreement on the need for Joint Force Air, Land, and Naval Component Commanders under the theater commander before Desert Storm can be interpreted as a joint service endorsement of the Air Force position that one commander should have centralized command and/or control over all air-related assets used or available for use in the theater of combat operations. For example, the opening salvo of Desert Storm involved B-52s flying from the United States firing conventional air-launched cruise missiles, Navy Tomahawk Land Attack Missiles (TLAMs), Army helicopters, stealth fighters, and other aircraft attacking specific targets that dramatically reduced the Iraqi air defense system's ability to defend against successive waves of coalition aircraft. However, the Joint Force Air Component Commander (JFACC) position itself is no longer the automatic purview of the Air Force, although the Air Force has traditionally provided the command and control system for theater-wide planning, directing and controlling air-related systems. The current name for the JFACC's centralized headquarters for preparing plans, issuing the air tasking order, and controlling current operations is the Combined Air Operations Center (CAOC). The CAOC, which typically tends to be concentrated at one location, has a big staff of intelligence personnel, operators turned planners and monitors, administrative and technical staffs, and frequently, liaison officers from all major units and services affected by the family of orders concerning air operations, which include, among others, the daily air tasking orders, airspace control orders, and special instructions.

The CAOC also has extensive communication equipment, with data-link feeds from command and control sites and aircraft, as well as from reconnaissance aircraft or unmanned aerial vehicles (UAVs). AWACS provides the big-picture radar view of the friendly and enemy aircraft. This air picture can be shared with other AWACS, command and control facilities, and the TACC (now CAOC). For example, the *Gulf War Air Power Survey* reports that, at least occasionally, the TACC was able to talk via secure communications to all four orbiting AWACS simultaneously, while also receiving and displaying the air picture "from coast to coast."[24] Consequently, during Desert Storm or NATO operations over the Balkans, the JFACC could theoretically, at any time, look at a screen and see where all the friendly and other known airborne radar contacts were. Improved reconnaissance platforms like the RC-135 Rivet Joint also provide real-time information on hostile aircraft and other targets to the command and control system at large, and can also provide important threat calls to aircraft in peril. In addition, satellites for reconnaissance, missile warning, and communications support have been increasingly integrated into theater air operations.

The ABCCC was still in use in Desert Storm and over the Balkans, coordinating close air support with the ground forces. In Desert Storm, the E-8 Joint Surveillance Target Attack Radar System (JSTARS) aircraft was used operationally for the first time on a test basis. JSTARS' own radar produces a picture of vehicles and targets on the ground. This picture is data-linked, thereby directly increasing the command and control system's situational awareness and targeting ability for close air support and interdiction missions. FACs still play a role in close air support missions, but the platforms have changed to the OA-10 and F-16. The change in aircraft gives them an armed reconnaissance capability, since they are no longer the unarmed, exclusively command and control node of the past. This change leans toward the heroic warrior archetype. However, weapons technology also plays a large role in the evolution of the command and control of close air support missions, pulling them toward the visionary archetype. First, the development of buddy lasing by FACs and later of hand-held laser designators, both of which still required the pilot to place the missile in a position to acquire the designator's reflection, gave the target selection and aiming responsibility to the command and control system. The GPS-navigated Joint Direct Attack Munition (JDAM) just requires the aircrew to load or monitor the automatic input of the target coordinates and release the munition when in range, which further reduces the aircrew's involvement in the process.

Currently, at least in the campaigns in Afghanistan and Iraq, the technology of hand-held laser-designators and GPS calculators for JDAMS targeting has given personnel who are integrated in ground units direct control over the actual targeting of munitions launched in their support. For example, the particular circumstances of the campaign in Afghanistan created instances where a Special Forces unit essentially had a B-52 tagging along, dropping JDAMs wherever and whenever the enlisted terminal attack controller asked and sent up the coordinates. No intermediary FAC was used. It was in many ways the epitome of a transformed military, at least from an Army perspective. Small, light ground units, moving across terrain, encounter fire. They quickly identify the target coordinates and make a radio call. Minutes or seconds later, a JDAM falls out of the empty sky, destroys the resistance, and the unit moves on. The B-52 pilot is irrelevant with respect to the management of the organized violence. Conceptually, the B-52 could just as easily have been a drone JDAM carrier.

IMPLICATIONS FOR AIR FORCE COMMAND AND CONTROL

The practical application of airpower does not rest on individual combat but on independent air operations. Independent operations means that aircraft and missiles should be centrally organized, equipped, planned, and commanded to achieve specific objectives, which may or may not directly support ground and surface forces. This maximizes the effectiveness and efficiency of aircraft and missiles in attacking targets that are beyond the imagination of a traditional ground or surface commander, at least partly because the range of action is so much broader and the speed of reaction so much faster than anything possible on land or on sea. Without aircraft, missiles or radio-electronic means, a ground or naval commander cannot think of shutting down the enemy's electric power grid in its capital or isolating the enemy leadership from its forces and population. Consequently, the basis of independent air operations is the most centralized and controlled system possible over all air and missile assets. This allows the most flexibility and synergy in planning and achieving specific objectives.

The requirement for both centralized control and flexibility has led Air Force officers to become uniquely accustomed to fluid lines of command and control. In the traditional ground forces' and naval concepts of *command,* the commander is in charge of a unit or ship, both personnel and equipment. The commander is responsible for what the unit or ship does, and he leads his unit or ship to achieve its assigned tasks in combat and peacetime. He is responsible for operational or combat leadership as well as administrative management of the unit or ship. That unit or ship fits into a pyramid-style structure with several echelons of command, with each level amalgamating lower-level units under its command. Several squads form a platoon; multiple platoons form a company, and so forth. Orders come down the pyramid from higher echelons to lower ones. At each node, the orders are translated into information and orders for that node's subordinate units. Information generally flows upward in the same way, being consolidated at each node.

Officers' careers progress similarly upward, starting normally at the bottom and rising up through the levels, with periodic jumps to positions on higher-level staffs, followed by returns to command along the progression. In this way, officers gain an appreciation for the pyramid, as well as for their current place and role in the pyramid. The higher the echelon, the bigger the commander's supporting staff. There is also a baseline unit, below which no further division is traditional, practical, or possible.

Baseline or higher units can be broken off at the command nodes and assigned to other commanders, but the baseline unit remains the same in terms of personnel, equipment, and internal chain of command. It simply has a new chain of command at the higher levels.[25] The pyramid's primary direction for information flow in the traditional ground and naval forces model is vertical. After all, that would seem to be what traditional military command is all about: A clear-cut subordination of many to one. Each soldier or sailor can theoretically find his or her place in the pyramid and draw a line up the chain of command to the Commander-in-Chief, the President of the United States, as well as down through whatever subordinates the soldier, sailor, or marine has.

Although an airman can also theoretically draw a line up the chain of command to the President, the nodes along the line can change dramatically during the course of a single mission. In comparison to the more traditional ships and ground units, aircraft, satellites, and missiles can transit great distances quickly. Whereas it can take weeks to move a heavy Army division and its equipment from Germany to the Middle East, a bomber might conceivably fly a mission from the United States to drop bombs in the Middle East today, but be back in the United States serving as part of the nuclear triad the day after tomorrow. When taking off from the United States, the bomber crew's chain of command is different from when it is dropping the bombs, which may in turn be different from its chain of command at the base it which it lands.

Since the Air Force's baseline unit can be an individual aircraft, there is no automatic correlation between Air Force combat formations and administrative units like squadrons, groups, and wings. A squadron, group, or wing commander still organizes, directs, and trains his or her unit, and the commander still has responsibility for the health, welfare, morale, and discipline of the personnel, but the commander does not plan combat operations for his entire unit or lead his entire unit into battle anymore. Instead, the command and control system generates air tasking orders that assign missions to single aircraft and two- or four-ship formations that the squadron must provide, but the squadron as a whole does not fly as such. The command and control system orchestrates, or commands, the aircraft during the mission.[26] Consequently, there is a web of potential command lines depending on where and what a person is doing at any given time.

The system is widely distributed in terms of geography. Although there is usually a centralized staff somewhere to develop plans, issue air tasking orders, and control ongoing operations, the direction and controlling of operations requires communications, radar, intelligence, and other facilities and personnel that are spread throughout a variety of sites. Satellite controllers of communications and reconnaissance satellites might be located in the continental United States. A mobile ground-based air surveillance and control radar post might be set up in friendly territory close to the battle area, E-3 AWACS aircraft and other surveillance and reconnaissance aircraft could be operating out of airfields in adjoining countries or even flying in from out of theater.

Furthermore, the centralized staff or headquarters need not be geographically close to the battle zone. Planning and daily air tasking orders for operations in Afghanistan are done in the CAOC in Qatar. The air commander does not beef up a fighter wing's staff as an Army commander might do with a corps staff to plan the campaign, and there is no airborne flagship replete with battle staff in the middle of a tactical air operation.

In fact, the air commander's command and control system need not have any particular ties to any of the forces under its control. They are all viewed as interchangeable parts. Although some area experience may be beneficial, bombers bomb, fighters fight, and command and control system personnel generally provide control over ongoing operations. In theory, all can easily be rotated in and out of a theater. In addition, the command and control system is essentially a separate chain of command, providing the planning, the operational direction, and the control over the actual aircraft and pilots while they are flying the missions. These pilots, however, report up administrative chains of command to whoever has operational control or full command over them. These chains may intersect at the Joint Forces Air Component Commander, or they may not. During the Vietnam War, for example, SAC never relinquished command or any real degree of control over its bombers flying bombing missions over Southeast Asia, although ground radar sites in Vietnam often controlled their actual bomb runs.

The Air Force relies on a myriad of systems and aircraft to successfully conduct operations. As weapons and the C4ISR system improve, fewer aircraft are required to provide more air-to-ground and air-to-air capabilities than in previous wars—but more *types* of aircraft and systems are required to counter improvements in adversaries' weapons and C4ISR. A multitude of aircraft and satellites provide support to a given raid package, or even to a stealth fighter or stealth bomber flying solo. For example, air-to-air refueling tankers may provide the raid package with aircraft fuel before or after the strike, electronic warfare aircraft may jam enemy surveillance and control radars during the strike, intelligence-gathering aircraft may be monitoring enemy communications during the raid, command and control aircraft oversee the entire operation, and satellites might provide navigation, communications, and additional pre- and post-strike reconnaissance. A theater air commander might have full command over some provisional wings made up of fighter and attack aircraft, operational control over some of the command and control aircraft, and only tactical control over bombers coming in from outside the theater for a few hours.[27] The theater air commander controls them all in combat and operations primarily through the *command and control system*.

The amount of command and control exercised by the system outside the individual cockpits has evolved over time and is closely tied to technological advances. The entire CAOC system, as the focal point of C4ISR, has become the basis of Air Force operations. The resources in terms of personnel and equipment required to coordinate, to plan, and to control the execution of the Coalition's 2,400–3,100 sorties per day during Desert Storm were immense. And there has been no letdown in the centralization of the CAOC-based command and control system, with an infusion of new systems such as the Predator UAV feeds, and more control over space-based assets. Technology both justifies and allows the growing intrusion of the C4ISR system into the cockpit, with the simultaneous decrease in the potential realm of pilot decision making. This in turn elliptically calls for a reevaluation of whether piloting provides the skill set that should dominate the officer corps' sense of expertise and leadership.

The heroic warrior archetype naturally is not receptive to this shift. The heroic warrior sees the pilot and the manned aircraft as the crux of airpower. The pilot is the ultimate decision maker, the final man in the loop, the one who takes a bad plan and, through flying skill and ingenuity, makes the mission a success. He is the one there in the midst of battle, dodging flak and enemy fighters. He knows what needs to be done and what can be done, instantly assesses the situation, makes his decision, and stands by it. His view is summed up by the phrase "centralized planning, but decentralized execution." He would admit that it is important in the independent Air Force that airmen have the ability to centrally control all aircraft so that maximum effort can be applied to the various target sets. Consequently, air headquarters should make the air plan but leave it to the pilots flying the missions to actually implement the plan. Unexpected things always come up, and flexibility is the key to airpower. And that flexibility rests on pilot initiative.

However, from the visionary point of view, improvements in technology make more information available for centralized decision making during combat operations. Furthermore, technology makes it possible to make potentially more effective and efficient decisions outside of the cockpit, as for example by air battle managers or by FACs on the ground or in the air directing close air support strikes. Furthermore, as unmanned combat aerial vehicles become a reality, the ultimate decision maker, the final "man in the loop," the one who takes a bad plan and, through flying skill and ingenuity, makes the mission a success, need not be pulling 9-Gs in an aircraft on the scene. It can be someone sitting at a console in an aircraft or on the ground controlling a part of the battle for the commander. And if the situation warrants, it could even be the commander him- or herself.

The CAOC is an Air Force product, largely manned by Air Force personnel, but with some degree of command and control over all airborne assets in a theater of operations. A CAOC C4ISR system orchestrated the opening attacks of Desert Storm, which included B-52s flying from the United States, Navy Tomahawk Land Attack Missiles (TLAMs), Army helicopters, and a variety of Air Force, Navy, Marine, and allied aircraft stationed throughout the Gulf region. This expertise is the bedrock of modern airpower, and it clearly embodies the concept of managing an organization achieving objectives through the application of, or the threat of, violence.

In order to ensure its professional survival, the Air Force must not only maintain and expand this expertise; it must seek to expand its near monopoly of jurisdiction against competition from other services. It must also be able to defeat potential enemies. Despite lingering jurisdictional disputes with the other services on seam issues such as the exact amount of subordination to or coordination with the CAOC over Army helicopter operations or Marine close air support missions, the Air Force appears to have a near monopoly on the jurisdiction of the joint air and space C4ISR system. In many ways, this jurisdictional claim is much more unique than Air Force claims to jurisdictions over aircraft, missiles, and satellites in general. In addition, the basic expertise and jurisdiction over the joint air and space C4ISR system provides the basis of the Air Force's expansion beyond electronic warfare into information warfare in order to counter potential enemy integrated air defense systems and to continue to have the capability to strike deeper and faster against less orthodox targets in the enemy's hinterlands than other services can. The C4ISR system is the bedrock of air, space, and cyber warfare.

CHAPTER 3

Aircraft/Weapons Technology Shifts the Locus of Decision Making to C4ISR

The issue separating the heroic from the visionary warrior is not one of technology per se. Heroic warriors are not anti-technology. The airplane, after all, was the symbolic culmination of humankind's technological progress for most of the twentieth century. The Air Force heroic warrior does not advocate a return to warfare with spears, nor even to the wind-in-the-wire biplane era. The heroic warrior archetype likes modern aircraft and is enthralled with the idea that succeeding generations have ever more capabilities.[1] However, the heroic warrior sees the pilot, with his airplane strapped on, as the centerpiece of modern battle. The visionary warrior, on the other hand, has modified the joy of constantly evolving technology for aircraft into a general embrace of continuous technical revolution, which need not center around an onboard pilot. The visionary warrior has an open horizon before him, but the heroic warrior faces a dilemma. The heroic warrior and the profession in toto must embrace new technologies. Maintaining the edge against both potential enemies and jurisdictional competitors requires that neither be allowed to gain a technical advantage over the Air Force officer corps.

The public and the government could potentially take away the Air Force officer corps' jurisdiction, or at least intervene in the profession and force changes, if the public perception changed to the view that the Air Force could not fulfill its missions, or that the Navy, for example, could do the job better. However, it is difficult to embrace only technologies that specifically support human pilots in the cockpits of combat aircraft. It is not a matter of accepting some technological improvements, like air-to-air missiles for example, but not others, like an integrated command and control system. Each improvement making the combat aircraft more effective and more efficient is potentially another step toward the demise of manned combat aircraft.

The heroic and the visionary warrior are both caught up in the technological landslide. The same basic concepts and technologies that guide an air-to-air missile from a fighter aircraft can be used on a surface-to-air missile, and the same GPS-type navigational improvements that are added to a long-range bomber could be used on a long-range cruise missile or surface-to-surface missile. Continuous technical developments will eventually make human pilots flying in aircraft cockpits on reconnaissance or combat missions redundant in many cases, if they have not done so already. Keeping the onboard pilot the centerpiece constrains technological development to the abilities of the weakest link—the person in the cockpit. Consequently, the heroic warrior must find new justifications and new jurisdictions for human pilots, while visionary warriors simply search for new ways to synergistically harness and command the emerging technologies.

This chapter is the second of two that examines the interplay between technology, jurisdiction, and the migration of combat decision making out of the cockpit into the command and control, or C4ISR, system. This chapter focuses on how technological improvements to aircraft and weapons indirectly lead to the shift in decision making. The first area to be examined is the increased safety and survivability of aircraft. As fewer aircraft are lost in accidents and during peacetime, the Air Force requires fewer aircraft. However, as the numbers of aircraft decrease, the importance of controlling them increases, since the margin for error decreases. The second area is the differing rates of change per aircraft types. Officers who fly in types of aircraft that experience greater technological change are more accustomed to both changing technology and modern technology, and this potentially makes them more visionary in outlook. The third area is Air Force weapons. As weapons become more capable, there is a greater reliance on accurate and up-to-date intelligence and less dependence on pilot flying skills to employ them. The net result is that the locus of combat decision making is migrating away from the cockpit and into the C4ISR system, whether to the air battle managers or to the Forward Air Controller (FAC).[2]

SAFETY AND SURVIVABILITY

Technology has been a key factor in increasing the safety and survivability of aircraft. *Safety* is measured in terms of major accidents, lost lives, and lost aircraft, primarily in non-combat operations. Moreover, aircraft safety also falls into the bailiwicks of jurisdiction and responsibility. The public expects a defense that is both efficient and effective, and high aircraft accident rates do not support either. The public does not want to spend excessive sums of money on bad aircraft. Finally, the public does not want to send its children into a profession with an inordinate death rate—before combat is even considered.

The Air Force's major accident rate dropped from approximately 40 per 100,000 flying hours in 1948 to 5 in the early 1960s and then eventually leveled out at around 1.5 in the mid-1980s (see figure 3.1). Actual fatalities peaked in 1953 with 1,274 fatalities from aircraft accidents, and were typically well below 50 per year in the 1990s. These shifts occurred despite the major changeover to a predominantly jet Air Force. In addition, as the Air Force officer corps shifted its combat emphasis from bombers to fighters, more officers flew fighters. Fighters, however, were not just sleek, fast, and fun; they were also more dangerous simply to fly, even in peacetime. This added to the mystique of being a heroic warrior. As technology and training improved, the accident rates fell, and succeeding generations of aircraft became safer. Nevertheless, a portion of the heroic warrior ethos is firmly grounded in the inherent dangers of flying faced by *past* generations of pilots.

Survivability refers to the aircraft and crew's ability to perform their mission and return home. It does not refer to the basic flying and accidents covered by safety but the ability to survive in combat situations. Aircraft survivability has increased dramatically over the life of the Air Force. In fact, it appears to be a peculiarity of Air Force operations that aircraft accident and fatality statistics for combat operations do not vary dramatically from those for in-theater non-combat operations. For example, in both Korea and in Vietnam, combat deaths accounted for 55% of the total in-theater fatalities, and aircraft accident fatalities accounted for the remaining 45%. In Desert Shield/Storm, the Air Force lost 14 aircraft in combat and 12 due to accidents. Since there are no big differences between losses due to combat and to aircraft accidents, there is no compelling reason for the Air Force to invest in large numbers of unnecessary

Figure 3.1
Air Force Flying Safety Rates

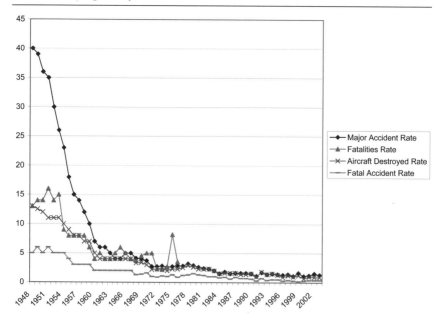

aircraft to be maintained as combat reserves. The officer corps can meet its needs with fewer aircraft, not just because they are more capable but also because fewer are lost in accidents or in combat. One important reason that they are more survivable in combat is that the C4ISR system has improved. This leads to better intelligence on enemy threats, better situational awareness, and better integration of electronic warfare and anti-command-and-control warfare. On the other hand, since there are fewer but more capable aircraft, they are harder to replace and consequently more valuable. It becomes more important to the air component commander to have control over each aircraft.

IMPACT OF DIFFERENT RATES OF CHANGE IN AIRCRAFT TECHNOLOGY

Technology has produced aircraft that can fly higher, faster, and farther, that can carry more ordnance, and that are safer and more survivable. However, the Air Force officer corps has implemented new technologies at different rates in different types of aircraft. Although the officer corps faces the traditional trade-offs, such as that between investing for tomorrow or buying for today, it must remain conscious of its social responsibility to defend the nation as well as jurisdictional competitions. The officer corps' general declining weight of effort applied to the strategic attack jurisdiction, along with the increasing weight of effort applied to the tactical jurisdiction, is reflected in the different rates of change in the application of new aircraft technology. This is important, because officers who fly in types of aircraft that experience greater and more frequent technological change are more accustomed to both changing and modern technology. This also means that they have potentially had more experience with the increasing impact of C4ISR on Air Force operations.

The difference in historical technological development between Air Force bomber and fighter aircraft is dramatic. In the case of bombers, the B-52 stands out. The B-52 flew and stood nuclear alert during the Cold War, and bombed conventionally in Vietnam, Desert Storm, the NATO operations in the Balkans, and the ongoing operations in Afghanistan and Iraq. By June 1956, for example, the Air Force had 63 B-52 crews and 35 B-52 aircraft on hand. On-hand crews peaked at 1,065 in 1964, and on-hand aircraft peaked a year earlier at 613 (see figure 3.2). The B-52 has remained the backbone of the Air Force bomber fleet since that time. Deliveries were completed in 1963, with most modifications since that time primarily designed to accommodate new weapons, navigational systems, and electronic warfare systems. The B-52's mission and weapons profiles have changed, the tail-gunner has been moved up to the cockpit and given remote controls, and the importance of the electronic warfare officer for survivability has skyrocketed. However, for the pilot, flying, that is, manipulating the yoke, rudder pedals, and throttles, has changed very little.

The story is quite similar with tankers, whose primary mission has always been to stretch the range of the strategic bombers. The KC-135 became

Figure 3.2
Number of Air Force Bombers by Type and Year

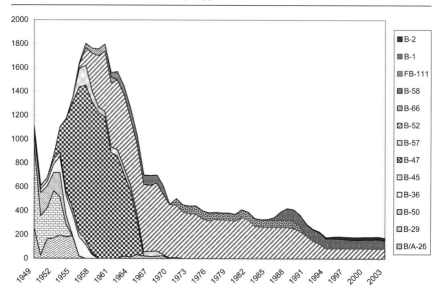

operational in 1958, eclipsed the KC-97 in terms of quantity by 1963, and has remained the Air Force's primary tanker through today. Although there have been modifications, including re-engining, the aircraft's structure and controls remain essentially unchanged. In the case of the B-52 and KC-135, colonels or generals can fly the same plane they flew as lieutenants, and possibly the same plane their fathers flew, with no major changes to the flying controls and handling characteristics of the aircraft. To a pilot, the work and the tools remain essentially unchanged.

By comparison, fighters have undergone dramatic changes over the same time periods. First of all, the tactical Air Force has cycled through airframes at a much faster rate. In 1957, for example, the Air Force had over 1,500 F-86s on hand, but also over 1,000 F-100s, 495 F-84s, and 470 F-89s. In 1969, the Air Force had almost 1,000 F-4s on hand, still over 400 F-100s, roughly 200 F-102s, 200 F-106s, 140 F-105s, and 100 F-101s. By 1978, the Air Force had on hand 1,200 F-4s, approximately 130 F-106s, 300 F-111s, 120 A-7s, 280 F-15s, and 120 A-10s. By 1997, the Air Force steadied out with over 600 F-15s, 130 A-10s, 800 F-16s, and 50 F-117s (see figure 3.3). In addition to the obvious changes in aircraft types, except in the case of the two-seaters like the F-89, F-94, and F-4, every modification for weapons and new technologies has affected the pilot as well. There is no bombardier or electronic warfare officer to handle the modifications—the pilot does it all.

This leads to a certain level of technological complexity, which is quite evident in software changes. For example, modern fighters are designed to

Figure 3.3
Number of "Fighters" by Type and Year

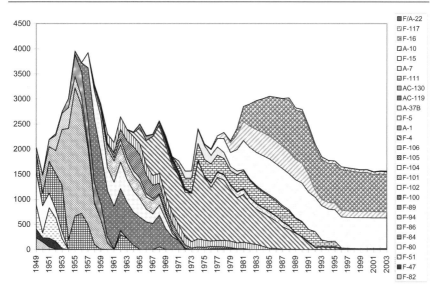

minimize the time for which a pilot is required to take his hands off the controls. The throttles and stick are full of toggles and switches, and major software upgrades may change the purposes of various switches or switch sequences. Squeezing the trigger does different things in different modes as well as in different software packages.[3] Flying the F-16 is not the same in 2003 as it was in 1983, and it is generations ahead of the F-86s of 1957. The work may be very similar, but the tools have changed dramatically.

Consequently, there is a difference between pilots of bombers, tankers, and fighters in terms of exposure to changing workplace technology. This different rate of technological innovation between aircraft types is amplified by exposure to the C4ISR system. Fighters have traditionally had more interface with air battle managers and the command and control system in flight while on training and combat missions than bombers have had. This creates a firmer tie to technological improvements in command and control systems such as AWACS and JSTARS. This in turn means that the evolution from bombers to fighters indirectly fosters further improvements in C4ISR, since the fighter generals have been directly affected by the synergy of new fighter technology and C4ISR improvements.

WEAPONS AND TECHNOLOGY

Technology has not only affected aircraft and the C4ISR system. It has had a major affect on weapons development, which in turn has radically altered the way war is fought. Aerial warfare traces its roots to the first attempts to use balloons to survey terrain and to observe enemy troop movements and emplacements. The human eye was the key to the surveillance operation. Military airplanes initially served as very mobile balloons, but during World War I they also became armed. Throughout World War I, however, the technology of combat airpower rested on the two pillars of the human eye and the pilot's ability to fly the plane. The human eye remained dominant in World War II and in Korea, although radar was used to control fighters intercepting enemy aircraft, range antiaircraft artillery (AAA) fire, and occasionally aim bombs. In the air-to-air arena, air defense radars were used to direct fighters into a position from which they could visually acquire the targets and attack them.

The weapon was still the gun, and it was still aimed by maneuvering the fighter. Although fighters might attack a bomber raid from the front, side, or rear, the standard dogfight between fighters was marked by intense maneuvering as each fighter tried to get to the adversary's 6 o'clock (behind the tail) position.[4] Since guns have a rather limited range, this position provided longer periods for firing the guns than did hit-and-run attacks from the front or side. In addition, it is difficult to shake someone who is on your tail. Wingmen played an extremely important position in defending the leader. Keen eyesight, flying skill, and the ability to perform under stress were critical attributes for successful air-to-air fighter pilots.

By the late 1950s, however, airborne radars had advanced sufficiently to be used in bombers for navigational assistance and targeting, and in fighters for long-range searches and target selection. The development of air-to-air guided missiles that were tied to the fighter's radar and fire control system led to a potential beyond visual range capability in the air-to-air arena. Radar bombing also meant that certain targets, that is, those that made good radar presentations on the scope, could also be bombed without ever being seen visually by the aircrew. The pilot's or aircrew's eye was no longer a limiting factor. These capabilities were sufficiently developed for use during the Vietnam War.[5] Electro-optical (television), infrared, and laser homing or steered glide bombs and missiles were also used during Vietnam. In addition, several systems that did not require the pilot, let alone his eyes, were also developed or refined. The Air Force's surface-to-air missile and the long-range surface-to-surface missile, or the intercontinental ballistic missile (ICBM), became operational in the 1960s, and variations of the cruise missile concept continued to be refined. Radar and inertial navigation systems provided the guidance, and atomic warheads made up at least partly for navigational inaccuracies. Consequently, by the end of the Vietnam War, the Air Force's foundation for precision guided munitions was established. The pilot or crewmember's eye and the pilot's flying skill no longer needed to be the pillars of aerial combat.

Weapons used in aerial warfare are typically divided along the lines of the technology used or the environments or mediums in which they are deployed, as is the case in the standard categories of air-to-air, air-to-ground, surface-to-air, and surface-to-surface. However, for this discussion it makes more sense to divide weapons into categories representative of crew involvement in terms of both the technical skills required to deliver the weapon and the decision-making skills with respect to acquiring and selecting targets and determining the best employment techniques to maximize the chances of destroying the targets.

Weapons can then be classified according to the following four categories. The first is aircraft-aimed weapons. The bullets, bombs, or missiles go wherever the ballistic trajectory of the aircraft at launch takes them. The second deals with precision guided munitions (PGMs) that require operators to acquire the target, lock the system onto the target, and then either "fly" the weapon to the target or else keep radar or other energy directed at the target for the weapon to home onto. These are "lock, launch, and monitor" weapons. The third category involves PGMs that require operators to acquire the target and lock the system to the target, but once launched, the weapon has no further contact with the launching platform or its systems. It is a "lock, launch, and leave" weapon. The fourth category is one in which the operators are never required to "see" or acquire the target. At most, the operators update coordinates or a flight path, then launch the weapon. The weapon is totally self-guided to the target. It is truly a "launch and leave" weapon.

CATEGORY 1: AIRCRAFT-AIMED WEAPONS

In the first category, the pilot or crewmember must visually acquire the target. Then the pilot must maneuver the aircraft to an optimum position to shoot or release weapons. Examples of this category include fixed machine guns or cannons in the wings or nose of an aircraft, "dumb" bombs, and unguided rockets.[6] Aircrew may have some minimal technological assistance in terms of a bombsight or gun sight, or perhaps even a ranging-radar as in the F-86, but the crewmember is primarily responsible for determining the release point for bombs or when to fire rockets or guns against airborne or ground targets. Guns in general, even those with sights integrated into complex fire control systems as in modern F-15s and F-16s, which incorporate radar information and other factors, still fall into this category. Manual bombing modes with such systems also fall into this category. A high degree of flying skill is required, but once the bombs, rockets, or bullets are away, the crew has no control over them and need not fly any prescribed path. The crew is free to re-attack the same target, attack a new target, or depart from the area. The flight path of the ordnance is subject to gravity, wind, launch conditions, and its own power, if it has any.

This category most closely aligns with the archetype of the heroic warrior. The delivery aircraft is integral to the weapon, and the pilot (together with the crew if there is one) is responsible for the entire process. Whether on an air-to-air or an air-to-ground mission, the pilot or crew must navigate to the area, acquire the target, determine the best way to attack the target, and deliver the ordnance. Although there may be considerably more maneuvering in a fighter, a bomber pilot must be able to keep the aircraft under firm control and within parameters to have any hope of hitting a ground target with gravity bombs. There is minimal technical assistance, and no apparent micromanagement from the command and control system.[7]

There still are roles for both conventional and nuclear gravity bombs as well as guns, and the heroic warrior has successfully equipped all late model F-4s and follow-on Air Force fighters with an internal gun, because situations occurred in the Vietnam War where missiles could not or did not work and it might have been possible to attack the Migs with a gun. However, there is no gun on the F-117 stealth fighter, since this would ruin its stealth characteristics. Visionary technology trumped the heroic warrior desire for an internal gun.

CATEGORY 2: LOCK, LAUNCH, AND MONITOR

The second category consists of PGM systems in which a crewmember must actually "see" the target, "lock" the system or weapon on the target, and take action to maintain the "lock" or "fly" the weapon into the target. This category can apply to ground-based systems such as SAMs, as well as to airborne weapons. A crewmember or operator can "see" the target visually through the cockpit canopy or via a television, radar, or infrared screen. "Locking" the target means that the weapon system requires some sort of designation of the correct target and some period of tracking the target before, during, or after firing the weapon. With a flexible gun, the gunner must adjust the gun as the target flies by, in order to keep the target in his sights. With a semi-active radar missile, the firing system's radar must continue to periodically scan the target, so that there are sufficient radar returns for the missile to follow until it hits the target or comes close enough for its proximity fuses to work. With a data-link command system, the control system must continue to track the target and the missile, and either send that information to the missile for its internal intercept calculations or compute the intercept and send course corrections to the missile. With laser-guided bombs, the firing aircraft or another aircraft or person on the ground must maintain the laser on the target after an aircraft launches a laser-homing weapon.

In an airborne system, some degree of flying skill is still required, since the pilot must maneuver the aircraft to get the target into the weapon's firing envelope, and perhaps execute maneuvers to keep the target locked on. However, the envelope is typically larger in this category of weapon than in the first. Examples of this category include the VB-3 Razon bomb, the AGM-12 Bullpup air-to-surface missile, the various laser-guided bombs, and the AIM-7 semi-active radar air-to-air missile. The Air Force officer corps took an early and visionary interest in these types of weapons. Visionaries in the Army Air Force embraced this type of technology during World War II, supporting research into a series of different types of controlled bombs, which were the forerunners of contemporary guided glide bombs.

However, only the radio-controlled VB-1 Azon saw combat. The VB-1 was used in Europe and in the Mediterranean, as well as in the China-Burma-India Theater, where it had its greatest success, destroying 14 bridges in seven missions.[8] This figure indicates that there were multi-target missions per raid, if not per aircraft, almost 45 years earlier than Desert Storm. Bridges were very difficult to hit with regular bombs because of the large Circle Error Probable (CEP) associated with them.[9] The use of the VB-1 also highlighted the visionary aspects of aerial warfare, including precision, relative bloodlessness, limited collateral damage, and the striking of targets to create desired and synergistic effects.

The VB-3 Razon, a derivative of the VB-1, did not see combat in World War II but was used in Korea, with some success in destroying bridges.[10] After the Razon came the TM-61 Matador ground-flown surface-to-surface missile or "unmanned bomber" in 1953, with 300-odd Matador missiles in 1956. By 1980, the Air Force had over 58,000 "lock, launch, and monitor" weapons in its inventory.

The next major operational conventional guided air-to-surface category-two Air Force weapon was the AGM-12 Bullpup. The Bullpup actually was developed by the Navy, and the Air Force accepted its first Bullpup missiles in 1960. The Bullpup was powered, and was "flown" into the target by means of a joystick that generated data-linked commands to the missile. It had a range of roughly seven miles, giving the launch aircraft important stand-off range, which was countered to an extent by the need to visually "fly" the missile to the target.[11] Although the Bullpup continued in service through the mid-1970s, the Air Force began moving to laser-guided bombs during the Vietnam War. These bombs are "semi-active" laser-homing, meaning that the launch aircraft, another aircraft, or a person on the ground must illuminate the target with a properly coded laser while the bomb is in the air, homing onto the reflected laser returns coming from the target.

The laser-guided bombs fundamentally altered the responsibility for (command and control over) a bombing mission, at least in certain circumstances. In the past, whether working with a FAC or not, the pilot or bombardier on board the aircraft had had to find the target, position the aircraft within the weapon's parameters, then aim, release, and perhaps track the bombs. Now someone else, off board, could select the target and designate it with the appropriate laser as the bomb homed in. The pilot (or bombardier) flying the launch aircraft was relieved of the responsibility to find, evaluate, and hit the target. Instead, he only had to launch the laser-guided bomb within the parameters necessary to get it to the target. When the laser designator was either a FAC flying over the target area or on the ground with the troops, the command and control system deliberately shifted these targeting responsibilities and decisions away from the raiding aircraft itself to the people with the best tactical situational awareness and most self-interest in a successful strike.

In the air-to-air arena, the Air Force began development work on the GAR-1, later redesignated the AIM-4A Falcon, in 1947 and was testing versions of the missile during the Korean War. However the Air Force did not begin accepting the first operational Falcon missiles until 1955. The Falcon became the world's first operational guided air-to-air missile in 1956.[12] The Air Force officer corps was not reticent about moving from the gun to air-to-air missiles, and accepted over 2,800 operational AIM-4As in 1957. The AIM-4A was a semi-active radar-guided missile, which meant that the launch aircraft had to lock the radar on to the target so that sufficient radar energy bounced off the target for the missile to track. Consequently, the pilot had to maneuver the plane in such a way that the target stayed within the fighter's radar coverage.

The missile was designed for the air defense fighter-interceptor force, which would be attacking bombers flying relatively straight and level, so it was not particularly maneuverable. It was not a dogfight missile. However, the missile could be fired from any aspect, that is, from the front, side, or rear of a target, and with a radar lock-on, the pilot did not need to visually acquire the target. Consequently, the missile could be fired day or night, or in inclement weather, and most important, the range of effectively engaging a target jumped overnight from thousands of feet to miles, making it potentially a "beyond visual range" weapon, meaning that the enemy aircraft might never visually see the launching aircraft. The AIM-4 Falcon semi-active radar guidance missile went through several iterations and remained a mainstay on Air Force long-range fighter-interceptors (e.g., the F-101, F-102, and F-106) until their demise in the early 1980s.

However, for tactical fighters, the AIM-7 Sparrow III was the Air Force's main semi-active radar guidance air-to-air missile. The AIM-7 was developed by the Navy in conjunction with the F-4 and entered service with the Navy in 1958. The Air Force began receiving its first operational AIM-7s in 1964. Having semi-active radar guidance, the AIM-7 Sparrow also required a radar lock on the target to ensure enough radar energy to home on. However, the Sparrow was more maneuverable, and has been modified over the years to increase its range and ability to resist ground clutter and enemy electronic countermeasures.[13] The AIM-7 had (and has) true "beyond visual range" capability, but two things are required before this capability can really be exploited. First, the fighter's radar must acquire the target and lock on to it.[14] Second, the Rules of Engagement (ROE) must permit beyond-visual-range firings as they did in Desert Storm, as opposed to Vietnam.[15] This limitation is at least partly political. In addition, it also connects to the command and control system since fighter radars are limited in coverage and somebody has to have the authority to declare radar blips as hostile before they can be shot beyond visual range.

Consequently, the second, "lock, launch, and monitor," category of PGMs did not free pilots from the C4ISR system. In fact, the reverse was true. Air-to-ground missions required better intelligence to be able to quickly and accurately find, identify, lock on to, and maintain the lock on the target. The idea was no longer to send a bunch of airplanes to flood the target area CEP with bombs and hope a few actually hit the target. The concept had changed to a small flight of aircraft with a high probability of hitting the target. Aim points also became critical as accuracy increased. One or two small bombs accurately hitting the wrong part of a building might have no affect on the target's ability to operate. Intelligence had to meet this new requirement. In addition, the ability of a FAC or person on the ground to designate targets took the target identification and aiming out of the cockpit and placed it in the C4ISR system. In the air-to-air arena, the longer-range command and control radars and the C4ISR system told fighters where to look for enemy aircraft, played a role in sorting out friendly and enemy aircraft, and enabled beyond-visual-range shooting.

CATEGORY 3: LOCK, LAUNCH, AND LEAVE

The third category is similar to the second, except that after locking the weapon on the target, the weapon is "launch and leave." For example, with a heat-seeking or anti-radiation missile, control systems must ensure that the missile is targeted at the correct target and that the target is within parameters before launching. Once the weapon is away, however, there is no external control over the weapon. Examples of this category include the AIM-9 infra-red heat-seeking air-to-air missile, the AGM-65 Maverick television-guided air-to-surface missile, or the AGM-45 Shrike radar-homing missile. The Air Force moved into this category with operational weapons in 1957. Air Force stocks rose from over 800 AIM-4B infrared air-to-air missiles in 1957 to over 38,000 "lock, launch, and leave" weapons by 1980. Many short-range SAMs also fall into this category. "Smart" aircraft with dumb bombs, as was the case with the F-16s in Desert Storm, also fall into this category. In certain modes, for example, the pilot can designate the ground target. The fire control system then computes the optimum flight path, and releases the selected munitions when it, the fire control system, determines. In an airborne system, demands on the pilot are less than in the second category, since there is no requirement to keep the aircraft in a specified relationship to the ordnance and/or target once the missile has been fired.

The Air Force came out with what was later designated the AIM-4B Falcon shortly after the AIM-4A semi-active radar air-to-air missile. The AIM-4B was the Air Force's first infrared (IR) guided air-to-air missile. Air-to-air in-frared missiles have a seeker in the nose that tracks infrared energy from jet engine exhausts. The missile seeker can typically search for targets on its own, or be slewed to the radar to search for a target that the radar has locked on, or bore-sighted through the front of the aircraft. Once it is clear that the infra-red missile has acquired the correct target, and that the target is within range parameters, the missile can be launched. Once it is launched, the seeker leads the missile to the target.[16] The AIM-4B was designed to be carried by fighter-interceptors against bombers, so it was not a dogfight missile. However, the Air Force procured the AIM-9 Sidewinder, originally developed by the Navy, and the AIM-4D infrared missiles, both of which were designed to handle the maneuvering engagement typical of a dogfight between two or more fighters. Both versions were used in Vietnam, although over the long run, the AIM-9 Sidewinder became the Air Force's standard fighter (e.g., F-4, F-15, F-16) short-range infrared missile.

The earlier, rear-aspect-only versions of the air-to-air infrared missiles had many attributes that were more representative of the heroic warrior archetype than of the visionary. First of all, being rear-aspect and close range, they required a high level of pilot skill, as the pilot would have to maneuver behind an adversary and get into a firing position. Although the missile's envelope was typically larger than that of an onboard gun, there was some overlap. Consequently, as a test of piloting skill, it is very popular among fighter pilots conducting air-to-air training engagements to limit the simulated on-board weapons to only infrared missiles and guns. The winner of the "knife fight" earns bragging rights at the bar. In addition, because of the rear-aspect limitation, the missile fusing characteristics, and the infrared countermeasures, an early infrared missile was more likely to damage or destroy the adversary's aircraft without killing the pilot in combat than a semi-active radar-guided missile fired into the front of an adversary aircraft. This linked the infrared missile's requirement for pilot skill with an allusion to early chivalrous World War I dogfights.

The heroic warrior perspective was also furthered by the fact that in the F-4, which was a two-seat fighter, the AIM-9s could be fired without the weapons system operator's assistance.[17] The AIM-7 semi-active radar missiles required both crewmembers. Nevertheless, in Vietnam, over half the Air Force air-to-air kills were made with AIM-7 Sparrows.[18] The longer-range, all-aspect ability of the Sparrow was more effective against Mig-21s employing high-speed hit and run tactics, since the Sparrow could run the Mig down in certain circumstances. Downing the Mig was more important than upholding the warrior image and missing the kill.

In addition to air-to-air missiles, category three also includes anti-radar missiles. The Navy began development of the AGM-45 Shrike radar-homing missile in 1961, and the missile became operational with Navy aircraft in 1964. The Air Force began receiving and using operational missiles in Southeast Asia in 1966. The joint Navy–Air Force AGM-78 Standard ARM (Anti- [radar] Radiation Missile) became operational and was used briefly in Southeast Asia in 1968. Its numbers never rivaled those of the Shrike in Vietnam, but it did have additional program algorithms to keep it on course to the radar site, even if the radar was shut down while the Standard ARM was in-flight to the radar. This capability rectified a problem with the Shrike that the North Vietnamese had quickly learned to exploit—the Shrike would go ballistic and usually miss the radar site if it lost the enemy radar signal in flight.

Degrading or destroying the enemy's command and control system became a critical prerequisite for effective and efficient use of the air medium. Anti-radiation missiles continue to be important. The HARM, or High-Speed Anti-Radiation Missile, added speed to the missile's flight. It is critical for

Wild Weasel aircraft, designed to detect and destroy enemy surface-to-air missile (SAM) sites, not only to detect and engage but most important to destroy critical parts of a SAM system before the SAM hits the trolling Wild Weasel aircraft. Technology is indispensable in this modern game of chicken. The enemy command and control system must be degraded, suppressed, or destroyed via electronic jamming, bombing, or information/computer attacks before aircraft can freely roam over enemy territory.

The "lock, launch, and leave" category did not significantly alter the relationship between combat aircraft and the C4ISR system beyond what had already been seen in the "lock, launch, and monitor" category with respect to air-to-ground and air-to-air warfare. The C4ISR system was most important in the target identification and selection phases of an engagement. The ability of the pilot to leave instead of monitoring reduced the demands on pilot skill. The addition of the anti-radiation missiles placed new burdens on intelligence, while simultaneously moving in the direction of more active anti-command-and-control warfare.

CATEGORY 4: LAUNCH AND LEAVE

The fourth category is often thought of as referring to a high-technology type of weapon. However, this need not be the case. In fact, the "Air Force's" first such weapon was developed in World War I. The Kettering Aerial Torpedo, known more affectionately as "the Bug," was the forerunner of the German V-1 flying bomb and cruise missiles in general. It was an unmanned biplane filled with explosives, launched from a dolly riding a track, and with a range of 75 miles.[19] The ground crew would set up the rail track, which provided direction. The Bug would be prepared for flight, and its timer would be set, based on the target's range. At the set time, the motor would shut down, the wings would drop off, and the Bug would dive to the ground. Although the war ended before the Bug could be used in combat, the concept illustrates the pure "launch and leave" category of weapons, although the "precision" aspects of the Bug are open to debate.

In the "launch and leave" category, unlike the other categories, crewmembers are not required to acquire or "lock" the target in any way. The target need never be seen, even with radar. Operators may need to load target information, which in the Bug's case was simply direction and range. Today, target coordinates, terrain maps, or flight plans may be preloaded, or uploaded shortly before the weapon is launched. However, once the weapon is fired, its own navigation systems fly it to the target. Examples of this category include ground-launched cruise missiles (GLCMs), air-launched cruise missiles (ALCMs), and the Joint Direct Attack Munition (JDAM) family of munitions guided by an inertial navigational system/Global Positioning System (INS/GPS). It also includes most but not all surface-to-surface missiles, including of course ICBMs. With an ALCM or JDAM, the mother aircraft transports the weapon to a point inside the weapon's range and launch envelope for a given target, but no particular piloting skill is required to launch the weapon. As in the case of the category two and three weapons, the Air Force officer corps made an early and substantial commitment to the fourth category of weapons. In 1959, the Air Force already had 40 TM-76 Mace tactical surface-to-surface missiles.

The "launch and leave" weapons of category four are important for a variety of reasons. First of all, they tend to provide great standoff ranges, thereby increasing the survivability of aircrews or missile launch crews. In addition, they reduce the need for pilots, crewmembers, and operators to develop specialized skills. Neither pilot nor bombardier has to try to positively identify the target through radar, television, or infrared imagery while flying in combat conditions. There is no need for a pilot to undertake any special maneuvers to obtain a lock-on of the target, no need to limit maneuvers in order to keep the lock-on, and no particularly demanding pop-up or diving maneuvers required to launch the weapons. Furthermore, the onus of target selection falls on the command and control system. It is no longer a pilot, crew, or operator decision. It is entirely possible that, for example, a Special Forces team under fire will set and send the coordinates for JDAM strikes to crewmembers in aircraft flying nearby, who have no insight into the targets or battle situation below. Consequently, the locus of control or targeting decision making is swinging dramatically from the pilot to the command and control system. This, of course, reemphasizes the point that the command and control system is more dependent than ever on accurate and up-to-date intelligence.

IMPLICATIONS

Technology is making aircraft better. Today's generation of combat aircraft can generally fly higher, faster, further, and more safely than its predecessors. Operationally, today's generation of combat aircraft can bomb more accurately, even with dumb bombs. In the air-to-air arena, fighters clearly have beyond-visual-range capabilities with the Advanced Medium Range Air-to-Air Missile (AMRAAM), with the AIM-7 Sparrow, and in some instances even with the AIM-9 Sidewinder missile. In addition, onboard technology, the command and control system, and the ensuing Rules of Engagement now tend to make this capability a reality in combat operations. PGMs, with better stand-off ranges and the launch and leave capabilities of JDAMs, HARMs, and conventional armed cruise missiles, dramatically increase aircrew survivability. However, each step away from the basic gun is a step toward more intrusive command and control system involvement. Each step is also a step toward potential unmanned combat air vehicles (UCAVs), as more of the flying and combat phases are computed and controlled by computers and electronic presentations that can be data-linked off-board.

Although it can be argued, as the *Gulf War Air Power Summary* does, that there still is a place for B-52 carpet bombing of enemy ground combat units, and A-10 fans say that there is nothing like its 30mm gun, the trend is clearly toward PGMs.[20] And it is not just toward generic PGMs, but toward the PGMs of the fourth category—the "launch and leave" weapons, which place the lowest demands on piloting skills. The heroic warrior cannot use his gun in most air-to-air situations. An enemy fighter would kill him with a beyond-visual-range missile while he was still just a dot on the radar scope. Enemy SAMs will do the same thing unless they are jammed or diverted by automatic onboard systems or other specialized aircraft. Heroic warriors understand this and realize that they cannot survive without relying on modern technology and modern weapons, and this indirectly creates a greater reliance on the C4ISR system.

Although heroic warriors realize that they cannot compete and meet their social responsibility to defend the nation in older, more heroic aircraft, the review of weapons technology indicates that Navy air was often more visionary than the Air Force officer corps in the tactical air jurisdiction. The Air Force eventually purchased and used large numbers of Navy-developed technologies. For example, the F-4, armed with the AIM-7 and AIM-9, became the Air Force's frontline fighter for a generation, and the Air Force used that combination as well as Bullpups and Shrikes in Vietnam.

Part of the Air Force officer corps' less than visionary approach to these rather important technical advances can be traced to the jurisdictional divisions of the 1950s. The Air Force officer corps' clear priorities were strategic offense and strategic defense. Consequently, its investments were directed in these jurisdictions. For example, the Air Force AIM-4 Falcon air-to-air missiles were designed for strategic defense interceptors to use against non-maneuvering bombers. This was a simpler technical problem than dogfight-capable missiles, and the AIM-4 was operational long before the AIM-7. Navy air, having no jurisdiction for strategic air defense or strategic bombing, could direct all of its investment into its tactical air mission.

On the other hand, since naval air is but one of several communities competing within the Department of the Navy and because space is a very limiting factor on a carrier, naval air is perhaps driven more toward the visionary perspective in order to maximize its effectiveness and efficiency. When defending the carrier, the objective is to destroy enemy aircraft from as far away and as quickly as possible. Maneuvering dogfights are not the first choice. They take time and increase risk. When attacking ground targets, the objective is again to shoot from as far away as possible, to minimize the risk to the aircraft and to minimize flight time. Time is important because takeoffs and landings must be choreographed into a tight, almost unalterable schedule. Reducing risk is important, because there are no spare aircraft on the carrier. The Air Force officer corps, blessed with more aircraft and more time, was perhaps more able or willing to tolerate the heroic warrior archetype and less visionary tactical weapons, at least until Vietnam made it clear that what was once visionary had moved to the category of necessity.

From the visionary warrior's perspective, the Air Force's use of camera clips of PGMs hitting targets so perfectly in Desert Storm, in the Balkans, and in

Afghanistan and Iraq has contributed to the public's awarding of a jurisdiction of sorts on precision in warfare to the Air Force. Concurrently, however, this has raised public expectations that survivability and accuracy will continue to increase and that collateral damage will continue to decrease. Although this requires the officer corps to continue to improve its weapons, it places a bigger burden on the C4ISR system to find, identify, and orchestrate attacks on specific targets. It also carries an inherent endorsement of the effects-based operations concept. Carpet bombing causes immense and random destruction and wreaks havoc, chaos, panic, and terror. Precision attacks on a relatively small number of targets can only be effective if the attacks result in a specific and predictable effect. This, in turn, places a new requirement on the C4ISR system. It must be able to overcome cultural and technological divides and reasonably predict the fallout from different attack scenarios.

As the precision of weapons increases, the number of aircraft, bombs, or missiles required to suppress, damage, or destroy a particular target has decreased. As then Brigadier General David Deptula pointed out in 2001, a one-thousand B-17 aircraft raid in World War II attacked a single, somewhat broadly defined target and had a CEP of 3,300 feet. A "dumb" bomb attack against a single target during the Vietnam War required a "package" of 30 F-4s, and had a CEP of 400 feet. By Desert Storm, the ratio of aircraft per target "flipped" to targets per aircraft, with a single F-117 being able to bomb two separate targets, with a CEP of 10 feet for each target. In the air war over Serbia in 1999, a single B-2 could attack 16 separate targets, each with a CEP of 20 feet.[21] Increases in the range of weapons (or standoff range in the case of aircraft-delivered ordnance) mean that the depth of the potential battle area has increased.

However, these two factors also combine to mean that requirements for pilot "hot stick" flying decrease, while pilot survival rates increase since fewer pilots (because fewer aircraft are required) are exposed to fewer threats (because of increased standoff ranges). Furthermore, since surface-to-surface missiles are also increasing in range and precision, there is a growing jurisdictional dispute as, for example, Navy Tomahawk Land Attack Missiles (TLAMs), as well as Army Tactical Missile Systems (ATACMS) and artillery provide overlapping capabilities to attack some targets. In the opening hours of Desert Storm, TLAMs, conventional air-launched cruise missiles, stealth fighters, fighters, and helicopters were all used to attack targets.

If there is no requirement for pilots or weapons system operators to visually acquire and identify targets through the canopy, the aircraft only serve to bring the weapons close enough to be within firing range. Then the issue becomes one of whether it is more efficient to have flying warehouses of air-to-surface missiles or to fire them individually from the surface. At the extreme end of the weapons progression, the ICBM and its shorter-range cousins could replace the manned bomber and fighter-bomber, and SAMs could replace the manned fighter-interceptor. In the middle lie solutions like unmanned combat air vehicles (UCAVs), which provide long loiter times over targets, and which could serve as fighters, actually engaging targets, or flying warehouses—all with "pilots" safely on the ground "flying" the UCAVs via joysticks or computer keyboards. At the near end, heroic and visionary warriors continue to fly aircraft, use as many launch and leave weapons as possible, and watch as combat decision making continues to migrate out of the cockpit and into the C4ISR system.

CHAPTER 4

A Flying Culture Obscures the Changing Air Force Missions

Although most Air Force officers profess ignorance with respect to the rising importance of C4ISR transformation, the trends are not only clear with respect to historical development but are also supported in Air Force statistics. This chapter briefly reviews data on the various self-described Air Force fields of expertise and jurisdictions—not by examining what is said in speeches and statements but by looking at the way the Air Force has presented its organizational structure and weights of effort over the years in the annual *United States Air Force Statistical Digest* series. This methodology also reveals a flying culture bias in the Air Force's reporting of its missions and structure. However, despite the near exclusion of non-flying combat and operational units, there is ample data demonstrating the rising importance of C4ISR systems and people in the Air Force's ability to execute its missions. As Abbott notes, a profession's expertise evolves in response to jurisdictional competition, the creation of new jurisdictions, and the demise of old ones.

THE CHANGING AIR FORCE SENSE OF MISSIONS

The 1947 USAF *Statistical Digest*, which covers the Air Force's establishment as an independent service in September 1947, is divided into the following parts: (1) Combat Groups; (2) Personnel, Military and Civilian; (3) Training; (4) Aircraft and Materiel; (5) Flight Operations; (6) Miscellaneous; and (7) Civilian Components (Air National Guard, Air Force Reserve, Air Force Reserve Officer Training Corps).[1] This is a relatively straightforward view of how the Air Force officer corps saw its major activities. The USAF *Statistical Digest* led off with the Air Force's raison d'être, air combat units. The rest of the sections described supporting functions. The Air Force required people, who in turn required training. The Air Force also required aircraft and other materiel. The USAF *Statistical Digest* then provided a summary of the Air Force's flying operations, the heart of its perceived expertise and jurisdiction, and concluded with its reserve component. The simplicity of this approach was not continued in later volumes of the *Statistical Digest*. Nevertheless, it still forms a good starting point for the Air Force officer corps' view of its expertise.

The early Air Force officer corps initially possessed three areas of combat expertise, which coincidentally mirrored its three types of combat aircraft: (1) bombers, which were the basis of strategic aerial bombardment and long-range, bomber-based reconnaissance; (2) fighters, which were the basis of air-to-air combat, whether as bomber escorts, combat air patrols, or air defense; fighter air-to-ground attack; and fighter-based tactical reconnaissance; and (3) transports, which transported ground troops and equipment in the theater of combat operations, including transport for airborne assaults. In addition, specific types of flying units such as weather reconnaissance, air rescue and Military Air Transport Service (MATS) directly supported the combat forces.[2] These are examples of further fields in which the Air Force held some jurisdiction.

The Air Force officer corps had a monopoly jurisdiction over strategic aerial bombardment, the foundation for its claim for an independent Air Force. It would have been senseless for society to allow the creation of an independent Air Force officer corps without granting it this monopoly. However, the Air Force officer corps did not have a monopoly jurisdiction over fighter operations, since Navy and Marine Corps aviation had similar aircraft and missions. There was a division of labor within the Department of Defense that generally kept Navy and Marine Corps aviation with things "naval" and Air Force fighters with either independent Air Force operations or in support of Army operations. However, direct support of Army operations as in close air support missions ruptures a jurisdictional distinction between the Army and Air Force. Consequently, it remains a source of jurisdictional tension between the officer corps of the two services. The Army and Air Force have also periodically clashed over in-theater air transport for the same reason.[3] With respect to long-range air transport, Navy long-range transports and aircrews were subordinated to MATS, lending credence to the Air Force's claims to be both the lead and the dominant force in this jurisdiction. However, the Navy and Army both retained short-range transport aircraft, and MATS contracted out the transport of some military lift requirements to civilian air carriers.[4] In addition, the Navy provided its own weather and air rescue capabilities.

There was no indication of any C4ISR role in the early USAF *Statistical Digest* volumes, because at that time, Air Force tactical or combat units were by definition flying units. No ground-based units were listed. In addition, all other flying units were clearly of secondary importance. They and the unlisted ground-based units existed to support the "pointy end of the spear"—the flying combat forces.

However, by 1952 things began to change, and missions became the basis of differentiation instead of aircraft types. At the highest level, the table provided in the *Statistical Digest* was divided into three categories: the first was Combat and Airlift, the second was Support Forces, and the third was Separate Squadrons. By 1953, Combat forces were subdivided into strategic, air defense, and tactical. Strategic war assets included heavy and medium bombers, strategic reconnaissance, both heavy and medium, and fighter escorts, also known as strategic fighters. Air defense became a world unto itself with fighter-interceptors, which is interesting because the fighter-interceptors were almost useless without the ground radar and the command and control system's direction. Tactical war assets included light bombers, fighter-bombers, and tactical reconnaissance aircraft. The Airlift category contained the troop carrier wings. Support Forces were initially limited to air refueling and MATS.

Separate Squadrons included a "Pilotless Bomber, Light" listing.[5] The pilotless bomber squadrons received their own category in 1954, and in 1955, the separate squadrons were combined under Support Forces. The pilotless bomber squadrons (guided missile squadrons) were listed as a separate category under Support Forces because they were not yet operational. Nevertheless, this was an important but complex step. On the one hand, the inclusion of pilotless bombers indicated a rather visionary professional readiness to move beyond manned flight as a combat expertise. On the other hand, calling the surface-to-surface missiles pilotless bombers staked out a jurisdictional claim. Surface-to-surface missiles might appear to some people to be essentially artillery, but bombers, whether manned or unmanned, clearly belonged in the Air Force officer corps' monopoly jurisdiction. Calling the surface-to-surface missiles pilotless bombers also cast missiles in the role of things flying, with all the inherent mystique. Consequently, pilotless bomber units, and later tactical and strategic missile units, were included with aircraft units in the USAF *Statistical Digest* series.

The USAF *Statistical Digest* for fiscal year 1957 marked another change in the conceptualization of Air Force combat forces. Categorization by missions was beginning to give way to categorization by major command. At the highest level, Air Force combat-type forces were divided into Major Wings and Support Forces (Flying). Major Wings were divided into Strategic, Air Defense, and Tactical, and the guided missile squadrons were switched from support to tactical combat forces. The term Support Forces (Flying) indicates that there were indeed non-flying support forces that did not merit inclusion in the table. The Support Forces (Flying) included "troop carrier group, assault," air refueling squadrons, MATS units, which eventually contained the air rescue, mapping and charting and weather reconnaissance aircraft, and separate units. However, air refueling units were divided into SAC (Strategic Air Command) and TAC (Tactical Air Command) units. The troop carrier units were also split, with 10 squadrons going to the tactical forces, and two listed under separate units.[6] These changes resulted in a clearer categorization along the lines of the Air Force's major command structure.

Strategic bombing with tanker support, strategic reconnaissance aircraft, and some fighter escorts meant basically SAC. From World War II into the 1960s, SAC was the strategic force of the United States. SAC's bombers were the only force capable of providing the long-range delivery of nuclear or conventional weapons to targets deep in the enemy homeland. The Air Force officer corps had full and undisputed jurisdiction in this area.

The second area of potential jurisdiction was represented by the air defense interceptors of Air Defense Command (ADC). However, counting fighter-interceptor units without mentioning the ADC radar, command and control, and communications network that directed the fighter-interceptors was myopic and representative of a culture that measured importance in terms of aircraft and flying. Nevertheless, the EC-121 Airborne Early Warning and Control squadrons, which were a flying element of the ADC command and control system, began being reported under Separate Units in 1954. The Air Force held a near monopoly jurisdiction over the strategic air defense of the continental United States.

The third, but the most diverse, jurisdiction was the wide range of tactical air forces that ran the gamut from tactical bombers to fighters, tankers, transport aircraft, and the new-fangled tactical surface-to-surface missiles. The tactical surface-to-surface missiles gave the Air Force a new weapon in terms of technology and potentially stretched the conventional understanding of airpower, but the surface-to-surface missile was cast as one of many types of "flying" activities under the general jurisdiction of tactical air operations. The tactical forces were found in Tactical Air Command (TAC) or in the geographically based tactical commands of the Air Force in Europe (USAFE) and the Pacific Air Forces (PACAF), formerly the Far East Air Forces (FEAF). The Air Force continued to share the tactical air jurisdiction with the other services.

The fourth, and supporting, jurisdiction was strategic or long-range transport, embodied by MATS, with no change to the Air Force officer corps' jurisdictional dominance over Navy long-range air transport and control over contract civilian air transport. The rest of the Air Force supported these jurisdictional claims and forces.

In 1958, strategic missile units were included under strategic units. One could argue that this new technology formed a new jurisdiction. However, the Air Force officer corps had already switched from a platform-based differentiation of skill sets to a mission, or major command, based differentiation. From this new perspective, strategic missile units provided the same deep strike that bombers did. Consequently, the technology redefined the jurisdiction from strategic manned bombardment to simply strategic bombardment. Nevertheless, strategic offense was now on the way to being divided into three distinct fields as seen from a technology perspective, with each vying for the same work and competing for a piece of the same jurisdiction. The Air Force officer corps had monopolies over manned and unmanned strategic bombers (MRBMs/ICBMs), but the Navy officer corps was creating its submarine-launched ballistic missile (SLBM) jurisdiction.

In the USAF *Statistical Digest* for fiscal year 1959, combat flying support forces were also divided into strategic, air defense, and tactical forces for the first time.[7] This made clear the allocation of the airborne early warning and control, radar evaluation, electronic countermeasures, tow targets, and drone squadrons to air defense combat flying support forces. Fighters were removed from the strategic forces, and the rather visionary "intercept missile" units were added to air defense forces. The new categorization indicates that the air defense forces contained a wide variety of innovative fields. The airborne early warning and control aircraft (EC-121) squadrons were listed through the late 1970s.[8] The inclusion of the EC-121s was the first reference, albeit elliptical, to the command and control, or C4ISR, expertise.

The surface-to-air interceptor missile (unmanned interceptors) system introduced new technology that competed with manned fighters for jurisdiction over the downing of enemy aircraft as a subset of the broader air defense jurisdiction. Officers sitting in front of radar screens on the ground directed the fighter-interceptors and launched the surface-to-air missiles that would shoot down enemy aircraft. In addition, radar evaluation units and electronic countermeasures units worked in an area that eventually would be seen as a separate jurisdiction—electronic warfare, which also formed the initial basis of counter-command-and-control warfare. Finally drone target squadrons offered a capability that competed with towed targets briefly before replacing them entirely. The ability to control drones, however, offered the opportunity for the large-scale control or flying of unmanned aircraft or unmanned combat aircraft. Consequently, strategic air defense was heavily involved in C4ISR and visionary forms of warfare.

The USAF *Statistical Digest* for fiscal year 1966 used new category titles and provided definitions for the first time of the forces' primary tasks. Strategic combat and strategic combat flying support forces were lumped together under the title Strategic Retaliatory, which demonstrated the officer corps' interest in keeping pace with the political rhetoric of the day. The nuclear arsenal was now conceptually retaliatory. Previously, *strategic* carried the connotation of *offensive*. Strategic Retaliatory forces had "long-range weapons delivery" as their primary task. These forces included heavy and light bombardment, strategic reconnaissance, air refueling, the Post-Attack Command and Control System, missile augmentation (AGM-28 equipped B-52) squadrons, and strategic missile squadrons. The missile augmentation squadrons represent another example of acceptance of a visionary technology since the addition of cruise missiles changed the B-52 bomber employment scenario from that of the heroic warrior flying over the target to that of a launch vehicle simply bringing the second stage within range of its target.

Air defense and air defense flying support forces were lumped together under Continental Air and Missile Defense. Continental Air and Missile Defense forces' primary task was "defending the US against enemy aerospace attack." The Soviet Union's ability to attack the U.S. homeland from the air and from space was acknowledged. This indirectly implied a jurisdiction for ADC to develop technology in space to both detect and defend against enemy missiles and enemy exploitation of space. However, the only forces listed were the fighter-interceptor, airborne early warning and control, drone, defense system evaluation, and interceptor missile squadrons. SAC's Post-Attack Command and Control System and ADC's airborne early warning and control units were included in the table because they were aircraft-based. The rest of the Air Force's command, control, and communications systems, being ground-based, were not culturally considered combat or combat support forces.

Tactical combat and tactical combat flying support forces were combined under the title General Purpose. General Purpose forces had the primary task of "attaining air superiority over battle areas, providing close air support and interdicting enemy supply and communications facilities." These forces included tactical bomber, tactical fighter, tactical reconnaissance, tactical fighter interceptors in PACAF, USAFE, and Iceland, special air warfare (special operations), tactical air control system (forward air controller airborne), airborne command post (CINCS), and tactical missile squadrons. Tactical air refueling squadrons were eliminated.

The inclusion of the tactical air control system units is an explicit reference to the command and control system, or C4ISR, expertise. However, only Forward Air Control (FAC) units, which are flying units, were included. Nevertheless, the FAC category, which is just the tip of the command and control system, continued as a USAF *Statistical Digest* category through 2003 and beyond.[9] It is also noteworthy that the officer corps understood the importance of communications in modern warfare enough to warrant listing enemy communications facilities as a target, even though Air Force command, control, and communications units, being non-flying, did not merit inclusion in the table.

Airlift and Sealift became its own, equal category containing military airlift, aeromedical airlift, and special air mission military airlift squadrons. Airlift and Sealift had the primary task of "air logistics support." General Support contained the usual leftovers of mapping and charting, aerospace rescue and recovery, weather reconnaissance, and the National Emergency Airborne Command Post (NEACP, which began to be reported in 1963). General Support forces' primary task was vaguely defined as providing "specified technical services."[10]

The USAF *Statistical Digest* for fiscal year (FY) 1967 established tactical electronic warfare units in the General Purpose category and changed several category titles. The concept of strategic retaliation with its inherent denial of preemption was short-lived, and Strategic Retaliatory became Strategic—Offensive. Continental Air and Missile Defense became Strategic—Defensive. General Support became Intelligence and Communications, without changing the types of units listed or the category's definition.[11] Although Intelligence and Communications implied a much broader C4ISR category that could include a variety of ground-based units, non-flying units were still excluded.

In fact, the title Intelligence and Communications was misleading, since it still only contained mapping, charting, and geodesy, weather service, aerial target tow, aerospace rescue and recovery, and the NEACP units. The actual C4ISR intelligence and communications systems remained shrouded in mystery.

This categorization and the basic definitions of primary tasks remained in effect through the USAF *Statistical Digest* for fiscal year 1980, after which the USAF *Statistical Digest* was discontinued until the USAF *Statistical Digest Estimate* for fiscal year 1991. In the interim, the 1981 USAF *Summary* and the 1982 USAF *Summary* both contained essentially the same table, with the categories of Strategic-Offense, Strategic-Defense, General Purpose, and Airlift. The Intelligence and Communications category and units were no longer reported.[12] Then the table dropped out of the USAF *Summary* series until the 1986 USAF *Summary*, when it appeared under the title "USAF Flying Squadrons by Function." All categorizations were dropped in the new table. It simply listed the numbers of squadrons by type. However, the table included ground-based command and control units for the first time, despite the fact that the title specifically limited the table to flying squadrons.[13] The inclusion of the ground-based command and control units offers the first direct evidence that such units are a particular Air Force officer corps' expertise and a potential claim for jurisdiction in their own right, because these are the only ground-based, non-missile units ever included in these tables. Consequently, their inclusion is more significant than that of the airborne early warning and control aircraft and FAC flying units. This version of the table continued through the reintroduction of the *Statistical Digest (Abridged) Estimate* for fiscal year 1991.

There was a general consolidation of the table in 1997. In the process, the table's contents reverted to flying squadrons only, although the title, "AF Squadrons by Mission Area" no longer appeared to limit the table to flying squadrons. The table dropped all mention of ground-based command and control units.[14] In addition, ICBM squadrons, which had been reported since 1958 and obviously continued to exist and make up a major part of Air Force combat power, were also dropped. Some C4ISR and visionary warfare units were briefly exposed, but then covered up by a heroic warrior culture that stresses the airplane and manned flying as the pillars of the Air Force officer corps' expertise.

The review of the USAF *Statistical Digest* series reveals that the Air Force officer corps consistently made claims of jurisdiction in four areas: (1) strategic attack; (2) strategic air defense of the United States; (3) tactical air forces; and (4) air transport. From the USAF *Statistical Digest* perspective, the flying parts of the strategic air defense forces eventually merged into tactical forces, leaving three jurisdictions. However, another interpretation is that the strategic air defense jurisdiction has largely passed to the reserve forces, and its two active duty successors, space and C4ISR, are generally ignored by the USAF *Statistical Digest* series.

With respect to the degree of monopoly over the three remaining jurisdictions recognized in the USAF *Statistical Digest*, the Air Force provides the strategic bomber and the ICBM legs of the strategic triad, which is the complete strategic attack jurisdiction. Consequently, the Air Force officer corps shares, and to a degree therefore competes, with the Navy within the strategic attack jurisdiction. Air Force tactical forces continue to share, and therefore compete, with the other services in the tactical air force jurisdiction. The Air Force continues to provide the bulk of long-range air transport among the services, but is supplemented by contracted civilian air transport, which in turn must be seen as the biggest competitor in the long-range air transport jurisdiction. With respect to tactical, or short-range, airlift, there continues to be some overlap and therefore competition with the other services, although the Air Force retains a monopoly over airplanes capable of conducting a large-scale airborne assault.

Throughout the entire USAF *Statistical Digest* history from 1947 through 2003, satellite control, communications, and a variety of operational and operational support ground-based squadrons were never mentioned. It is as if these missions were never part of the Air Force or at least not important enough to be mentioned in any breakdown of combat and combat support squadrons by mission area. They may have been excluded because they were seen as providing purely support functions, somewhat akin to maintenance squadrons, which were never counted.

Of course, there is a difference between the space missions and maintenance support. For example, reconnaissance satellites do the same work as reconnaissance aircraft, whose units were consistently included in the USAF *Statistical Digest*. One might be tempted to argue that ignorance or a sense of secrecy might also account for the exclusion of space units. However, the table immediately following the "AF Squadrons by Mission Area" table is invariably the "Aircraft & Missile Procurement" table, which frequently contains information on ICBMs, space launch vehicles, or satellite procurement.[15] The information was clearly available. It simply was not included. It is also possible that the officer corps somehow considered ground-launched and ground-controlled satellites to be somehow non-flying, even though ICBMs, tactical surface-to-surface missiles, and SAMs were included in the table until the mid-1990s.

In any event, it is noteworthy that the Air Force devotes so much coverage to the largely flying-based fields of strategic offense, tactical, and strategic airlift in which it has no jurisdictional monopolies. By comparison, air defense and its byproducts of command and control and space get short shrift. A reading of the USAF *Statistical Digest* series for the Air Force officer corps' fields of expertise yields the conclusion that C4ISR does not appear to be the foundation for any Air Force jurisdictional claim, and space, where the Air Force has a near monopoly jurisdiction, is nonexistent. Consequently, the pervasiveness of the flying culture results in a skewed view of the Air Force and its missions. Fortunately, other statistics present a fuller picture.

SQUADRONS AS INDICATORS OF CHANGE

The numbers of squadrons the Air Force assigned to particular types of work provide a gauge of the relative weight of effort between different jurisdictions. Figure 4.1 shows the above-mentioned shift in the Air Force's weight of effort over time between the four amalgamated categories of Strategic Offense, Strategic Defense, Tactical, and Strategic Airlift.

Strategic Offense squadrons, the Air Force's original jurisdiction, were the early emphasis. Their numbers peaked with the Sputnik, heralding the introduction of strategic missiles, which are included in the strategic offense squadron count. The number of Tactical squadrons declined in 1950, partly because of the general post–World War II drawdown, but also because forces were siphoned off to create the rapidly growing Strategic Defense squadrons, which represented a new Air Force jurisdiction. The number of Tactical squadrons increased dramatically in response to the Korean War, followed by another steep buildup, which peaked during the Vietnam War. The Tactical squadrons remained the highest proportion of squadrons per jurisdiction from the mid-1960s onward.[16] The number of Strategic Defense squadrons climbed quickly but then declined in the face of the ICBMs. The fighter-interceptor force was useless against Soviet ICBMs, and the mission was eventually passed to the reserve forces.

That depicts the story as told in the USAF *Statistical Digest* series. However, using the same data but switching to percentages and removing all of the

Figure 4.1
Strategic Offense, Strategic Defense, Tactical, and Strategic Airlift Amalgamated "Flying" Squadrons Based on USAF *Statistical Digest* Reporting

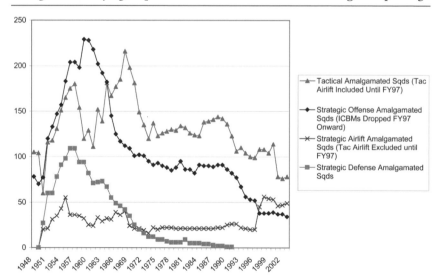

command and control—including the FAC flying squadrons—as well as the intelligence, reconnaissance, and electronic warfare squadrons and combining them into one new amalgamated C4ISR expertise reveals different trends. C4ISR now appears to be historically at least as important as Strategic Airlift. Furthermore, the relative weight of the C4ISR expertise in terms of squadrons shows an overall positive growth trend since its nadir in the early 1960s (see figure 4.2).

The USAF *Statistical Digest* series' exclusion of space squadron data presents a skewed, heroic warrior view of Air Force officer corps that does not reflect the real distribution of missions within the officer corps. Consequently, *Air Force Magazine*'s reporting on space squadrons, which reaches back into the late 1980s, presents a more accurate representation of the distribution of missions. In figure 4.3, active-duty Air Force space squadrons are amalgamated into Space Operations (space operations, launch, control, and aggressor squadrons) and space C4ISR (space communications, warning, and surveillance squadrons), which are then added to the existing C4ISR category. When the space squadrons are added to the mix, two things become evident. First, the total number of C4ISR squadrons now clearly exceeds the number of Strategic Airlift squadrons for the duration of the reporting. Second, the number of squadrons in the Space Operations amalgamation is getting very close to the number of squadrons in the Strategic Airlift amalgamation. This is fitting, since space operations exemplify a visionary form of warfare for which the Air Force officer corps is seeking a monopoly jurisdiction. Furthermore,

Figure 4.2
Strategic Offense, Strategic Defense, Tactical, Strategic Airlift, and C4ISR Amalgamated "Flying" Squadrons by Percentage, FY1948–FY1996

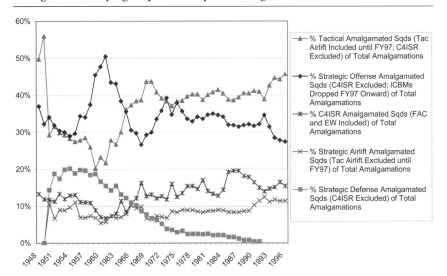

Figure 4.3
Strategic Offense, Strategic Defense, Tactical, Strategic Airlift, C4ISR, and Space Operations Amalgamated Squadrons by Percentage

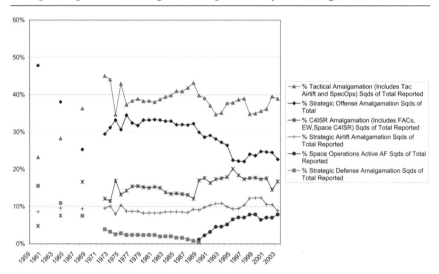

if one were to add the Space Operations squadrons to the C4ISR amalgamation, the resulting total percentage would rival that of the Strategic Offense squadrons.

AIRCRAFT AS INDICATORS OF CHANGE

It is also possible to look at the Air Force's aircraft for clues to the officer corps' changing jurisdictional claims, realizing that as in the preceding discussion, concentrating on aircraft largely ignores non-flying fields such as command and control, missiles, and space. Starting with a look at simple quantities of aircraft, it is apparent that active-duty Air Force total aircraft holdings peaked in the 1956/1957 time period (see figure 4.4). Despite the Vietnam War, the total number of active (i.e., not in long-term storage) aircraft generally declined until 1976, with another decline at the end of the Cold War.

In terms of the specific aircraft themselves, figure 4.5 shows the ratio of various types of aircraft to fighter/attack aircraft.[17] Although fighter/attack aircraft have dominated since the early 1960s, the C4ISR aircraft to fighter ratio has generally been close to the fighter to tanker ratio since the mid-1970s.

There are also qualitative issues involved with Air Force aircraft. For example, the B-52's long domination of the bomber world is indicative of a long-term shift in the Air Force officer corps' emphasis away from the manned bomber, supporting the jurisdiction of Strategic Offense, to the manned

Figure 4.4
Active-Duty Air Force Aircraft Inventory per Fiscal Year

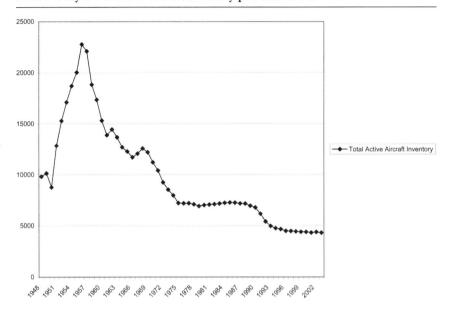

Figure 4.5
Ratios: Fighter/Attack to Other Types of Aircraft

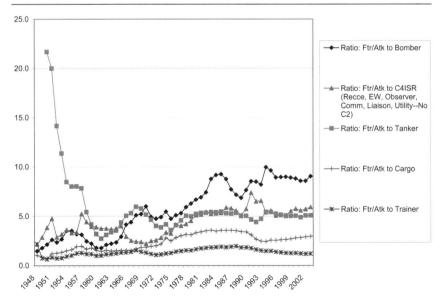

fighter, supporting the Tactical jurisdiction. Since a bomber cannot strike targets as quickly, as deeply, and with as much impunity as ICBMs, new strategic bombers have been a hard sell to the American public. New bombers are extremely expensive, and the B-52 platform has proven to be very adaptable. The competition that the Air Force's manned bomber faces for jurisdictional dominance over Strategic Offense comes not from other bombers but from its own cruise missiles and ICBMs and the Navy's SLBMs. The Army and Navy officer corps both gave up any rights to strategic bombers in the series of inter-profession agreements that led to the Air Force's independence, as well as in later agreements resolving jurisdictional disputes.[18] Furthermore, the SALT and START nuclear arms control agreements placed limits on the two Air Force legs (bombers and ICBMs) of the American nuclear triad.[19] Consequently, any bomber, old or new, arguably provides sufficient justification to maintain an Air Force bomber-based claim for a share of the Strategic Offense jurisdiction. Nevertheless, the Air Force has been able to continue to sell the need for a manned strategic bomber and procure limited numbers of B-1s and B-2s.

In addition, there has been a general blurring of the once clearly distinct *strategic* and *tactical* realms. This blurring is the result of improved, more bomber-like fighters with respect to combat radius and bomb loads on the one hand, and the ability of the Air Force's ability to achieve air supremacy so that bombers can be used in tactical roles without undue fear of losses on the other.[20] The post–Cold War and post-9/11 world offered opportunities for bombers in tactical, non-nuclear war. Bombers still can carry larger ordnance loads further, but they have also become more fighter-like by carrying precision-guided munitions (PGMs), which shift the emphasis away from simple bomb tonnage to the number of targets that can accurately be attacked per sortie. Culturally, the B-52 crew of six shrinks to four in the B-1 and to two in the B-2. In addition, the B-1 image of variable-wing and supersonic technology is quite fighter-like, and the B-2, with its stealth and flying-wing technology, is certainly not reminiscent of an old bomber—the biggest feasible box with wings to carry the most fuel and bombs possible. To be useful, however, all bombers must be able to provide not only strategic attack but a complementary role in the Tactical jurisdiction—specifically, in the blurred, non-nuclear, strategic/tactical air-to-ground area.

The tanker story is not quite the same as that of the bombers. Tankers cannot simply be replaced by ever-more-capable fighters. Although the KC-135 was originally tied to the B-52 intercontinental bombing mission, tankers have been instrumental in giving fighters the range to cause the blurring of tactical and strategic bombing. Furthermore, tankers no longer just service bombers and fighters. Today's Air Force tankers support cargo, reconnaissance, and command and control aircraft. In addition, Air Force tankers provide the fuel to extend the ranges of Navy, Marine, and a host of allied aircraft in flying operations and exercises conducted with the Air Force. In fact, the Air Force has a near monopoly in this jurisdiction—flying gas stations in the sky.

Naval tankers are much more limited in range, speed, fuel offload, quantities of aircraft, and types of refueling connections. Outside of the United States, few countries have more than a handful of big tanker aircraft. However, the long life of the KC-135 fleet, extended by modification and rejuvenation programs, is indicative of an apparent Air Force officer corps willingness to minimize investment in the supporting jurisdiction of air-to-air refueling. This could potentially be the result of a perception that it is in a safe professional or "market" position with its near monopoly holdings.

The story that fighter aircraft tell is quite different. The Air Force officer corps places a premium on possessing state-of-the-art technology in fighter aircraft and their weapons systems. This also means that fighter pilots are more accustomed to changing technology in their workplace. This is at least partly because competition is intense in the fighter world. First of all, Air Force fighters are competing with the other services for a slice of the Tactical jurisdiction. For example, Naval and Marine aircraft have participated in Desert Storm, the Balkan operations, and Operation Enduring Freedom and Operation Iraqi Freedom. These aircraft, flying from carriers or air bases, have capabilities comparable to those of the Air Force fighters. Army helicopters compete with the Air Force fighters in the expertise of close-air-support, and Army Tactical Missile System (ATACMS) and Navy Tomahawk Land Attack Missiles (TLAMs) compete with fighters for jurisdiction over deeper strikes. Naval and Army surface-to-air missile systems (SAMs) also compete with fighters for jurisdiction over portions of air defense. Furthermore, fighters compete directly with enemy aircraft and systems during times of conflict. Bombers do not compete with enemy bombers in head-to-head competition, nor do cargo aircraft. Instead, bombers penetrate enemy airspace and fall prey primarily to enemy fighters and SAMs. Bomber crews can do little more than shake their fists at enemy bombers bound in the opposite direction. They have their bombs to drop on ground targets and electronic and infrared countermeasures equipment to protect them from enemy missiles, but no air-to-air missiles. Cargo aircraft typically fly over friendly territory and seek to avoid both enemy fighters and SAMs, since they can do little more than run away and use their more limited electronic and infrared countermeasures equipment.

Fighters, however, hunt all enemy aircraft on both sides of the figurative border and must deal with enemy SAMs and antiaircraft artillery (AAA) in the border area and beyond as they attack aircraft or ground targets. At this level, however, competition is not over jurisdictional claims directly, but about survival. After survival, however, winning in an effective and efficient manner is still important because it provides the foundation for keeping or enlarging jurisdictional claims. Consequently, the high levels of competition against other services' aircraft and systems, the Air Force's own bombers, and enemy aircraft and systems result in a need for heavy Air Force investment in fighters simply to maintain its market share of the multifaceted Tactical jurisdiction.

The Air Force's C4ISR aircraft are critical parts of the larger C4ISR complex that provides command and control over the entire air war. However, the quantity of C4ISR aircraft is misleading, since it underrepresents Air Force C4ISR capabilities; some have been transferred to space-based systems and others remain ground-based. One might make a similar case for bombers vis-à-vis ICBMs, but none of the other aircraft missions have been transferred to space.

FLYING HOURS AS INDICATORS OF CHANGE

Flying hours are another Air Force metric that provides similar data on the evolution of a separate Air Force C4ISR expertise. The caveats remain, since flying hours are tied to aircraft and exclude space and ground systems. In terms of overall flying hours, the flying hours roughly parallel the number of active aircraft. However, dividing total active-duty active flying hours by total active-duty active aircraft yields a slightly different presentation of the story. Whereas total flying hours in 2003 are less than a quarter of the Air Force's peak total flying hours in the mid-1950s, the flying hours per aircraft ratio shows considerably less variation, and clearer peaks for the Korean War, Vietnam, and Desert Storm, suggesting a total peacetime ratio in the 400 hours per aircraft range (see figure 4.6).

Figure 4.6
Total Flying Hours per Active-Duty Active Aircraft per Year

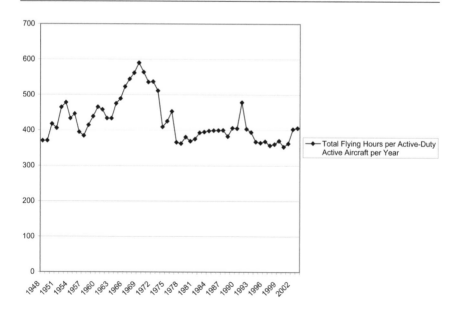

However, there is some variation by aircraft type. It is clear that cargo aircraft consistently fly significantly more hours per individual aircraft than any of the other categories.[21] This makes intuitive sense, in that cargo aircraft tend to fly long missions. Furthermore, the cargo hours per aircraft ratios demonstrate buildups for Korea, Cold War events, Vietnam, Desert Storm, and post–9/11 operations.

For an examination of the Air Force's allocation of the percentage of flying hours per aircraft type, see figure 4.7. This chart indicates a clear split in the Air Force's weight of emphasis. The allocation of the percentage of flying hours by aircraft type indicates that historically half or more of the Air Force flying hour allocation goes to trainer and cargo aircraft. Once again, the Air Force is allocating a large portion of a measurable resource to fields in which it has no monopoly jurisdiction. That is, there is considerable competition from the civilian world and other military services to train pilots and transport people and material with aircraft. The bomber aircraft flying hour allocation peaked in the early 1960s, and has generally been in decline since then. This indicates a shift and a gradual lowering of emphasis on manned bombers—despite the fact that manned bombers provided the Air Force with its original monopoly jurisdiction over Strategic Offense. The post-Vietnam boost in the flying hour allocation to fighter-attack aircraft to the 25%–30% range of the total Air Force flying hours indicates a clear shift in prioritization favoring the Tactical jurisdiction.[22] The relative allocation of flying hours to tanker aircraft has grown over the Air Force's history, indicating the growing importance of tankers beyond the role of supporting strategic bombers. The

Figure 4.7
Percentage of Flying Hours by Aircraft Type

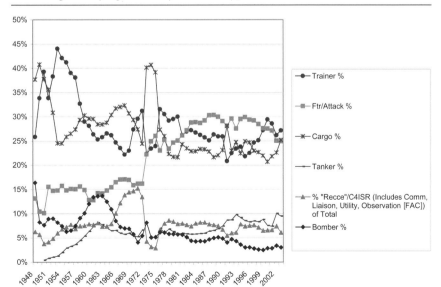

surge of tanker hours per aircraft ratio during Desert Storm and beyond is indicative of the importance of air-to-air refueling in the Balkan operations, no-fly zones over Iraq, and post–9/11 operations. Finally, C4ISR continues to be a relatively consistent and measurable categorization in the Air Force's flying hour allocation, in spite of the transfer of some C4ISR capabilities to space.

PERSONNEL CATEGORIES AS INDICATORS OF CHANGE

Another way to look at how the Air Force officer corps has changed its sense of mission or jurisdictional priorities is to examine the Air Force allocation of its officers between commands. Figure 4.8 shows that the C4ISR major command amalgamation (from Air Force Communications Command, the Air Force Security Service and various successor intelligence commands and agencies, and Air Force Space Command) shows relatively steady growth, from zero at the beginning of the independent Air Force to 9% of the total Air Force officers in 2003.

If one looks at officers by the career field specialty in which they are currently assigned, the combination of pilots and navigators, the majority of whom are pilots, has been the historic leader (see figure 4.9).[23] However, the percentage of pilots and navigator billets has been in a relatively steady decline, from 36% of the total officers in 1961 to 22% in 2003. The C4ISR officer career

Figure 4.8
Percentage of Officers per Major-Command-Type Amalgamated Groups

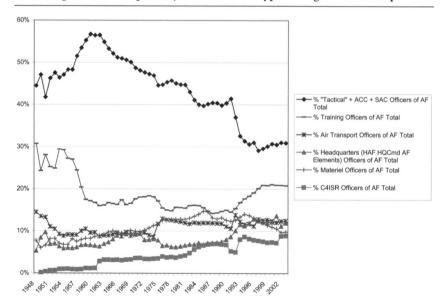

Figure 4.9
Percentage of Total Air Force Officers Serving in Various Amalgamated Career Field Billets

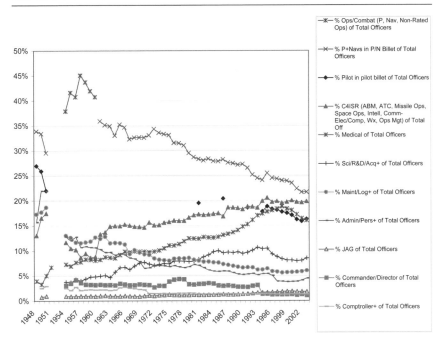

field billet amalgamation has been the second most populated amalgamated career field billet amalgamation for most of the Air Force's history.[24] In fact, the C4ISR career field billet amalgamation matched the number of pilots in pilot billets in 1991 and clearly exceeded them from the mid-1990s onward. The C4ISR billet amalgamation accounted for 20% of the total Air Force officers in 2003. The third leading officer career field billet amalgamation was medical.[25] The medical billet amalgamation accounted for 16% of the total Air Force officer corps in 2003. In fact, from 1998 through 2002, officers in the medical amalgamation billets actually formed a higher percentage of the total officer corps than pilots serving in pilot billets.

From the perspective of the Air Force's career field billet allocation, the Air Force officer corps prioritized its weight of effort in the following rank order: manned flying, that is, pilots and navigators, followed closely by C4ISR (including space and missile operations), and then medical care. From a jurisdictional perspective, manned flight is not a jurisdiction that the Air Force monopolizes, although it does of course have monopolies or near monopolies over certain areas within the jurisdiction, such as strategic bombers and air-to-air refueling tankers. The Air Force is dominant in the C4ISR/space/missile operations jurisdiction, at least within the confines of aerospace warfare, but there are competitors for pieces of the total jurisdiction. The Air Force certainly has no monopoly over the medical jurisdiction. At best, flight medicine might offer a niche expertise, but medical practitioners outside the Air Force officer corps also practice aspects of flight medicine. Furthermore, medicine is often taken as one of the original professions, which implies that Air Force doctors, for example, might already have a sense of professional responsibilities that might compete or at least coexist with those of the Air Force officer corps. Finally, with respect to developing, buying, and maintaining aircraft and other equipment, Air Force officers might have experience dealing with specific types of aircraft and equipment, but certainly not for the entire realm of activity in these fields. Furthermore, few in society would view the developing, buying, and maintaining of equipment as knowledge meriting the status of a profession.

BUDGET INFORMATION AS AN INDICATOR OF CHANGING JURISDICTIONAL CLAIMS

In accordance with the old auditor's advice to "follow the money," figure 4.10 shows the allocation of Air Force total obligational authority (TOA) by major force program, with data from 1964 through 2003. Once again, the graphs reflect the growth of C4ISR. The Intelligence/Communications category started out just below General Purpose Forces at roughly 15% of the total TOA in 1964, but began a climb from the mid-1980s, actually exceeded General Purpose Forces allocations in the early 1990s, and ended in solid second place at 24% of the total Air Force TOA in 2003.

CONCLUSION

The discussion and the various figures presented in this chapter reveal that the Air Force and its officer corps are not static. The weight of effort given to a particular mission varies over time, and new fields develop and are incorporated into the profession. As new types of work were developed and added to the profession, jurisdictions and the Air Force position within given jurisdictions changed. Overall, the biggest changes in the types of work performed by the officer corps are symbolized by the jurisdictions of strategic attack and strategic air defense. In terms of jurisdictional claims, the Air Force officer corps went from a monopoly on strategic attack in 1947 to a shared jurisdiction involving Air Force ICBMs and bombers as well as Navy SLBMs in the 1960s. This jurisdictional distribution still prevails today. Furthermore, within the Air Force, the declining importance of strategic attack relative to other missions, especially those of the tactical or general purpose forces, was evident in a number of the figures presented in this chapter. Many of the charts also captured what appeared to be the total demise of the strategic air defense jurisdiction as the fighter-interceptor mission passed to the reserve forces.

Figure 4.10
Allocation of Air Force Total Obligational Authority (TOA) by Major
Force Program

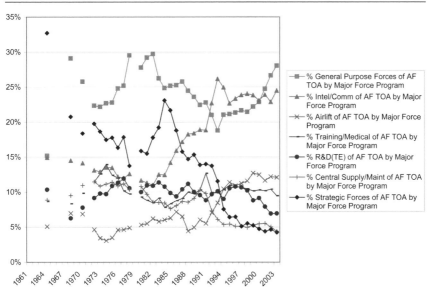

However, this also highlighted the fact that for most of the history of the independent Air Force, the organizational culture emphasized flying units almost to the exclusion of non-flying, ground-based combat and combat support units. For example, of the two active-duty successors of strategic air defense, space was completely ignored in the USAF *Statistical Digest* series, and C4ISR was only tangentially referenced.

Although Air Force reporting on its functional missions was skewed, shifting the metric to an examination of the number of squadrons assigned to a particular work still showed the growth in importance of C4ISR. In fact, in spite of the bias against non-flying squadrons, the number of C4ISR squadrons historically rivaled the number of Strategic Airlift squadrons using USAF *Statistical Digest* data. Switching to *Air Force Magazine* data to include space and C4ISR squadrons yielded two further conclusions. First, the number of C4ISR squadrons exceeded the number of Strategic Airlift squadrons for the duration of the reporting. Second, the increasing number of squadrons in the Space Operations amalgamation was approaching the number of squadrons in the Strategic Airlift amalgamation. Consequently, the data supports the argument that C4ISR is indeed a jurisdiction and that the Air Force office corps is moving to fill it, in combination with a potential jurisdiction for visionary types of warfare.

CHAPTER 5

The Long Shadow of Early Personnel Decisions

The explanation for why pilot general officers have been able to maintain their overrepresentation, while it has disappeared in the lower ranks, lies in structural factors and traditions that led to and maintained the pilot overrepresentation. This chapter in particular deals with two early Air Service and Air Corps stratagems to increase their independence that became public law, and thereby restricted the independent Air Force officer corps' ability to evolve further professionally. The first of these was the concept that the Air Service officer corps should be 90% flying officers, and the second was that only pilots could command flying units. This is followed by a look at a third issue that contributes to the pilot overrepresentation: the officer corps' tendency to equate piloting with officership as embodied in the Aviation Cadet Program.

STRATAGEMS TO INCREASE INDEPENDENCE RESTRICTED THE OFFICER CORPS' EVOLUTION

The revolutionary advocates of an independent air force were fighting to simultaneously create the expertise of airpower manifested in strategic bombing, the jurisdiction of independent air operations, and the profession to fill this new niche. All three aspects were interconnected. Strategic bombing depended on government funding to develop the aircraft, navigation systems, weapons, crews, and command and control system capable of conducting the big bomber raids of World War II.

Since the Army was not supportive of an independent air force, air power advocates turned early to the public and to its representatives to make the case for a new jurisdiction. European, Soviet, and Japanese armies could not march over the North Pole to strike Chicago, and enemy naval forces could do little more than harass the coasts before being driven off and sunk by air-craft and ships. Enemy long-range bombers on the fringes of development, however, would soon be able to strike deep in the American homeland. From this perspective, it was easy to recognize that there was now a significant void in the jurisdiction of national defense. The professions of the Army, Navy, and Marine officer corps had previously been granted specific pieces of juris-diction within the overall national defense umbrella, and none was willing to expend large amounts of its resources on what each considered to be a tertiary task. Only a new breed of cat, the aviator, could take on this newly emerging jurisdiction.

Neither the public nor the government bought the argument hook, line, and sinker, but it was clear where the airpower advocates wanted to go, and Congress took steps that moved gradually in the direction of an independent air force. In 1914, before there was any great interest in an independent air force, Congress established an aviation section within the Signal Corps of the Army, limiting it to 60 aviation officers and 260 aviation enlisted men, all of whom were extra and above the Signal Corps' old ceilings. Officer aviation students had a maximum of one year to prove "their fitness or unfitness for detail as aviation officers," and aviation officers were to be generally detailed for four years to the aviation section.[1] All officers within the aviation section were called *aviation officers*, and the aviation section was basically given all Army things flying with a minimum of guidance on what that would entail.[2] The act also created three ratings: junior military aviator (officer); military aviator (officer); and aviation mechanician (enlisted).

The term "pilot" never appears in the act. Indeed, it is not clear whether aviation officers were expected to be jacks-of-all-trades, flying an airplane one day, observing from a balloon the next, or if they might specialize in some way. Junior military aviators simply had to demonstrate in flights "that they are especially well qualified for military aviation service."[3] The rating of military aviator was restricted to 15 officers in the aviation section and required three years service as junior military aviator. Officer aviation students had to be un-married, lieutenants of the line, and not older than 30. Up to 12 enlisted men at any time could "be instructed in the art of flying," but it is not clear what rating they were to receive, if any. The danger of the activity was highlighted by the rewards. Officer aviation students and military aviators received higher pay, sometimes advanced rank, and a form of life insurance.[4]

The concept called for a rotation of young, unmarried officers through flight training, with the graduates having the opportunity to fill aviation sec-tion billets for up to four years. This was a beginning, but the restrictions on marriage, age, and rank, coupled with the rotational concept, could not provide the basis for the development of an independent profession. Flying was something that a number of junior officers should be exposed to, but their careers remained tied to their original branches in the Army.

In the National Defense Act of 1916, Congress specified that a colonel would command the aviation section within the Signal Corps. Flying also shed its monastic image—officers selected for flying training were no longer required to be unmarried, or to be of specific ranks or ages. The cap on enlisted flying was also removed. Furthermore, the grade of aviator, Signal Corps, was created for direct civilian entrants, to make up for any shortfalls in officer flying personnel, but it was tied to the rank of master signal electrician in terms of pay scales.[5]

The aviation section now had prospects for developing an independent officer profession. It could now generate aviators directly from civilian status, instead of being limited to lieutenants of the line already serving in other Army branches. In addition, legislation mandating aviation officer positions in the field grade ranks meant that at least some aviation officers could potentially stay in the aviation section and not return to their original Army branch. The removal of the age and grade restrictions had the same effect. Finally, removing the restriction on married officers also mainstreamed career prospects within the aviation section. However, except for the lieutenants, the 1916 Act did not specify that any of the captains or field grade aviation officers must actually have any rating, and the junior military aviator and military aviator ratings were still legislatively undefined.

The 1920 Amendment to the 1916 National Defense Act was a significant milestone in the development of an independent aviation officer profession. Congress elevated aviation's status by establishing the Air Service, independent of the Signal Corps, with the Chief of the Air Service having the rank of major general and his single assistant being a brigadier general. Flight pay for officers and enlisted personnel was standardized at 150% of the individual's pay. The Air Service was given 1,514 officer billets in the ranks of second lieutenant to colonel, and 16,000 enlisted billets, of which not more than 2,500 could be occupied by flying cadets.

In a new twist, no more than 10% of the officers below the rank of brigadier general "who fail to qualify as aircraft pilots or as observers within one year after the date of detail or assignment shall be permitted to remain detailed or assigned to the Air Service."[6] Consequently, the Air Service's officer corps was intent on making itself into a very flying-centric organization. If an officer could not qualify as a pilot or observer within one year, he should generally be thrown back to his original Army branch. The Air Service officer corps was to be populated by flyers, either as aircraft pilots or as observers, at the rate of 90% or more. At the time, the Air Service officer ranks were swollen with more than 25% non-flying officers.[7] However, the Chief of the Air Service and his deputy were not required to be flying officers.

The second new twist in the act was the statement that "Flying units shall in all cases be commanded by flying officers."[8] The term *flying officers* was not defined in the act, but the implication was that it included aircraft pilots and observers, since officers with those ratings could remain in the Air Service without restriction. The 1920 Amendment's section on the Air Service was formulated in accordance with the requests of the Air Service's leadership. The act's two new provisions set personnel courses that the Air Corps took to even further extremes, and that the independent Air Force has found difficult to alter.

OF THE AIR SERVICE OFFICERS, 90% SHOULD BE FLYING OFFICERS

The Air Corps did not present an explicit definition of the term flying officer until the 1926 Amendment to the 1916 National Defense Act. A flying officer was defined "as one who has received an aeronautical rating as pilot of service types of aircraft," during time of peace, but "in time of war may include any officer who has received an aeronautical rating as observer."[9] This definition made the term flying officer synonymous with the term pilot. The United States was at peace and expected to be so for the foreseeable future; so an observer rating became almost meaningless. The Air Corps, however, wanted to hedge its bets, realizing that in time of war, pilots might be scarce or inexperienced, so an experienced officer with an observer rating might be better than a new pilot or totally ground-bound officer. The 1926 Amendment further restricted the definition of future peacetime flying officers to pilots of heavier-than-air craft with a minimum number of career total flying hours, while concurrently grandfathering in all officers in the Air Corps with any type of pilot rating, including airship pilots, as flying officers.[10] Officers possessing only observer ratings became a dwindling commodity as the Air Corps implemented a system in which observer training and ratings were given to officers only after they had qualified and earned pilot wings.

The Air Service, together with Congress, continued to tweak the wording of provisions that required that a minimum of 90% of the officers in the Air Service be flying officers. This goal proved to be impossible to meet during World War I, but the 1920 Amendment to the 1916 National Defense Act was effective in reducing the number of non-flying officers or non-pilots to well under the 10% allowable maximum level. When Major General Patrick testified before the Senate Committee on Military Affairs on this issue and on the wording in the House resolution proposing to amend the 1916 and 1920 National Defense Acts, he reported that the Air Service in the spring of 1926 only had 12 non-flying officers—out of approximately 900 total officers.[11] That is, 98.7% of the total Air Service officers were flying officers, that is, pilots according to the 1926 definition. In addition, the 1926 Amendment continued the 1920 Act's specification that officers detailed from the rest of the Army to the Air Corps for flight training had to be qualified as flying officers within one year or be returned to their original branch, unless the Air Corps wanted a particular officer to stay and occupy one of the up to 10% of the total officer billets that could be held by non-flying officers.

Furthermore, the 1926 Amendment restricted the number of officers in any military service that received flight pay to 1%, "exclusive of the Army Air Corps, and student aviators and qualified aircraft pilots of the Navy, Marine Corps, and Coast Guard."[12] This provision clearly limited the ability of officers outside the Air Corps to gain or maintain any flying skill. Congress effectively restricted the expert knowledge of flying to the Air Corps and the flying elements of the Navy, Marine Corps, and Coast Guard. This concurrently supported the development of a professional sense of corporateness specific to the Air Corps, separate from the Army officer corps at large.

Finally, Major General Patrick adamantly maintained in the face of several senators' incredulity that the Air Corps did not need or want 10% of its officers to be non-flying, even in times of war: "In the mobilization plans we have made and where we have figured in the amount of nonflying personnel we need, the number is less than 10 per cent."[13] In fact, when pressed on the percentage of non-flying officers in World War I, Major General Patrick replied, "That is scarcely a criterion. I can not answer the question; but they were learning to fly. Probably half of them."[14] In spite of a wartime track record of half of its officer corps performing non-flying functions or in training, the Air Service/Corps officer corps was insistent that a pilot rating was all but a requirement for admittance to the profession. The entrance requirement did not translate to a requirement for all pilots to maintain their flying currency, however. Once an officer received a pilot rating, he was considered a pilot, regardless of whether he was currently qualified, current and receiving flight pay, or not.[15]

In his *Annual Report* for FY1930, Major General J. E. Fechet, Chief of the Air Corps, reported that on June 30, 1930, 94% of the Air Corps' commissioned officers were pilots, 6% of whom were airship pilots. Only 1% of the commissioned officers had no flying rating, another 1% of the commissioned officers were observers, and the remaining 4% were currently in flying training.[16] The general concept that over 90% of the Air Service/Corps officers be flying officers continued through the 1936 Amendment to the 1916 National Defense Act. The long-lasting effect of the 1926 stipulation that only pilots were considered flying officers in peacetime can be seen as late as 1939, when the Air Corps consolidated the requirements for aeronautical ratings and established the new ratings of command pilot and senior pilot. The requirements for being a combat observer were either to already have the airplane observer rating and be grandfathered in, or to first earn a pilot rating and then establish observer credentials. Since the National Guard granted the observer rating to non-pilots, "Combat Observer ratings awarded federally recognized officers of A.C. [Air Corps] units of the N.G. [National Guard], who are not rated pilots, will be recognized only during the tenure of their commissions as federally recognized officers of A.C. units of the N.G."[17] The combined effect was to make the terms flying officer, rated officer, and pilot synonymous, with non-pilot observer ratings holding an anachronistic place in the hierarchy of non-pilot officers.

The Air Service/Corps officer corps' personnel policy goal, of a commissioned officer corps that consisted of between 90% and 100% pilots, was only practical given specific conditions. The first and perhaps most important factor was that the total Army officer corps was divided along functional lines into a myriad of branches. Consequently, the Air Corps could remain pristine and pilot-dominated but borrow officers from the Quartermaster Corps, the Corps of Engineers, the Chaplain and the Medical Corps, and so on, for support.

For example, figure 5.1 shows the growth of Air Force–type personnel as a percentage of total Army personnel, as well as the percentage of officers serving with the Air Corps/Force that actually belonged to other branches, corps, services, and eventually to the Army in general once the Air Force was independent. The first, generally ascending curve shows that the total "Air Force" percentage of Army personnel climbed steadily but moderately from 1919 to 1939, before it surged to almost one-third of Army personnel in 1943.

This percentage, however, included enlisted men as well as officers. Within the officer corps, it included not only pilots, navigators, and flying-connected officers such as those leading aircraft maintenance units but also generic officers providing administrative services as well as officers from other Army branches such as the Signal Corps. Consequently, this curve is inflated in the sense that the Air Corps/Forces/Force officer corps did not consider all these officers to be part of its membership, and from the Army's point of view, many of them were not. On the other hand, however, the Air Corps/Forces/Force could not operate without them.

The second, descending curve on the graph illustrates this flip side. In 1943, 24% of the officers serving with the Air Corps were actually officers from

Figure 5.1
Percentage of Total Army Personnel Serving in/with the Air Service, Corps, or Forces and the Percentage of "Air Force Officers" Belonging to Other Corps or Services

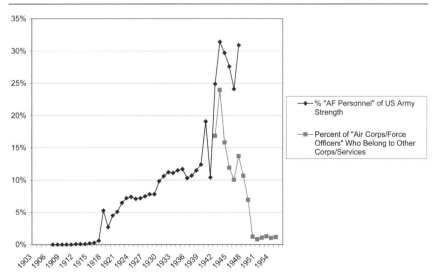

these different, supporting branches. In fact, the Air Force officer corps continued to rely on supplementary officers, primarily from the Army, through 1955. By that time, the Air Force officer corps had established its own officer training and career tracks to provide these services—but, of course, the Air Force officer corps could no longer aim for the ideal of 90% to 100% of its officers being pilots.

A very limited organizational size, limited technological change, and peacetime were three other factors that enabled the Air Service/Corps officer corps to cling to the ideal of 90% or more pilots in its ranks. During his testimony in 1926, Major General Patrick put the Air Service/Corps officer total at approximately 900. An organization of this size, with less than 9,000 enlisted men, allowed time for officer pilots to take on other duties, such as administration or maintenance, in addition to, or in some cases to the exclusion of, their flying. After all, the intent was to have every officer earn pilot wings, not necessarily that they all be qualified and current to fly combat missions every single day.

Technology did not become an issue until the Air Corps/Forces began to actually receive the big, multiengine bombers of the types used so successfully in World War II. If these bombers were indeed going to be flown hundreds of miles across oceans and deep into enemy territory, they could not rely on the enemy to place navigational aids along the way for the bombers' use. A crewmember was required to navigate and track the aircraft's position. Mastering this skill required considerably more training than that previously required for the observer rating. In addition, most bombers also required a crewmember to act as a bombardier. Although these crew positions could have been manned by pilots, the duties could not realistically be performed by the pilot and co-pilot flying the aircraft. It was economically inefficient to tie up two extra pilots, with high training costs, to perform other in-flight functions. Furthermore, pilots were not keen on performing non-pilot functions. After all, they were pilots![18] In addition, the navigator position in particular arguably required a more mathematically astute and therefore potentially an individual educated to a higher standard than the pilot candidate standard. As the inventory of large, crewed aircraft began to expand, the Air Corps began to train aviation cadets solely as navigators in 1940.[19]

Consequently, the big bomber, the aircraft that made the theory of strategic bombing a viable proposition, was ironically also a key factor in the Air Corps/Forces/Force grudging shift away from an all-pilot officer corps. World War II was the last factor contributing to the conceptual broadening of the Air Force officer corps' composition. The big buildup meant that every available pilot was required to fly, either as an instructor, an airlifter, or a combat pilot. A pilot doing administrative support work as his main task was a waste. Draftees with education and experience in a variety of fields could more effectively and efficiently become, for example, statistics officers, financial officers, or intelligence officers, than pilots performing these duties part-time or as a hobby.

The pre–World War II buildup and the war itself clearly demonstrated that the Air Corps/Forces/Force officer corps could not function effectively or efficiently without significant percentages of non-pilot officers. Achieving and maintaining 90% to 100% of the officer corps as pilots was unobtainable in a large organization prepared for war to break out at any time. In 1948, pilots made up only 50% of the total Air Force officer corps, and the percentage never increased beyond 50% in the independent Air Force. Instead, it had decreased to fewer than 20% of the total Air Force officer corps by 2003. However, in 1949, 90% of the Air Force general officers were pilots, although only 88% of them were still on flying status. In a sense, this illustrates the fact that the Air Service/Corps' drive for an almost all pilot officer corps as one of several concurrent strategies to achieve independence worked. However, this image did not fit the rest of the Air Force officer corps, and the percentage of pilot general officers also decreased to roughly 60% by 2003.

ONLY PILOTS CAN COMMAND FLYING UNITS

This pilot bias is at least partially explained by another aspect of the Air Service/Corps officer corps' strategy to achieve professional independence after World War I. This strategy was to enshrine in national law that only pilots could command in the Air Service/Corps. At the highest level lies the issue of command over the entire organization, or the position that today is called the Chief of Staff of the Air Force. Although Congress had passed several pieces of legislation dealing with the Air Service, it was not until 1926 that Congress wrote into public law the requirement that the Chief of the Air Corps shall be a flying officer.[20] In addition, at least two of the three assistants to the Chief were also required to be flying officers, that is, pilots. The emerging Air Service/Corps officer corps pushed for this restriction in order to prevent the Army officer corps, whose postings were seniority driven, from sending more senior colonels over from other branches like the cavalry or quartermaster corps to take over the senior Air Service/Corps billets.[21] The 1926 Act also carved out a seven-year period through July 1, 1933, that exempted the pool of candidates for the post of Chief of the Air Corps from being limited to colonels, which was the Army requirement. Instead, the Chief of the Air Corps could be drawn from more junior ranks. In addition, the 1926 Act also reinforced the existing notion that the candidates for Chief of the Air Corps must "have demonstrated by actual and extended service in such corps that they are qualified for such appointment."[22]

Even a colonel of cavalry who had a pilot rating but had only spent a year or two in the Air Service might be excluded from competing for the Chief of the Air Corps position. Instead, an Air Service/Corps officer pilot of any rank, perhaps a lieutenant colonel or major, but with as little as 15 years of active service with most if not all of the service in the Air Service/Corps could be appointed Chief of the Air Corps and given the temporary rank (with pay and privileges) of major general. Such an officer was also eligible to be a candidate for one of the three brigadier general postings as assistants to the Chief.

This antipathy towards the Army officer corps' seniority-based system, a preoccupation with youth, and an emphasis on piloting were traits upon which the Air Service/Corps officer corps was founded. Major General Patrick was clear in his testimony with regard to the 1926 Act's sections on increasing the number of Air Corps officers that the Air Corps did not want any sort of normal distribution of ranks in the officers to be transferred from the other Army branches. He would take all second lieutenants if he could get it that way. Officers above the rank of lieutenant brought baggage with them, had difficulty in pilot training, and would not be as hard working or as hard flying as young lieutenants.[23] The Air Service/Corps could never reach its potential in terms of mastering flying and flying combat operations if its mid-grade to senior leadership positions were filled by way of a revolving door for old, non-flying officers. Furthermore, the Air Service/Corps officer corps could not create its own sense of professional corporateness unless it had a closed membership with entry primarily by way of one path—pilot training. Whether by statute or tradition, it is inconceivable that the Chief of Staff of the Air Force could be a non-pilot.

The need for non-pilot (observer) rated officers was very limited, given the aircraft of the time. However, as the Air Corps continued to grow, it opened the exciting theoretical possibility that an observer in a strategic bomb unit could command the unit in time of war. Of course, the day the theoretical war ended, the observer would have to relinquish command. In 1940, Congress eliminated the distinction between wartime and peacetime definitions of flying officers. In fact, the definition of flying officer became quite liberal: "A flying officer is defined as one who has received an aeronautical rating as a pilot of service types of aircraft or one who has received an aeronautical rating as an aircraft observer or as any other member of a combat crew."[24] Observers, navigators, bombardiers, and other officers serving in crew positions were now classified as flying officers even in peacetime. In fact, in 1942, flight surgeons, as well as commissioned and warrant officers in flight training, were also classified as flying officers for the duration of the war plus six months.[25] However, this liberalization was meaningless, since the 1940 Act closed the old wartime exception—now only pilots with heavier-than-air ratings could command flying units. However, with war on the horizon, these pilots could now come from the larger Army and were no longer specifically restricted to the Air Corps officer corps.[26]

The initial implementation of the 1940 Act by the World War II Army Air Forces was even more restrictive. The August 1942 Army regulation stated that no officer but a pilot "Will command tactical units of the Army Air Forces, posts, camps, stations, depots, schools, and other commands, the primary functions of which are so connected with flying operations as to call for a comprehensive knowledge of flying on the part of the commander."[27] However, since every air base with a flying strip or navigational aid was conceivably so connected to flying that it required a pilot, the wartime Air Forces could not hope to fill all of these billets with pilots. Consequently, in 1943, the Army Air Forces tightened the definition of flying units to units with actual aircraft assigned or units that could issue flying orders.[28] This limited the number of units requiring pilot commanders.

On a practical level, the ramifications of a policy that only pilots could command flying units were immense. From the top down, all major commands, numbered air forces, and units down to the squadron level were authorized to issue flight orders, even those without direct flying tasks such as Technical Training Command. From the bottom up, as squadrons were amalgamated into groups, groups into wings, and wings into air divisions and/or into numbered air forces, non-flying units were quickly subsumed under the wings of a flying organization. Functional units performing tasks like maintenance, supply, air traffic control, tactical air control, or policing were technically open to command by non-rated officers serving in these career fields up to the squadron or even group organizational level. However, sooner or later they would be amalgamated into a group, wing, or higher command that owned aircraft and/or was authorized to issue flight orders. From that point onward, only a pilot could be in command. Since flying units could only be commanded by a pilot, all key positions in that particular level of unit were reserved for pilots, so that they could be prepared for command. Non-pilot officers were explicitly prohibited from operational commands and implicitly forbidden to command pilot officers.

This policy, which the senior officer leadership of the Air Service/Corps initially pushed into law to free itself from an Army preoccupied with seniority as a selection criterion for command, was maintained as the natural order of things. However, this action also effectively placed a glass ceiling over all non-pilot officers and restricted the profession's ability to make use of potentially good leaders. Whether they were observer/navigators, air battle managers, missileers, maintenance officers, or communications officers, these officers were legally barred from the pinnacle of their profession and in practice prohibited from career progressions that approached the summit, that is, positions of command in operations and operations support. The policy, which limited the upward mobility of non-pilot officers, created a two-class system of pilots and non-pilots within the officer corps.

PILOTING AND OFFICERSHIP

The officer corps' policies linking successful completion of flying training with officer qualification present a third strand of explanation for the overrepresentation of pilots in the general officer ranks. The Aviation Cadet Program was the core embodiment of the belief that piloting was synonymous with officership, and the belief was reinforced by the Air Corps/Force's reduction of academic qualifications in order to satisfy its insatiable need for pilots. If pilot wings are the key to admission to the officer corps, college degrees and non-flying officer skills appear to be of secondary importance. In the independent Air Force, it has never been a question as to whether pilots need to be commissioned officers. They simply are. However, that was not always the case in the Air Force's predecessors.

One of the Army's earliest personnel decisions with respect to aviation was that enlisted men should provide a major part of the pilot pool. The anticipated revolving door of enlisted pilot trainees would permit the aviation section to build up a pilot pool independent of the interest of Army officers in other branches in pilot training and aviation service. Furthermore, civilians could be directly recruited into the aviation section to fill officer manning shortfalls. World War I saw the first mass application of the principle of turning civilians directly into pilots and flying officers.[29] This training program produced both pilots and observers.

In July 1918 during the World War I buildup, Congress made clear that medical qualification and physical skills, not education, were the prerequisites for flying officers. "No person otherwise qualified for service as a flying cadet, pilot, or other officer in the aviation service, shall be barred from such service by reason of not being equipped with a college education."[30] In 1919, Congress statutorily established the grade of flying cadet, and stipulated that the Air Service could have at any one time a maximum of 1,300 flying cadets, 500 of whom could be enlisted. The 1919 Act also statutorily established that upon satisfactory completion of a flying cadet course, each graduate could choose to be discharged and then accept a commission as a second lieutenant in the Reserve Officer Corps.[31] However, the commission in the Reserve Officer Corps was not an active duty position, so if an enlisted man wanted to remain on active duty, he stayed enlisted. Consequently, enlisted men in small numbers continued to be rated pilots.[32]

The Secretary of War, the Army at large, and Congress continued to push for more enlisted pilots. The 1926 Amendment to the 1916 National Defense Act stipulated that "on and after July 1, 1929, and in time of peace, not less than 20 per centum of the total pilots employed in tactical units of the Air Corps shall be enlisted men, except when the Secretary of War shall determine that it is impractical to secure that number of enlisted pilots."[33] However, Major General Patrick, Chief of the Air Service, had previously told the Senate Committee on Military Affairs that he was not a proponent of the provision and that he had already conveyed this opinion to the Secretary of War. General Patrick maintained that:

Legislation is not necessary to provide for the training of enlisted men as pilots. I am training now as many enlisted men as I can find who are competent to take that training. We have at the present time, I think it is about 55, enlisted men who have been trained as pilots and who are acting as such. It is a question as to what makes a man capable or qualifies him for this pilot training. I think he is more than just an aerial chauffeur. I think he must have a certain amount of intelligence and he must display that by his ability to pass proper examinations before we are justified in spending time and money in training him. The flying cadets are taken in after an examination which necessitates not more than an ordinary high-school education. Many of the candidates fail. Any enlisted man may now apply for appointment as a flying cadet. If he passes that examination, he may come in and be trained. Unless they pass at least this qualifying examination, I think it is a waste of time to teach them to fly. . . . I am qualifying now all the enlisted men I can find who can take this training.[34]

General Patrick went further and explained that he was not really interested in producing large numbers of enlisted pilots. Instead, he stated, "I want to get in young men from colleges and schools and men of that kind to learn to fly—really officer caliber. Those are the ones I would like to have."[35] The Chief of the Air Service in 1926 had a clear preference for college men, not merely high school graduates, as the foundation of his pilot trainees, because the college men were *really officer caliber*. If these men were not available, then the minimum requirement for entrance into pilot training, whether for enlisted men or civilians, was to pass the flying cadet examination.

During World War II, piloting was still not automatically equated to commissioned officership. In fact, there were enlisted pilots, warrant officer pilots, flight officer pilots, and commissioned officer pilots.[36] Enlisted men and warrant officers with current ratings as pilots or observers could be appointed flight officers. Civilians who were qualified for pilot or observer ratings could also be directly appointed to the flight officer rank.[37] Flight officers could in turn be recommended for appointment to commissioned status as second lieutenants. A flight officer had to serve for at least three months as a flight officer before being recommended for commissioned status. Each recommendation had to include the flying officer's military record with the Army Air Forces, including training courses, and of course, his ratings. The promotion was not automatic.[38] Aviation cadets received their wings and active duty commissions upon graduation. However, this also was not an automatic process, at least in theory.[39] Cadets not meeting the standards for obtaining an officer's commission would become flight officers at graduation.

Pilots (and observers/navigators) who were not commissioned officers quickly disappeared after World War II. The Army Air Forces reported 32,413 flight officers in 1945, making up 8% of the total commissioned, warrant, and flight officers. The number of flight officers dropped to 1,510 in 1946, and only three in 1947. The independent Air Force dropped the flight officer category entirely.[40] The independent Air Force officer corps' decision to limit piloting to an officer career path elevated the status of piloting. However, the Air Force did not change the prerequisites for pilot training, which had become a major and automatic portal to membership in the officer corps. For civilians and enlisted personnel, the route to pilot wings and a commission was still the Aviation Cadet Program. Candidates had to pass physical and academic examinations, designed to weed out those medically disqualified or lacking in aptitude, but college degrees were not a requirement. Successfully completing pilot training earned an automatic commission. From 1939, when the size of the program doubled in the pre–World War II buildup, through the mid-1950s, the Aviation Cadet Program was the major provider of the rated force (see figure 5.2). The program ended in 1965. Aviation cadets provided over half of the Air Force's annual Undergraduate Pilot Training (UPT) graduates from 1948 to 1955.

Although the pilots and navigators in the independent Air Force were all commissioned officers, most were not the *really officer caliber* college-educated men that General Patrick envisioned in 1926. The officer corps' reliance on the Aviation Cadet Program for so long had two major side effects. First, it permitted large numbers of men without college degrees to join the officer corps, and second, it established a clear correlation between piloting and officership. Since General Patrick's preference for college-educated men had set the pace until the Air Corps buildup began in 1939, the senior (colonel and general officer) leadership of the officer corps was predominantly composed of officers with bachelor degrees through World War II and into the 1960s. In fact, a combined effect of World War II and the Air Force's independence was that some relatively young pre-1939 officers were quickly promoted to senior rank and actually served at the highest ranks for the duration of the period from World War II into the 1960s.[41]

The generally less educated mass of aviation cadets entering training between 1939 and 1945 served primarily in the junior officer ranks during World War II. For example, in 1951, 73% of the Air Force's rated officers did not have a bachelor's degree.[42] From the mid-1960s on, officers who were former aviation cadets rose to senior ranks by sheer weight of numbers. However,

Figure 5.2
Aviation Cadets and Air Force Academy Cadets, 1922–2003

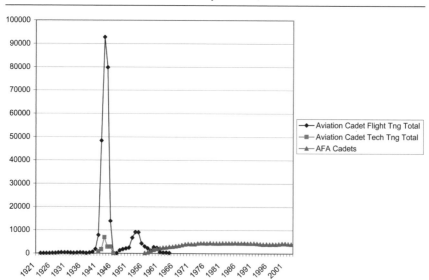

it was not just numbers alone that accounted for their rise to senior ranks. These officers were pilots, and it was intended that they serve full careers, unlike their ROTC-educated colleagues, who were expected by and large to serve shorter stints on active duty before transitioning to reserve status. Furthermore, the high percentages of aviation cadets without college degrees were not a World War II or even a Korean War phenomenon.[43] Between 1951 and 1955, that is, when aviation cadets provided more than half of the UPT graduates, the percentage of aviation cadets without bachelor's or higher college degrees climbed from 66% to over 90%. All of the UPT graduates became officers (see figure 5.3).

The Aviation Cadet Program cast a long shadow over the officer corps' professional development. Some aviation cadet UPT graduates from 1955 could reasonably expect to be promoted through the ranks to general officer. Such an officer would hit 35 years on active duty in 1990. Aviation cadet graduates from the last pilot aviation cadet classes in 1962 would hit the 35-year mark, if they made general officer rank, in 1997.

This led to the perplexing professional problem that the leadership of the Air Force, which prided itself on being the most technological of the armed services, was transitioning to a group of relatively uneducated general officers and colonels. This would make it difficult to convincingly sell the members of the Air Force officer corps as masters of technology before Congress and the public. The military service with the nation's ICBM force, with the lead in military space activities, and with large investments in C4ISR as well as very

Figure 5.3
Percentage of Aviation Cadets and Officers with Less than a Bachelor's Degree, by Rank

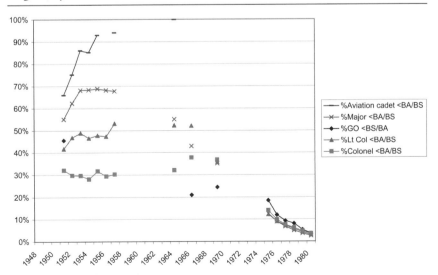

sophisticated aircraft could not claim to run everything with a single management tool based on seat-of-the-pants flying experience. In fact, over 20% of the general officers and over 35% of the colonels did not have bachelor's degrees in 1966 and in 1969.

Part of the problem was that the Aviation Cadet Program was based on the idea that a college education does not contribute to a person's ability to learn to fly. In fact, the percentages of officer and aviation cadet UPT fatalities roughly mirrored the percentages of officer and aviation cadet graduates in the experience of the independent Air Force (see figure 5.4).[44] Of course, the real issue was not whether 18- and 19-year-olds or college-educated officers made better pilots. The real issue concerned the linkage of piloting to commissioned status. The Air Force needed pilots, but it also needed officers.

If a college education was immaterial to pilot training success, piloting did not appear to fit into the general bailiwick of a professional expertise as defined by Huntington and others. Instead of having a liberal arts college education form the foundation upon which professional education rested, piloting would be seen largely as a physical or athletic-type technical skill. In addition, pilot training was obviously not an exclusive jurisdiction of the Air Force officer corps. After all, initial training and initial flying training/screening had been performed by civilian contractors for the Air Force. Furthermore, even if piloting was indeed a trade skill and a bachelor's degree did not help, the fact

Figure 5.4
Percentage of Officer Student-Graduates for Pilot (UPT) Training versus Percentage of UPT Fatalities That Are Officers (the Rest are Aviation Cadets), FY 1948–1965

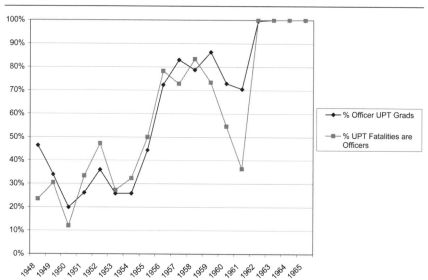

that only pilots could command flying and important non-flying units meant that the Air Force officer corps was building itself a pool of uneducated future commanders. To further complicate issues, the draft brought more college-educated officers into the Air Force in non-flying positions, leading to a potential imbalance, with well-educated junior officers being led by minimally educated, but pilot, senior officers.

One can argue that education does not make the man, but this argument runs contrary to the generally accepted Huntington perspective on officership. The argument also runs against General Patrick's assessment that a college education was indeed an indicator of officer caliber material. The extra four years of maturation and broader intellectual exposure may not improve hand-eye coordination, but they may improve critical thinking, problem-solving skills, and leadership abilities. In General Patrick's day, it was clear that being a pilot did not equate to being an officer or having any particular leadership skills. Not all officers were pilots, and obviously not all pilots had those somewhat intangible characteristics required of officers. The Army Air Force also clearly made that distinction, with the flight officers and enlisted pilots embodying the fact that piloting did not equate to commissioned officership. However, the independent Air Force officer corps' simultaneous awarding of wings and officer bars to aviation cadets indicated a belief that piloting skills directly correlated with officership skills.

Graduates from the aviation and flying cadet programs would appear to be the epitome of the Air Force's heroic warrior archetype. For an aviation cadet graduate, flying was in many ways the measure of all things. Such an individual enlisted in the aviation cadet program in order to learn to fly. Aviation cadets who failed pilot training were in a sense punished, because they reverted to enlisted status in the Air Force.[45] Flying ability was the sole criterion for the decision as to whether a cadet would become an officer or an enlisted man in the Air Force. Successful completion of flying training, that is, being awarded pilot wings, not the completion of a degree or service academy program, was the qualification for an officer's commission. Educational background, experience, and leadership skills were immaterial in defining an aviation cadet's fate.

Once commissioned, it was clear that rated officers were given preference over non-rated officers for regular commissions. They were paid more as long as they continued to fly, and they usually stayed in the Air Force longer. This paradigm could not help but be at least partially subsumed into the officer corps' concept of membership, and particularly into its concept of who formed the membership core. Just as his pilot rating made an aviation cadet an officer, his pilot rating made the officer eligible for command, and eligibility for command made the pilot officer eligible for pre-command jobs, which were in turn more promotable positions with more responsibility. A pilot's rating was the key to opening doors as an officer progressed through the system. The Aviation Cadet Program was a vestige of a world in which 90% of Air Force officers should be pilots.

The Aviation Cadet Program was a relatively simple way to provide the Air Force with a large pool of pilots and navigators, but it did not necessarily provide the Air Force officer corps with the mix of academic backgrounds and life experiences that could best translate into the leadership qualities that the officer corps needed to run the independent Air Force and successfully compete with other professions for jurisdictions. Flying was obviously important to the Air Force, but things like radar, electronic warfare, guided air-to-surface bombs, cruise missiles, medium-range ballistic missiles, and the atomic bomb were all used operationally during World War II. The basic tools for building an air force devoid of piloted aircraft, or for building an independent *ether* force, were already present. The Air Force officer corps needed pilots and navigators, but it also needed men with vision—a vision that would take the officer corps beyond strategic bombing and piloting.

IMPLICATIONS

The early officer corps' decisions covered in this chapter have truly cast long shadows over developments within the Air Force officer corps. The requirements that 90% of the Air Service officer corps be pilots and that commanders of the Air Service and all of its flying units be pilots were critical to creating an independent officer corps for the new profession. They clearly set the tone within the officer corps and society that the Air Force was all about pilots. In addition, the independent Air Force's equation of the completion of UPT with officer's bars and wings in the Aviation Cadet Program further reinforced the connection between officership and piloting. Consequently, it should be no surprise that non-pilot officers felt themselves at a disadvantage since they did not fit the model and were legally barred from senior positions within the profession.

CHAPTER 6

Revolutions in Personnel

The three personnel policies discussed in the previous chapter continued to evolve with the officer corps. Total inflexibility on these issues would limit the profession's ability to remain competitive in its jurisdiction and to discover and adapt to emerging jurisdictions. The requirement that 90% of the officer corps be pilots proved impossible to maintain during the World War II buildup, and the independent Air Force has been pulled in the opposite direction. Common sense and practical issues limited the realization of the principle that 90% of the officer corps be pilots. Nevertheless, its shadow still colors the perception of the officer corps and the public with regard to what the composition of the officer corps, and the general officer ranks in particular, should be. The legacy of the Aviation Cadet Program is somewhat similar, in that the perception remains pervasive that piloting and officership are intimately connected. In this case, however, the officer corps of the emerging aerospace force actively combated a major byproduct of the Aviation Cadet Program when it switched almost overnight to an extreme emphasis on bachelor's and graduate degrees at the termination of the Aviation Cadet Program as the Air Force Academy came on line. The officer corps has even shown itself over time to have some limited flexibility on the issue of command of flying units.

EDUCATION BECOMES IMPORTANT

Over the long run, college-educated officers, and West Point graduates in particular, were not likely to retain dominance in the top leadership positions in the independent Air Force, since the majority of pilots were former aviation cadets. In order to ensure a pool of quality officers available for selection to its most senior ranks, the officer corps of the independent Air Force could have raised the academic standards required of aviation cadets or reverted to the previous model, in which not all pilots were officers. The officer corps might also have argued for a change in the law restricting command of flying units to pilots, because the implementation of the law resulted in a general skewing of promotable billets to pilots.[1] However, the history of the struggle for independence precluded the option of letting non-pilots command flying units or exercise responsibility and decision making in any operational, and therefore, key positions.

The independent Air Force officer corps would arguably never reach its full professional potential if its most educated and most rounded members continued to be initially shaped by an Army institution. The Air Force officer corps needed its own service academy, and giving up the Aviation Cadet Program was part of the price of professionalization. An Air Force Academy would allow the Air Force officer corps to take the best of the aviation cadet candidates and educate them in a totally Air Force environment.[2] They would be exposed to the traditional academy mix of a heavy emphasis on engineering with some rounding liberal arts course work. The cadets would graduate with a bachelor of science degree and a firm grounding in airpower, before being sent to pilot training.[3] This would help establish Air Force flying and the exercise of airpower as an intellectual or mental expertise, not merely an athletic skill. Simultaneously, it would lend credibility to the Air Force officer corps' claims for jurisdiction in the fields of developing and applying state-of-the-art technology affecting air, space, and communications.

After a generation, the officer corps' senior professionals would be at least as well credentialed, academically, as the junior officers they led. Air Force general officers would not have to rely on a stratum of technical advisors. The generals themselves would have some understanding of technical and other non-flying issues for which they assumed responsibility. An academy was not all positive, however, for it meant a relatively fixed number of graduates per year based on the number admitted four years earlier, without the Aviation Cadet Program's flexibility, which enabled it to quickly adjust the number of pilots in training. The loss of the aviation cadets also resulted in a more even distribution of pilot training slots between the remaining commissioning sources. Nevertheless, pilots, and presumably Air Force Academy graduate pilots in particular, would still provide the core of the profession's senior leadership.[4] In the meantime, the officer corps began to stress the importance of academic degrees.

Since the Air Force Reserve Officer Training Corps (AFROTC) program and the academies produced only officers with bachelor's degrees, the Officer Training School (OTS) was the last major source of commissioning outside of the Aviation Cadet Program allowing non-degreed people to become officers. However, OTS was indirectly helped by the draft from the Korean War through the end of the Vietnam War. A voluntary tour in a non-flying, non-combat position in the Air Force was seen by many young men as preferable to a tour in the Army. Consequently, the Air Force could be more selective in its OTS candidates and require bachelor's degrees by 1966. The phasing out of the Aviation Cadet Program led to a steady fall in the percentage of officers without a bachelor's degree. In the intermediate ranks, the Air Force encouraged officers to earn college degrees, both at the bachelor's and the graduate levels. In fact, the Air Force would pay for officers to go to college.

Officers' academic credentials also appeared to play a role in promotion selections. From the mid-1960s onward, Air Force reporting of promotion board results often included statistics on the academic credentials of the newly selected promotees, directly stressing the importance of degrees in the promotion process.[5] The initial emphasis was on general officer promotions and possession of a bachelor's degree, but the focus gradually worked its way down through the field grade ranks, while simultaneously shifting to the possession of master's degrees as the initial group of officers who had all entered with bachelor's degrees reached consideration for major in the mid-1970s. By the early 1980s, a master's degree was generally considered a prerequisite for promotion to major.[6] Figure 6.1 captures the essence of this transition in the officer corps' informal requirements for advancement to mid-level and senior ranks.

As seen in figure 6.2, the history of the Aviation Cadet Program loosely parallels the decline in officers with less than a bachelor's degree. The percentage of officers with a bachelor's degree captures the shift to the requirement for a bachelor's degree at accession into the officer corps. The rise in the number of officers with master's degrees indicates the informal requirement for a master's degree to be promoted to field grade rank, and the record of

Figure 6.1
General and Field Grade Officer Postgraduate or Professional Degree Levels by Percentage

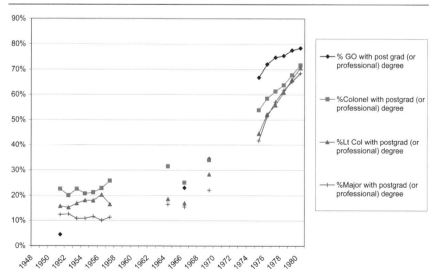

Figure 6.2
Officer Highest Education Level by Percentage

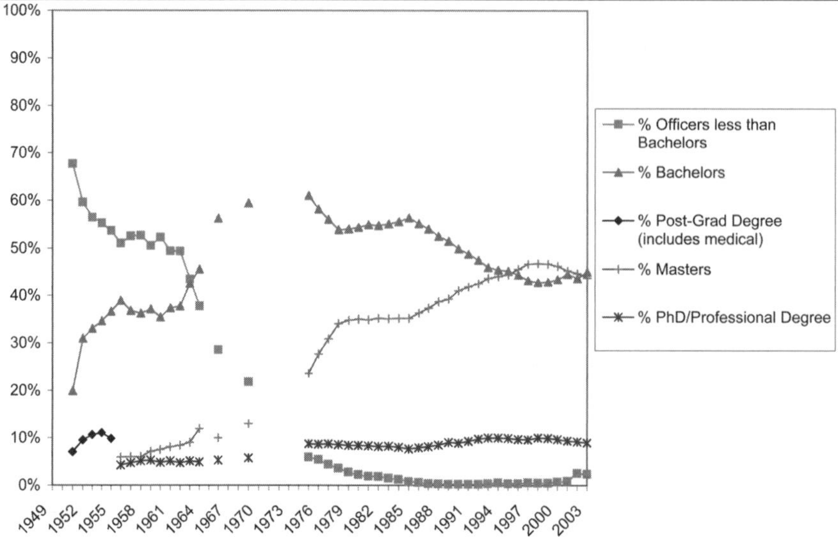

PhD/professional degreed officers generally captures the non-line officers.[7] As a general rule, field grade line officers are expected to have a master's degree, but not a PhD, since a doctorate signifies an investment of too much time in things academic, and not enough in things flying or operational, or in supporting these endeavors.

The profession prides itself on the high percentages of officers with advanced degrees. Education, as evidenced in the accumulation of bachelor's and higher-level degrees, was pushed across the board, but the effect was to bring pilot credentials in line with those of the rest of the officer corps. The end result was that the pilot class leading the officer corps of the new aerospace force could continue to command and serve in non-flying billets across the board, without the need for specialist or technical advisors. Instead of relying simply on flying credentials, they were now pilots with advanced degrees, worthy to lead the technologically advanced air and space force.

NAVIGATORS ARE PERMITTED TO COMMAND FLYING UNITS

The Air Force officer corps has not been completely blind to the implications of a policy that only pilots can command flying units. For example, in March 1949, Major General Laurence Kuter, the commander of Military Air Transport Service (MATS), requested that General Vandenberg, the Air Force Chief of Staff, grant him authority to appoint non-pilot officers to command positions in MATS. Major General Kuter included limitations in his request, for example, the specification that he would not put non-pilots in charge of units with wartime missions, and he even briefly described the analogy between MATS and civilian airlines, which did not rely entirely on pilots for management. Furthermore, General Kuter stated that his non-pilot commanders would obviously use pilots for advice where and when needed.

The request was denied, and a staff study supporting the denial indicated that non-pilots already had enough command opportunities, since they were theoretically eligible for consideration for 71% of all Air Force command billets. Furthermore, 85% of field grade billets could theoretically be held by non-pilots. The study did not make a distinction between *other-rated* (navigators) and non-rated officers. They were for all intents and purposes the same, and only pilots could command flying units.[8] Pilots were eligible for 100% of the line command billets and could compete for 100% of the field grade line billets, which they continued to dominate. In 1953, pilots occupied about 2,400 command and directorate positions, while other-rated (navigator) officers held only 15.[9]

MATS and Air Training Command later requested that the Air Staff take another look at the possibility of using other-rated officers in command positions. An Air Staff study in 1953 outlined the problem, but did not result in other-rated officers being allowed to command flying units. However, in October 1953, units that did not have flying as a primary function, but only as a collateral or support function, were opened to non-pilots, with a preference given to other-rated over non-rated officers. If a non-pilot was selected, though, his operations officer deputy was required to be a pilot. In the case of ground-launched missiles, command was not opened to non-pilots until 1956. Other-rated officers were not given any priority over non-rated officers for missiles, presumably because they did not have even tangential experience with ground-launch missiles and, of course, they presumably lacked the pilots' inherent leadership skills. Nevertheless, pilot experience was still listed as the desired experience for command of ground-launched missile units until 1960.[10] Consequently, other-rated appeared to be the equivalent of non-rated, which in turn meant non-pilot or perhaps simply lacking in leadership.

The requirement for commanders of Air Corps/Forces/Force flying units to be pilots was set in place in 1926 and continued throughout World War II, Korea, and Vietnam. Then, amid the post-Vietnam drawdown and tremendous social upheaval within the services, the Air Force officer leadership went back to Congress in 1974 and presented a draft bill "to amend title 10, United States Code, by repealing the requirement that only certain officers with aeronautical ratings may command flying units of the Air Force."[11] The Air Force asked Congress to strike all requirements for command of flying units.[12] Statutorily, from December 1974 on, any Air Force officer could command Air Force flying units.

While the bill was making its way through Congress, a "high-ranking Headquarters official" acknowledged to an *Air Force Times* reporter that non-rated officers, including women, who were excluded from rated status, could become commanders of flying units with the passage of the act, but maintained that "for the time being, the possibility will remain theoretical."[13] The Air Force officially maintained that it was only asking for the change in order to provide equal career opportunities to navigators by allowing them to command flying units. However, instead of proposing an act changing the requirements from allowing only pilots to command flying units to allowing rated officers, or perhaps rated line officers in order to exclude flight surgeons, the Air Force simply proposed abolishing all restrictions on command of flying units. The confusion between the terms rated, other-rated, and non-rated, and the question of where exactly observers, navigators, and flight surgeons fell, complicated discussions of the bill and clouded the Air Force's implementation of the law.[14]

Because all jobs that were seen as building blocks toward command had been reserved for pilots for generations, some Air Force officials implied that it could be a long time before a navigator could actually take command of a flying unit.[15] First, commander billets that navigators could fill had to open up. Navigators would only be permitted to command units flying aircraft with navigator positions, although there was no statutory basis for this restriction.[16] Second, qualified navigators would have to be found that could compete against pilots for the billets.[17] Field grade navigators had already missed the required steps in flying units. There was talk about some sort of training for command positions, but pilots of course did not require or receive such training. Consequently, the long-term emphasis would be on growing brand new navigators who could compete for and win intermediate positions, such as flight commander and operations officer slots, along the way to command. This process, however, would take 15 to 20 years.

That notwithstanding, the Air Force announced its ice-breaking navigator commander in February 1975 when Colonel (Brigadier General-select) Eugene D. Scott was named commander of the 47th Air Division at Fairchild Air Force Base (AFB), Washington. The 47th Air Division commanded a B-52 wing at Fairchild AFB as well as a missile wing at Malmstrom AFB, Montana. Colonel Scott had never served in the B-52, but the assignment made sense from the perspective that he was arguably better defined as a missileer with navigator experience. Although he had served as a navigator from 1950 through roughly 1962, his career from 1963 through 1975 was largely in missiles. In fact, he was commander of a missile wing when selected for command of the air division.[18] Such a career was not atypical for navigators who reached more senior ranks, because they could realistically only achieve higher rank outside the flying world. Although they were second-class citizens in the flying world, second-class wings often trumped no wings in the non-rated world. By September 1975, roughly a year after the Air Force first introduced the bill allowing non-pilot officers to command flying units, the Air Force reported that navigators commanded "three operational flying units and seven flight training squadrons" out of the Air Force's 350 total flying units.[19]

Several factors were at work in shaping the Air Force officer corps' decision to ask Congress to repeal the requirement that only pilots could command flying units. One factor was the general tendency in the Air Force and society at large to recognize existing discrimination and to attempt to redress it. The discussions on the issue of navigator command frequently painted the picture using words like discrimination and second-class status, and the discrimination was obvious. For example, from the Air Force's birth into the 1960s, pilots in some units wrote the performance reports on higher-ranking navigators that happened to be in their crew. In this case, rank meant nothing in the air, and also nothing on the ground. The pilot function overrode all other hierarchies. In addition, it was not unheard of to have "pilot-only" rooms in base operations facilities. Furthermore, there was a major lag between the Air Corps/Forces' implementation of wings showing the bearer's rating and seniority for pilots versus those for navigators, and the highest rating for navigator was master navigator versus command pilot. After all, only pilots could be associated with *command*.[20]

Prior to 1974, navigators who stayed in flying units, by choice or under compulsion, were on a dead-end track. No matter how experienced and competent they were as navigators, they could not command. Since they could not command, they were not given promotable jobs. Since they did not serve in promotable positions, they did not get promoted. However, if they left flying units, they could get commands and positions of responsibility in the non-flying world.

Figure 6.3 shows that after the wave of senior World War II navigators pushed through the Air Force's general officer ranks in the early to mid-1950s, the number of general officers who were navigators on flying status dropped to zero until 1965. Then, as the war in Vietnam, protests against the war, and civil rights protests increased, the Air Force officer corps increased the numbers of its navigator, black, female, and other minority general officers. There appears to be some correlation between the total number of general officers who were navigators, black, female, or from other minority groups. The curve for each group tends to rise and then fall between roughly 1970 and 1990 of a second wave of growth in all categories but "other" (other minority) from roughly 1990 to 2003 also indicates a correlation between these groups. Consequently, a general social awakening may have played a role in the Air Force officer corps' decision to let navigators compete for command of flying units.

A variety of other factors are also involved in the navigator case. Overall navigator manning levels played a role. The Air Force experienced two clear successive waves of navigator intakes that progressed through the ranks. The first wave began with a big influx of navigators in the lieutenant ranks between 1953 and 1961, during the Cold War bomber and air defense ascendancies. The percentage of Air Force lieutenants who were navigators on flying status peaked in 1961 at 22%. As the lieutenants were promoted to captain, the percentage of captains who were navigators on flying status peaked in 1966 at 21%. The same wave peaked for majors in 1971/1972 at 21%, for lieutenant colonels in 1977 at 20%, for colonels in 1979 at only 12%, and for general

Figure 6.3
Air Force Navigator, Black, Female, and Other (Minority) General Officers

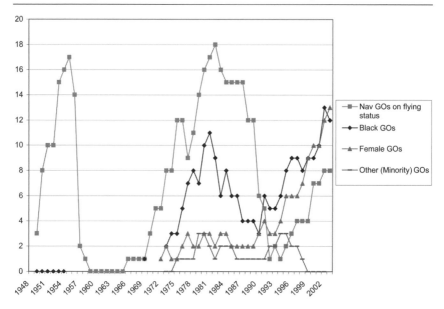

officers in 1982 at just 5% of the total general officers. The second wave, the Vietnam buildup, started with lieutenants in 1968 and peaked in 1975 when navigators made up 16% of lieutenants. The Vietnam wave played through, but the end of the Cold War distorted it and created a new pattern. In 1974, when the Air Force brought the draft to Congress and the bill became law, the percentages of generals, colonels, lieutenant colonels, and captains who were navigators on flying status were still climbing. This flood of navigators across the ranks potentially created a general atmosphere of increased tolerance for navigators and support for navigator issues within the officer corps. After all, the navigators were being promoted at consistent rates through lieutenant colonel by promotion boards consisting of Air Force colonels.

Another reason for the Air Force officer corps' support for the law allowing navigators to command flying units was that, quite simply, the Air Force needed navigators and the assorted specialties captured under the term *navigator*. Navigators proved indispensable in the Vietnam conflict. The new technology for waging war required navigators. For example, the F-4 became the Air Force's top fighter in terms of both quantity and quality during the war. The Air Force's front-line fighter through the early 1980s required equal numbers of pilots and weapons system operators (WSOs) to operate it. Furthermore, pilots and WSOs had to function as a team in order to get ordnance on targets, whether in the air-to-air or air-to-ground arenas.

In recognition of this fact, when the Air Force set the rules for determining air-to-air "kills" in Vietnam, it decided to give a kill credit to both crewmembers in the F-4 for downing an enemy plane. This decision was made in 1966 when both crewmen were still pilots, but the Air Force did not change the kill policy when it changed F-4 manning to include WSOs.[21] After all, the WSO, who ran the radar system, was critical to the plane's operation.[22] The WSO frequently acquired the "bandits" on the radar scope before the pilot saw them visually, and the WSO locked on the enemy aircraft so that the pilot could fire the air-to-air missiles. By the Vietnam War's end, the leading Air Force ace, with six kills, was a WSO, and two of the Air Force's three total aces were WSOs. WSOs were not just indispensable; they were the Air Force's heroes.[23]

Although not as lionized, navigator electronic warfare operators (EWOs) played critical roles in Wild Weasel fighter aircraft battling SAMs as well as in B-52s. In the B-52, three of the five officer crewmembers were navigators (navigator, bombardier, EWO), and no one would go home if the B-52 EWO could not electronically divert the SA-2 "flying telephone poles" streaking toward the bomber. The new technology of warfare required navigators, and the wartime experience emphasized in a personal way to pilots how much they were dependent on navigators not only to complete the mission, but simply to survive. Navigators indeed demonstrated that they too could have the right stuff, and this in turn, broke down some of the barriers to non-pilot command of flying units.

In addition to their importance in the aircrews of modern combat aircraft, navigators also provided a more steady level of flying experience in the officer corps. Whereas the total number of pilots with the most experienced command pilot rating began a steady decline in 1962, the number of master navigators remained more level (see figure 6.4).

And in fact, when examined in terms of percentage of pilots and percentage of navigators, the percentage of navigators with master navigator ratings first exceeded the percentage of pilots with command pilot ratings in 1976 (see figure 6.5).

Navigators made a flatter curve with respect to the percentage of navigators who stayed until retirement, in comparison to the percentage of pilots or percentage of non-rated officers staying until retirement (see figure 6.6).[24]

By the 1960s, navigators did not possess a job skill in demand in private industry, but pilots and many non-rated officers did. Consequently, the steady experience of the navigator pool potentially offset the large increase in inexperienced pilots caused by the Vietnam buildup (see figure 6.7). This also boded well for an upping of the general status of navigators in the mid-1970s.

Finally, the Air Force officer corps may have consciously tried to buy navigators in before it lost them. In 1974, the Air Force was on the verge of a dramatic change in regulations on flying status and flight pay. In order to cut costs, the Air Force and other services were being forced to give up the old system of flying four hours a month in practically any aircraft to maintain flight currency and pay and move to the gated system. Pilots and navigators would only fly when they were in a flying billet, that is, when they were part of a flying unit. Meeting the flying requirement for each gate would also mean

Figure 6.4
Pilots and Navigators with Command Pilot or Master Navigator Rating (1948–1980)

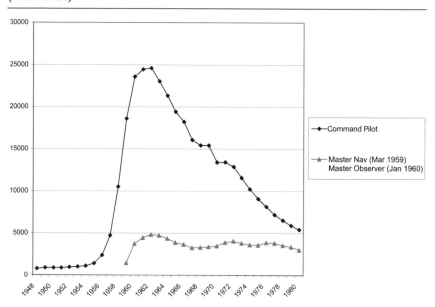

Figure 6.5
Percentage of Total Pilots and Navigators with Command Pilot or Master Navigator Rating (1948–1980)

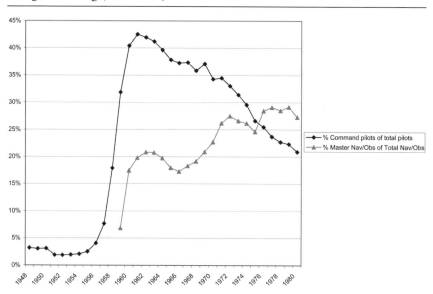

**Figure 6.6
Retirement-Eligible Losses for Pilots, Navigators, and Non-Rated Officers
(1953–1980)**

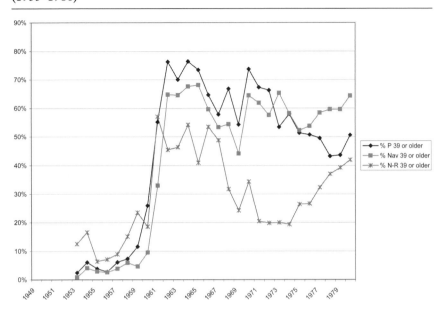

**Figure 6.7
Pilots per Pilot Rating (1948–1980)**

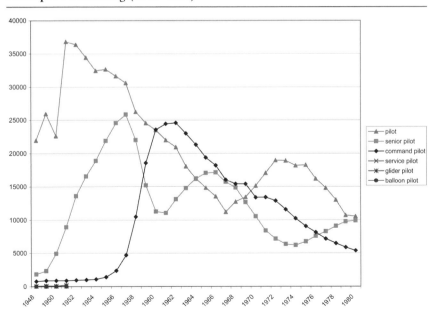

a lot more flying assignments, potentially including some in the field-grade ranks. Consequently, the old navigator's dream of flying for a few years as a line flyer in a squadron then escaping to non-flying jobs, but with the potential to still fly for proficiency four hours a month and collect flight pay, was over. Navigators at the rank of major or even lieutenant colonel might be forced to return to full-time flying under lieutenant or captain pilots in order to meet their final gates. This might be more digestible if the navigator had at least the theoretical possibility of earning positions of authority and command in the flying unit. Furthermore, there was potential competition from the Navy, which offered a better deal for potential navigators since naval flight officers (navigator equivalents) were already commanders of flying units. The Air Force officer corps needed its navigators, and it had to take steps to make navigator membership more than a second-class option.

NON-RATED OFFICERS AND COMMAND

Although the Air Force officer corps appeared somewhat interested in re-dressing navigator claims of discrimination in 1975, it ignored the issue of dis-crimination with respect to non-rated officers. In August 1975, the Air Force had a total of 3,691 command billets (flying and non-flying, from squadrons and detachments up to bases, wings, and installations) for the rank of colonel and below. Pilots filled 1,505 (41%) of these billets, navigators 422 (11%), and non-rated officers 1,764 (48%).[25] As of 30 June 1975, the Air Force officer corps consisted of 32% pilots on flying status, 14% navigators on flying status, and 54% non-rated (including pilots and navigators not on flying status and flight surgeons, in addition to purely non-rated) officers. From a proportional standpoint, pilots were overrepresented in command billets, while navigators and non-rated officers were underrepresented. Flying officers were also given priority over non-rated officers for non-rated commands.

In its report on the 1974 Career Motivation Conference, issued in the sum-mer of 1975, the Air Staff reported that, as a consequence of the new law eliminating the restriction that only pilots could command flying units:

Air Force policy is *now* that *all* Line officers will be eligible to command Line units. Only the best qualified Line flying officers (pilots and navigators) will be selected to command flying units. Only the best qualified Line officers will be selected to com-mand other Line units.[26]

The policy reflects not only the change to allow navigators to command fly-ing units but also a broader possibility for non-rated line officers to compete more fairly for command of non-flying units. However, that possibility hung on the phrase "best qualified." If best qualified meant qualified in terms of knowledge and experience in carrying out the unit's mission, then the non-rated maintenance officer, for example, would always appear to be best quali-fied. If best qualified was measured in terms of mastery of the Air Force's primary mission and the officer's potential for further command and promotion, pilots and navigators would get the nod, at least until the Air Force ran out of rated officers to take the non-flying commands. After all, some rated officers had to command flying units, serve on staffs, and fly, so the supply of rated officers was not unlimited. Non-rated officers had to be able to fill in when rated officers simply were not available or interested.

This was still the profession's dominant conceptual framework in 1974. However, the statistics already belied that framework. The percentages of the officer corps that were pilots and navigators, that is, the percentage of rated officers on flying status of the total Air Force officer corps, crossed 50% in the downward direction for the final time in 1965 (see figure 6.8).

From that point on, not just pilots but rated officers on flying status in total were a minority in the officer corps. In fact, pilots had been a minority within the line officer category since 1950 (see figure 6.9). Even with large numbers of pilots serving in non-rated billets, the Air Force still needed more non-rated officers than pilots.

Faced with its clearly increasing need for non-rated officers, in 1965, the Air Force investigated its inability to retain larger numbers of non-rated officers. The investigating committee found a variety of reasons for the non-rated officer exodus, centering around non-rated officers' limited opportunities for career advancement. In particular, non-rated officers voiced discontent with the practice of placing rated officers in non-rated supervisor billets ahead of

Figure 6.8
Rated Officers on Flying Status versus Non-Rated Officers by Percentage of Total Officers

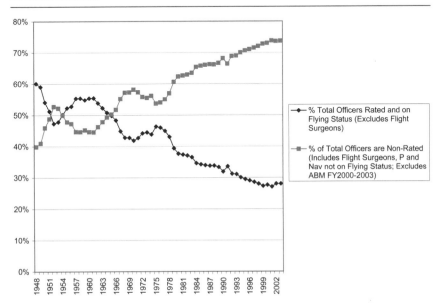

Figure 6.9
**Pilots on Flying Status as Percentage of Total Officers versus Pilots
as a Percentage of Line Officers**

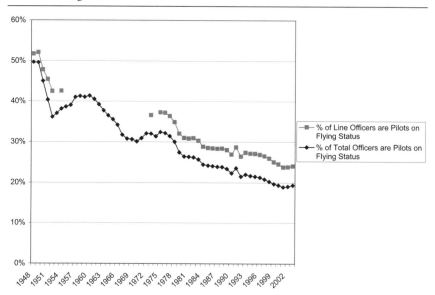

more qualified non-rated officers. In addition to shutting non-rated officers out of promotions, this practice also adversely affected units' abilities to meet mission requirements. Non-rated officers also reported that the term non-rated was pejorative and that the lack of non-rated specialty *badges*, in comparison to the *wings* worn by rated officers on their uniforms, symbolically and visually reinforced the separation and thereby lower status of non-rated officers.

The committee recommended that the term non-rated be dropped, that assignment policies be changed to give non-rated officers better opportunities for career advancement, and that badges be developed for all officer specialties. However, the committee did not attribute the number of rated officers serving in non-rated billets to any sort of Air Force policy to maintain a reserve pool of rated officers to handle an initial wartime surge or to career-broaden future pilot leaders. Instead, it saw the problem as one in which poor non-rated retention rates forced the Air Force to use rated officers in non-rated billets.[27] That conclusion, however, implied that if the Air Force could retain enough non-rated officers, it could cut its pilot levels even further.

AIR BATTLE MANAGERS PERMITTED COMMAND OF FLYING UNITS BEFORE BEING RATED

The origins of the air battle manager (ABM) career field dates back to the Battle of Britain in World War II. The ABMs are the descendants of the intercept controllers on the ground directing the fighter scrambles and the interception of the German bomber raids. Although they were initially ground-based, the concept of an aircraft carrying a large-area surveillance and aircraft control radar with intercept controllers aboard dates back at least to the closing days of World War II, when Admiral Nimitz pursued the creation of such aircraft to augment ship- and shore-based radar defenses against Japanese kamikazes for Operation Olympic, the invasion of Japan.[28] The Air Force's first operational command and control radar aircraft was the EC-121, which remained in the active inventory from the mid-1950s through the mid-1970s and was primarily designed to augment the ground-based air defense coverage. Although weapons controllers were part of the crew, the vast majority of the officers in the weapons controller (later renamed the air battle manager [ABM]) career field worked on the ground, either in fixed, strategic air defense centers or in mobile, tactical radar and command and control units. EC-121s demonstrated the utility of airborne command and control aircraft in tactical warfare during Vietnam, so the EC-121's successor, the E-3 AWACS, was placed under Tactical Air Command instead of the decaying Aerospace Defense Command. Weapons controllers also provided the backbone of the ABCCC system, which flew as a capsule inside specially modified C-130 aircraft. The ABCCC also proved to be a critical piece of air-to-ground operations in Vietnam, and its successor, the E-8 JSTARS, is also crewed by ABMs. With the advent of AWACS in the late 1970s, the percentage of ABMs in flying positions began to climb steadily. This process was accelerated when the Air Force turned the strategic air defense mission over to the Air National Guard, when JSTARS started to come on line during Desert Storm, and as the Air Force retired ground-based radar command and control units in the 1990s.

Previously, ABM officers earned the weapons controller badge upon completion of the basic course. ABMs typically commanded the mobile ground radar squadrons, although these squadrons tended to be amalgamated into fighter groups and wings with an ensuing glass ceiling. Fixed, strategic defense operations centers were commanded by pilots, with ABM deputies. ABMs serving in flying positions for the odd tour or two were awarded officer non-rated aircrew wings to wear in addition to, and above, their ABM badge. As early as 1982, however, the Air Force began to send 2nd lieutenants directly from the basic weapons controller course and without ground ABM experience directly to AWACS assignments, with the prospect that these officers might only serve one or two ground ABM tours in a 20-year career. For these officers, aircrew duty was not going to be an exotic experience but their career emphasis. These officers would fly as many hours as their rated navigator and pilot colleagues, they would fill more of the onboard AWACS crew positions, and they would perform the aircraft's primary mission, but they could not command the aircraft or the squadron; nor were they eligible for flight pay or bonuses.[29] Non-rated ABMs were paid hazardous duty pay on a lower scale and without the rated gate system. ABMs were only paid when on flying status and logging four hours a month (with a limited carryover of hours).

The situation was certainly as bad as it had been for navigators, and it was further complicated by the high operations tempo of AWACS. As General Ralston later explained, "We started flying AWACS in Saudi Arabia in 1979 and kept guys flying there 24 hours a day, 365 days a year for 10 years."[30] Additionally, AWACS flew in support of every operation and major exercise, so aircrews and maintenance crews spent large amounts of time away from home. Desert Storm and the resulting no-fly zones accentuated the problem. As General Ralston said, "If you had been in the AWACS community" before 1994, "all you had known was 200 days a year away from home. It was driving AWACS into the ground."[31]

However, there was an important difference between the flight crew (two pilots, one navigator, and an enlisted flight engineer) and the mission crew (ABMs and enlisted communications, radar, and computer technicians). Pilots and navigators could more easily rotate tours between AWACS and other aircraft such as tankers, but ABMs and the enlisted aircrew members, as well as the AWACS maintenance and computer-support personnel, were increasingly stuck in AWACS or in JSTARS units, which fared no better. Of course, an ABM could break up the pace of the high operations tempo in AWACS by opting for a one-year assignment without family to a remote radar post. Seeing a future full of time away from home, no hope for advancement to positions of responsibility, low promotion rates, and flight pay inequities, ABMs resigned. The officer corps had undervalued ABMs, had undersold the career field to officer recruits, and did not significantly adapt the training pipeline to meet the AWACS and JSTARS demand. There was a perpetual shortage of ABMs. As more resigned, the remainder had to do more, creating a snowball effect. ABMs could not leave the career field, could not be spared for broadening or schools to enhance their promotability, and of course could not take promotable positions from future pilot leaders. Consequently, as ABMs' promotion chances continued to decline, more would leave.

The Air Force's responses were varied. An early action, taken in the mid-1980s, was to create a non-flying training squadron within the AWACS wing so that there was at least one AWACS squadron command for ABMs. This was a small offset to the number of disappearing ground ABM commands. Perhaps the most innovative solution was the decision to introduce enlisted weapons controllers in 1991. The enlisted weapons controllers would overlap with officers in the lower ABM crew positions. Only officers could fill the highest ABM positions in aircrews, but lieutenants, for example, could serve functionally under noncommissioned officers as they learned the tools of the trade. This was a radical variation of the concept that rank has no meaning in the air, and it symbolically devalued the ABM career field. After all, Huntington purposefully excluded enlisted personnel from his definition of the military profession. Furthermore, enlisted weapons controller trainees occupied officer trainee spots since the training was the same; so the process did not speed up the replacement process. In addition, the enlisted weapons controllers frequently came from the surveillance technician career field, so there was an element of musical chairs in filling the gap, rather than bringing totally new personnel into the field. Nonetheless, the enlisted weapons controller solution has remained in force in the ABM case. Curiously enough, though, the independent Air Force has never implemented an enlisted solution to resolve pilot and navigator manning difficulties.

Another solution was the development of an AWACS reserve unit to help man the active aircraft along the lines of the model already in use with cargo aircraft. JSTARS went to an even more extreme form of mixed active duty and National Guard personnel on National Guard–owned aircraft. These solutions once again press or exceed the bounds of Huntington's definition of the officer corps as a profession, since reservists are in a quasi-professional state. The Air Force has also implemented "stop-loss" on occasion to maintain its ABM force, as well as its pilots and navigators. Stop-loss prevents personnel in general, or in a specific career field, from leaving active duty during times of war or tension.

Finally, in the late 1990s, after the other solutions had already been implemented, the Air Force officer corps returned to the 1974 navigator model. If the profession needs the skill, it should value those that provide it and embrace them within the profession's core membership. Consequently, the senior Air Force officer leadership implemented a series of actions to raise the status of ABMs. Since the 1974 act abolished all requirements for command of flying units, it was suddenly found possible to name a non-rated ABM to command of an AWACS flying squadron. This occurred in January 1997 when Lieutenant Colonel John Kennedy, an ABM, was selected to command the 963rd AWACS. This made him the first non-rated officer to command a flying unit in the Air Force's history. Furthermore, the 963rd was an operational, not merely a training, squadron, which gave the event a bit more prestige.

Lieutenant Colonel Kennedy was followed by other ABMs in command of AWACS squadrons and even the Operations Group, but on October 1, 1999, ABM became a rated career field.[32] This step did not require Congressional intervention, only the "discovery" of existing law. The 1940 Amendment to the National Defense Act had already defined a flying officer as an officer "who has received an aeronautical rating as a pilot of service types of aircraft or one who has received an aeronautical rating as an aircraft observer or as any other member of a combat crew under such regulations as the Secretary of War may prescribe."[33] The change to rated status resulted in new ABM wings, as well as flight pay and the gate system used for pilots and navigators. Furthermore, it opened the possibility of using ABMs to fill rated staff positions, which could then free other rated officers, that is, pilots to return to flying or command positions. However, this was unlikely, since the ABM career field remained undermanned. Only 74% of ABM billets were manned in October 1999.[34]

The last part of the anti-discrimination package appeared in 2002, when the Air Force offered bonuses for the first time to non-pilot aviators. Both ABMs and navigators were offered bonuses, although ABMs and navigators received a maximum of $15,000 per year for a five-year service commitment extension, compared to the $25,000 given to pilots. Nevertheless, non-pilots saw it as recognition of the importance of their role in the profession, and the Air Force saw it as a way to keep up retention, in particular with an eye to placing many of the committed navigators in staff positions to free up pilots for non-staff duties.[35]

THE SPACE "WINGS" SAGA

The Air Force continued to use the term non-rated because the distinction between rated and non-rated was real in terms of command and promotion opportunities, status, and income. The Air Force did adopt badges for non-rated officer specialties, although General McConnell, as Air Force Chief of Staff, seemed opposed to the general idea.[36] In addition, there are important distinctions between wings and badges. Flyers (pilots, navigators, air battle managers, flight surgeons, flight nurses, and non-rated officer aircrew members) are awarded wings, which are required to be worn on all uniforms. Astronauts of course wear wings. Non-rated officers have career specialty badges, and their wear is optional. Wings look like the outstretched wings of a falcon, ready for flight, with one of various shields centered where the bird's body would be. Badges typically have some sort of symbol indicating the career field or functionality of the bearer and are often surrounded by compressed wreaths. The only exception are the parachutist wings, which actually look like a badge.

Badges, like wings, can be awarded at two advanced levels. The first advanced level is senior, with the star on top of the badge. The highest level is marked by the star encircled by the wreath, but as in the case of navigators, for non-rated officers, this level is called master, not command. In addition, the qualification times to achieve senior and master levels were much shorter for badges than for wings, to the tune of 3 instead of 7 years for senior and 7 instead of 14 for command/master. One effect of this shorter period to the awarding of senior status was the implication that badge-type jobs were easier to master than wings-type jobs. In addition, using shorter periods for the award of advanced badge levels also let rated officers collect merit badges that implied the wearer had gained a higher level of expertise in a non-rated field while on non-flying tours. Furthermore, the qualifications for badges vary; the wearing of some badges can be somewhat misleading. For example, the space/missile badge could be awarded for operations, maintenance, or acquisition work.

The saga of the wings versus badges with respect to the bearer's status and closeness to the core of the profession continues. Every career field is now potentially covered by some sort of wings or badge, and two have made the jump from being a badge-type job to a wings-type job since 1998. The first is the air battle manager career field. The second is the space/missile career field. It is not coincidental that officers serving in both of these specialties form a large part of the C4ISR personnel. The space/missile story carries cultural overtones since the career field has not been given rated status.[37]

Nevertheless, in a major break with tradition, the Air Force allowed the non-flying space/missile badge to take on the appearance of wings in 2006. Although certain wings like those worn by flight nurses and non-rated officer aircrew members have never been associated with an aeronautical rating per se, the wearers of those wings served on aircraft. The space wings, or "swings" as they are pejoratively called by some officers, are awarded to operators, maintainers, and acquisitions officers associated with space and missile systems. The swings are an indication of the officer corps' recognition of the importance of the space/missile field to the profession. The symbolic elevation of this career field to "flying" status is one more indication of the evolutionary broadening of the inner core of the profession's membership.

IMPLICATIONS

The navigator, ABM, and space/missile cases demonstrate the non-linear evolution of the Air Force officer corps' concept of itself and its inner core membership. The combination of issues captured under the concepts of wings, ratings, and the profession's inner core will continue to be problematic for the officer corps. In essence, the problem is that the Air Force officer corps is struggling with the status of non-pilot operators. The non-pilot operators have been increasing in number and in importance, and in order to develop or maintain its jurisdictions in space, cyberspace, and the air, the Air Force officer corps must incorporate the C4ISR officers across the entire range of its rank structure. Heroic leaders at the top will limit the influence of visionary officers below.

The officer corps is also aware that adopting policies similar to its earlier policies on command and the composition of the officer corps could destroy the Air Force. If only space officers could command and man space units, only ABM officers could command and man Combined Air Operations Center (CAOC) and command and control forces, only cyber officers could command and man cyberspace forces, and only pilots and rated officers could command and man flying forces, the Air Force officer corps might as well devolve into four professions. Permitting only pilots to command and to serve across the board in all specialties, while restricting other officers to narrow career stovepipes, could foster strivings for independence. Consequently, the navigator, ABM, and space wings cases reveal an increased willingness by the officer corps to broaden prestige and concepts of command, moving away from a pilot-centric world toward a more C4ISR-embracing perspective.

CHAPTER 7

The Heroic Warrior Counterrevolution

It is clear that C4ISR has been increasingly important to the Air Force officer corps, but the visionary versus heroic struggle does not end with the navigator, ABM, and space wings cases discussed in chapter 6. As the officer corps was opening command to more officers on the one hand, it was taking steps to reemphasize piloting on the other. One might be tempted to label attempts to reinvigorate the heroic warrior ethos as pushback against the rise of C4ISR officers, but this does not appear to be the case. Pushback would require that the pilot group actually felt threatened by the rise of C4ISR officers. However, the Air Force officer corps does not treat C4ISR officers as a group. Instead they are viewed as members of small, isolated, career fields. Nevertheless, as the Vietnam War ended and the Air Force switched to the gated flying pay system, Air Force general officers seemed increasingly to place an emphasis on piloting and traditional types of command. Defining leadership using these two characteristics creates significant hurdles for non-pilot officers to overcome, as is evident in the long-standing promotion system bias in favor of pilots and the resulting overrepresentation of pilots in the general officer corps.

FLYING/COMBAT HOURS—INDICATORS OF PILOT SKILL, LEADERSHIP, AND DECISION-MAKING?

Sample data from Air Force general officer biographies indicate that relatively little emphasis was placed on a general officer's pilot skills prior to the Vietnam War.[1] Few of the earlier general officers reported their total flying hours. The categories are pilot-centric, but navigators and some non-rated line officers also had opportunities to accumulate flight hours and combat hours or sorties.

The inclusion of a general officer's total flying hours in his biography provides no new information in most cases, since the overwhelming majority of general officer pilots and navigators in the samples had already identified themselves as command pilots or master navigators.[2] These are the highest ratings, they include very high minimum flying hour requirements, and they indicate that the holder spent the majority of his career on flying status and/or met his flying gates. Fewer than 10% of the general officers reported any total flying time until the 1968 sample, but this climbed to 72% in the 1983 sample, and afterwards the curve loosely followed the percentage of general officers sampled who were pilots (see figure 7.1).

Several factors explain the curve. Close to 90% of the general officer corps were pilots in the early years of the independent Air Force. There was no apparent need to reinforce the fact that an officer was a pilot by listing total flight hours. There may have been a sense of modesty, or at least a sense of no need to brag about one's numbers of hours. After all, simply writing "command pilot" was sufficient in and of itself as the ultimate confirmation of flying skill. In fact, in the independent Air Force, the percentage of pilots who held the command pilot rating was less than 5% through 1956. Furthermore, large parts of the initial Air Force general officer corps had been general officers during World War II with staff and planning responsibilities. Many did not actually accumulate that many new hours in modern combat aircraft during the war, at least in comparison to their junior colleagues in flying units.

Figure 7.1
Line General Officer Flying Hours Listed in Biography by Percentage

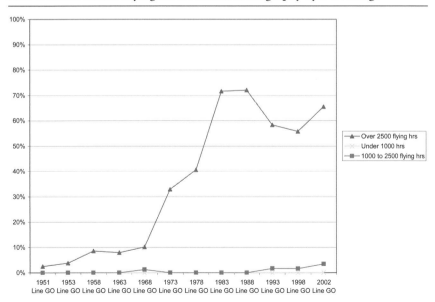

The 1973 sample indicates a large change in the reporting of total flying hours. General officers were now members of that crop of junior officers in World War II and Korea who had accumulated large numbers of hours, many of which were combat hours. Pilot general officers may have also been reacting to the growing number of non-rated general officers. Furthermore, as junior officers flying in Southeast Asia increasingly racked up large numbers of combat flying hours and sorties, general officers may have begun to list their total flying hours as a way to maintain credibility. From this perspective, the general officer biographies appear to send the message that some captain's 150 combat flying hours in Vietnam were of minimal significance in comparison to a general's 4,500 total flying hours.

Roughly a third of all Air Force pilots held the command pilot rating between 1959 and 1973. Reporting total flying hours may have been an attempt to gain increased status by showing how far a general officer had exceeded the standard. In addition, a biography with a sentence like "the general is a command pilot with 5,000 hours flying assorted fighter aircraft" strikes a chord within the officer corps. It stakes a claim that the general is a part of the inner corps of the officer corps, not only with respect to rank but also because each hour is another point in a tally of professional skill. More hours, in the absence of qualitative indications, signify more professional competence and, therefore, more credibility, showing that a particular officer has what it takes to make decisions and to assume positions of authority and responsibility within the officer corps.

At the same time, it is clear that there is more to becoming a general officer than accumulating thousands of flying hours. Many pilots with large numbers of flying hours do not become general officers. Nevertheless, career flying hours are significant. Sufficient hours to qualify for the command pilot rating or master navigator rating seem to be the desired minimum for rated officers to be considered for promotion to general officer rank. The apparent standardization since the 1970s of the inclusion of total flying hours in general officer biographies has had the powerful effect of highlighting the absence of flying hours in a biography. The absence of the flying-hour reference reinforces the point that the officer is not a pilot or navigator, and attempts by such officers to substitute a master-level non-rated badge in lieu of flying hours fall flat.

However, total flying hours may be trumped by combat flying hours or sorties. Although listing a single combat sortie appears insignificant in comparison to listing several thousand total flying hours, the inclusion of combat experience, however small, stakes a claim that that the flier is brave, has faced death at the hands of the enemy, and presumably has kept a cool head under the added stress of combat. To the heroic warrior, combat flying hours and missions are the epitome of the profession. It is no surprise, then, that larger percentages of general officers reported their combat flying hours or sorties in earlier samples than reported their total flying hours (see figure 7.2).

The combat hours/sorties curve also rises faster than the total flying hours curve, although it does not reach the same heights, since many officers rise to

Figure 7.2
Line General Officer Flying Hours versus Combat Hours/Sorties Listed
in Biography by Percentage

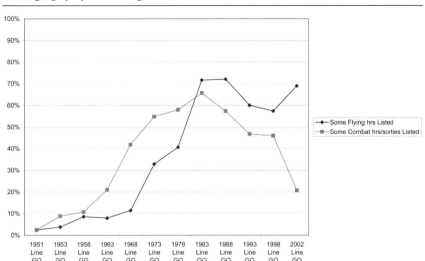

general officer ranks without combat experience. This is evidence of a vision-ary outlook within the general officer corps. It also appears to be somewhat subjective as to what is counted as "combat" experience. A FAC flying an O-2 along the front lines, a C-141 crew ferrying supplies to a rear base, and an EC-121 flying over the Gulf of Tonkin all faced quite different levels of risk during the Vietnam War, but all might have logged combat time.[3]

The curve is also somewhat paradoxical, since officers who were generals and colonels in World War II often did not fly that many combat missions in World War II or in Korea, because they served on staffs and in senior positions during those wars. However, many stayed on active duty into the 1960s; the increased reporting of combat hours in the mid-1960s reflects younger World War II fliers becoming generals, not young Vietnam fliers being quickly pro-moted to general officer ranks. Consequently the big hump in the percentage of combat hours/sorties reported between the 1968 and 1988 samples reflects a hodge-podge of combat experience by various officers from World War II, Korea, and Vietnam. Desert Storm experience had yet to make a significant impact in the 2002 sample; one can expect another large increase in the re-porting of combat hours as officers with combat experience in Desert Storm, operations in Southwest Asia and the Balkans, and the Global War on Terror are promoted to general officer ranks.

This in turn raises the question of the relevancy of reported combat hours/sorties that often reflect missions flown 20 years earlier. The officers un-doubtedly demonstrated courage and embody the heroic warrior archetype, but the actual experience may not be particularly relevant, given the changes in aircraft, command and control technology, weapons, tactics, and doctrine during any 20-year period in the Air Force's history. This gap between a general officer's actual combat experience and the technology and systems in contemporary use would seem to foster the division between the heroic warrior and visionary archetypes. The old ways invariably appear more heroic than the modern, technology-dependent systems.

Figure 7.3 illustrates a shift in the emphasis that the officer corps attaches to combat experience. No 4-star general officers sampled reported combat hours/sorties in the early samples. These officers had served as general officers during World War II and worked in strategic, or more visionary, roles during the war and had minimal combat experience. However, some of the 1- to 3-star generals, who had served in lower-level positions during World War II, had accumulated more combat hours and reported them in their biographies. They were no doubt proud of their accomplishments, and were perhaps implicitly arguing that the future senior Air Force officer corps leadership should belong to flying officers with combat experience.

Once members of this generation of officers began to reach 4-star ranks, they quickly surpassed the percentages of 1- to 3-star general officers reporting combat experience. Whereas the percentage of 1- to 3-star general officers reporting combat hours/sorties peaked in the 1983 sample at just over 60%, the 4-star percentages ranged from 80% to 100% from the 1978 through

Figure 7.3
**Four-Star versus 1- to 3-Star General Officers—Some Combat Hours/
Sorties Listed**

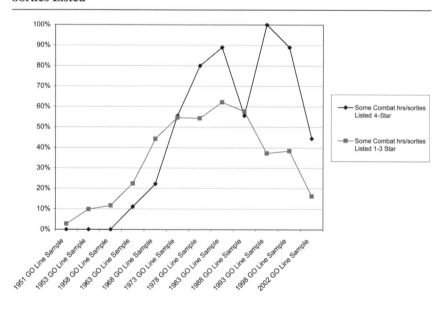

1998 samples, except for the anomaly of the 1988 sample. Consequently, the historic trend at the 4-star general officer level illustrates a shift from the visionary emphasis during World War II to nearly a requirement for heroic warrior combat experience, at least in rated 4-star general officers.

COMMAND: NOTHING IS MORE IMPORTANT, LITTLE IS LESS RELEVANT

The next characteristic concerns what levels and what types of units general officers have commanded. Although it is clear that command of flying units no longer has anything to do with leading flying units in combat, command is still an important variable, because it has become part of the standard biographical litany. General officer biographies from the 1980s onward almost uniformly contain an entry on flying and/or combat hours and another entry on command experience. These two entries have become so standard that the absence of either one is immediately apparent and signals that something is different with regard to a particular general officer. The implication is that the officer's claim of professional competence is incomplete, because it is not grounded in the twin pillars of flying experience and command. This subtly reinforces the status of pilots and places something akin to a "glass ceiling" over C4ISR officers, who may not have any flying hours and may have limited opportunities for command.

Realistically, neither flying hours nor command experience provide a credential of professional competence, but both have become associated with senior leadership qualifications in the Air Force officer corps.[4] At best, both traits serve as proxy variables for leadership skills, that is, the ability to make good decisions with incomplete or conflicting information in stressful situations and the other characteristics von Clausewitz termed "military genius," which are nearly impossible to quantify and measure.

The cultural acceptance of the proxy variables as actual defining characteristics of what the officer corps wants in its leadership runs into problems as the officer corps seeks to shift its emphasis and to broaden its jurisdiction in C4ISR, as technology continues to shift the character and nature of warfare away from onboard-piloted vehicles. Flying hours and combat sorties become meaningless in the traditional sense when the pilots are monitoring computer screens in Nevada while the aircraft are bombing targets in Iraq. Command of flying squadrons, groups, and wings has long lost meaning in combat operations, but it remains a pillar of professional competence, partly because the Air Force officer corps has failed to develop new, pertinent pillars.[5] On the other hand, the inclusion of command as a pillar means that non-pilots can also participate, although on an unequal playing field. Non-flying command has less prestige than command of a flying unit, but it still generally carries more prestige than no command experience at all.[6]

Figure 7.4 provides a comparison of the percentages of wing, group, and squadron as well as colonel-level center and program director command

Figure 7.4
Line General Officer Wing, Group, Squadron, Center, or Program Director
Command by Percentage

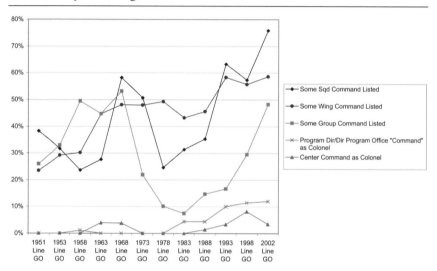

reported in the general officer samples. Center command and command as program director or director of a program office are included because the officer corps instituted them as commands in a visionary attempt to equate modern organizational structures with the older, more established squadron, group, and wing structures. Centers tend to be function specific, and positions as program directors or directors of program offices are part of the Air Force acquisition process. Neither a center nor a program typically has the manning, equipment, or aircraft of a group or wing, but center commanders and program directors frequently have rank and program responsibilities that are at least commensurate with group or wing command. Consequently, the Air Force officer corps has attempted to equate these positions to command of a group or wing and increase their status, perhaps partly as a way to encourage rated colonels to take such jobs.

The group command and wing command curves are reminiscent of the combat hours/sorties discussion above, in that many of the officers quickly elevated to general officer ranks in World War II skipped the group and wing command levels. Consequently, as more officers who were more junior during the war became general officers, the percentages of general officers with group and/or wing command experience increased. It was not until the 1993 sample that over 50% of the general officers reported some type of wing command, which indicates a rather late boost in the significance of wing command. In fact, this occurred when wing command opportunities were decreasing because of the post–Desert Storm and post–Cold War drawdown.

Nevertheless, wing command is particularly noteworthy, because there are fewer opportunities for wing command, with approximately three squadrons per wing, and because it is frequently the last stop prior to promotion to general officer rank. However, with less than 60% of the sampled general officers ever reporting some form of wing command, the apparent importance attached to command as a pillar of professional competence in modern general officer biographies may be misleading. The percentage of general officers reporting group command drops dramatically in the 1973 and 1978 samples, reflecting the demise of the group-level administrative and tactical role. The increase in group command from 1983 through 2002 reflects a reorganization of the typical wing structure into functional groups, for example, into an operations group or a logistics/maintenance group, each complete with a "commander" who has few of the earlier group command tactical and command functions.

Figure 7.5 provides qualitative data on the type of wing command first reported in an officer's biography. The initial importance of bomber wing commands is evident, as is the dominance of fighter wing commands from the 1973 sample onward. The decrease in the percentage of officers whose first or only wing commands were over bomber units may indicate a shift from the heroic to the more encompassing visionary warrior perspective, since fighter pilots have traditionally dealt directly with more rapid changes in technology and have long since grown accustomed to an evermore intricate interfacing with the C4ISR system during operations, whether via ground-based radar sites, AWACS, JSTARs, ABCCC, or FACs.

Figure 7.5
Line General Officer First Wing Command by Percentage

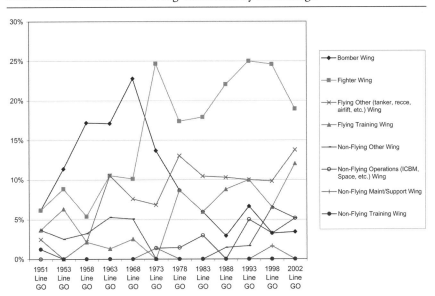

However, over the samples, the importance of flying other wings, which contain airlift, tanker, and surveillance and reconnaissance aircraft, for example, has steadily increased to the point where 14% of the line general officers reported this type of wing command. Command of a flying training wing and acquisitions "command" as a program director or director of a program office were both reported by 12% of the general officers in the 2002 sample. The later samples also show an increase in the percentage of officers reporting command over non-flying wings, although these wings are often commanded by fliers. In fact, in the 1988 sample, 31% of the line general officers reported that their first or only wing command was non-flying or a command over a center or as a program director or director of a program office (not presented graphically). In the 2002 sample, the figure was still 25%, which indicates a clear visionary trend in the last three samples. Officers with non-flying wing-level command experience were valued enough that they could be promoted to general officer ranks.[7]

In terms of differences between 4-star and 1- to 3-star general officers with respect to wing command, figure 7.6 indicates that once the rapid promotion effect of World War II diminished, a greater emphasis was placed on wing command at the 4-star than at the 1- to 3-star general officer level. The 4-star general officers appear to be more heroic warrior oriented, since only one, in the 2002 sample, reported a first or only command over a non-flying operations wing, and none ever reported a first command over a center or other type of non-flying wing. The percentage of 4-star general officers with bomber wing command approached 45% in the 1968 and 1973 samples, which grossly exceeded the 1- to 3-star general officer percentages, but no 4-star generals reported bomber wing command as their first or only wing command after the 1983 sample. The line 4-star general officers who were sampled also reported fighter wings as first commands at higher percentages than the 1- to 3-star general officers from the 1973 sample onward.

However, it is the late acceptance of officers whose first or only wing command was a flying training wing into the 4-star general officer ranks (first reported in 1993, when it was 33%, and reported in each successive sample), and an increased percentage of 4-star generals reporting flying other (tanker, airlift, surveillance and reconnaissance, etc.) wings (40% in 1978) that account for the large overall difference between the percentages of 4-star and 1- to 3-star general officers with wing command experience. These non-bomber and non-fighter wings, as well as 4-star reports of colonel-level command as program directors or directors of a program office (first reported in 1988 at 11%, and 11% in the 1993 and 2002 samples), indicate a potentially more visionary approach to wing level command.

The percentages of line general officers reporting squadron command across the samples are shown in figure 7.7. The initial decrease in reported squadron commands is explained by the fact that many of the officers quickly promoted to general officer in World War II had been squadron commanders, but then skipped group and wing command. More junior officers had not

Figure 7.6
Four-Star versus 1- to 3-Star General Officers—Some Wing Command

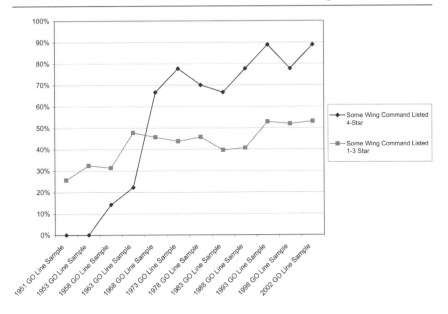

Figure 7.7
Line General Officer First Squadron Command by Percentage

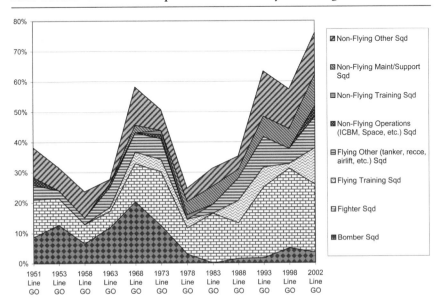

yet been squadron commanders and skipped over the squadron level to group or wing commands. They were followed by the World War II wave of aviation cadets who followed the more normal progression of promotions and command. These officers form the hump between the 1963 and 1978 samples.

The general increase in the percentage of general officers reporting a squadron command from the 1978 sample onward is accompanied by a dramatic decrease in the percentage of generals with bomber squadron command, an increase in the reporting of fighter squadron command that exceeds the earlier bomber peak, and an increase in the percentage of officers reporting initial squadron commands over non-flying squadrons. In the 2002 sample, for example, 27% of the line general officers reported that their first or only squadron command was over a non-flying unit. This indicates not only that squadron command in general was becoming accepted as a prerequisite for promotions to general officer ranks, but that up-and-coming rated officers were willing to command non-flying squadrons. That, in turn, indicates a shift toward the visionary warrior archetype.

PROMOTION SYSTEM BIAS AGAINST THE NON-PILOT MAJORITY

The emphasis on piloting and command in the traditional sense, along with the inherent bias in favor of pilots over flying commands, perpetuates a promotion system bias favoring pilots over the non-pilot majority of the officer corps.[8] Figure 7.8 shows the percentages of total general officers, colonels, lieutenant colonels, and majors who are pilots on flying status with a comparison to the percentage of total officers who are pilots on flying status. The difference between the percentage of general officers who are pilots on flying status and the percentage of total officers who are pilots on flying status has varied, but it generally remains between 40% and 50%. This 40%–50% overrepresentation of pilots on flying status in the general officer ranks remains real, even as the overall percentage of pilots on flying status in the Air Force officer corps has decreased.

Furthermore, figure 7.8 indicates that as a general trend the overrepresentation of pilots in field grade ranks is shrinking, while it remains constant in the general officer ranks. This trend is particularly apparent at the rank of colonel, which earlier formed a clear step between the percentages of the other ranks and the general officer percentages.

Previously there was a semblance of a general pattern indicative of a gradual weeding out of non-pilots (or of higher promotion rates for pilots) through the progression of ranks. Higher percentages of pilots would be promoted in stepwise fashion, culminating in a final weed-out at the general officer level. The colonel rank retained its position in this pattern until roughly 1984. From that point onward, the semblance of a step-wise building of pilot overrepresentation disappeared, as the percentages of colonels, lieutenant colonels, and majors who

Figure 7.8
**Percentages of Field Grade and General Officer Ranks That Are Pilots
on Flying Status**

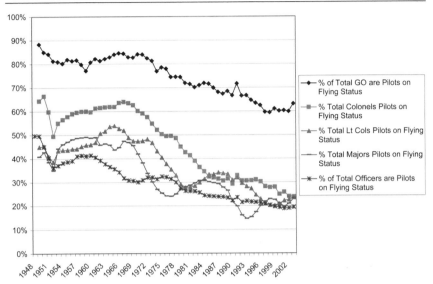

were pilots on flying status began to approach one another. From 1997 on, the proportion of field grade officers who are pilots on flying status appears to have consolidated in the 20–25% range. The over-proportional promotion of pilots now occurs primarily in one fell swoop between colonel and brigadier general.

This is noteworthy, because general officers sit on the promotion boards that decide which officers are promoted to the rank of colonel and the general officer ranks, and colonels man the promotion boards that select officers for promotion to the ranks of captain through lieutenant colonel. Consequently, general officers, as a group, have used promotions to lower the representation of colonel pilots on flying status to a level approaching the Air Force average, but they have not done the same within their own ranks.

Figure 7.8 also indicates higher levels of variation in the percentages of majors and lieutenant colonels who have been pilots on flying status. In fact, the percentages of majors and lieutenant colonels who have been pilots on flying status have dipped several times below the percentage of total officers who have been pilots. Consequently, one would expect to see more variation in promotion data bias for promotions to major and lieutenant colonel than for promotions to colonel. Finally, since the bias is obvious in the colonel promotions, and to a lesser extent in the major and lieutenant colonel ranks, from 1949 to 1984, the period from the mid-1980s onward reveals more complexity as the bias has shifted to a more subtle form.

An analysis of Air Force field grade line officer promotions from 1989 to 2003 shows that the bias is still present, although it is not as systemic as it once was in promotions within the in-primary-zone (on-time or normal) group.[9] However, the bias is clear and systemic in the below-primary-zone, or early promotion, groups.[10] Below-primary-zone selections are particularly important because the extremely small numbers of officers promoted early are identified as "fast burners" and are often given further promotable jobs, which leads to a cascading effect if they are promoted early through successive ranks.

For example, an officer entering the Air Force as a 2nd lieutenant in the early 1980s could have been promoted two years early to major, two years early to lieutenant colonel, and two years early to colonel, arriving at the rank of colonel six years earlier than his original peers. The numbers of below-primary-zone promotions tend to represent a selection pool equal to two to three times the annual number of brigadier generals selected, leading to the conclusion that the below-primary-zone promoted officers form the inner pool of contenders for promotion to brigadier general.[11]

The below-primary-zone promoted officers are also considered to be in a grooming process for that selection. Although they assume positions of responsibility with attendant risks of failure earlier, officers with multiple below-primary-zone promotions tend to move more often and spend less time in their duty billets. This exposes them to more aspects of the Air Force, but it limits their opportunities for both failure and learning at each duty station. They appear more rounded and experienced than their primary-zone colleagues, which in theory keeps them on the promotion fast track. Consequently, below-primary-zone promotions indicate a separate, less-traveled inside track that provides a better explanation of the bias in promotion to general officer rank than is provided by on-time promotions.

From 1989 on, the number of non-rated officers considered for below-primary-zone promotion to major greatly exceeded (ranging between the extremes of 3:1 to 6:1) the number of rated officers considered. More non-rated officers were being considered for below-primary-zone promotion to major, because they had better records and did better at the major command screening boards. As the rated officer initial commitment and back-to-back early cockpit tours climbed, rated officers had fewer opportunities for staff and other non-flying jobs before coming up for below-primary-zone consideration. Rated officers spent most of their time flying, and their records were largely indistinguishable from each other. Non-rated officers, however, had more opportunities for command positions over enlisted personnel, and often migrated into staff positions earlier. Consequently, larger numbers of non-rated captains had records with distinguishing characteristics such as command over a large maintenance or security police section and/or staff positions with responsibility for major programs and resources.[12]

As a class, these non-rated officers obviously did better at the major command screening boards, being pushed forward to the actual below-primary-zone board at rates exceeding 3:1 over their rated peers, but nonetheless doing much more poorly where it most mattered—at the actual promotion board. It is possible that the rated officers selected for below-primary-zone consideration formed a small, special group of rated officers with truly extraordinary records that stood above all other rated as well as non-rated records. If so, this could indicate an earlier fast-track selection process whereby only a very small, select group of rated officers were chosen and moved into positions that engendered outstanding records. They might also have been war heroes of some sort in Desert Storm or the post-war aerial occupation of Iraq. Or there could simply have been a professional bias favoring rated over non-rated officers at the boards. All three explanations are based on a bias of some sort. The only difference is with regard to whom and where the bias is exhibited.

In more recent times, the Air Force has provided data breakouts beyond the rated versus non-rated statistics. This allows the separation of pilots from the other rated categories and eliminates any skewing caused by the navigators and ABMs who are included in the rated numbers.[13]

Figure 7.9 uses trendlines to depict the percentage of pilots selected in-primary-zone for major, lieutenant colonel, and colonel.[14] By 2003, pilots comprised about 25% of the officers selected in-primary-zone for major, lieutenant colonel, and colonel. These figures are not particularly overrepresentative, since the percentage of captains who are pilots was 22%.

Below-primary-zone promotion selection statistics for promotion to major, lieutenant colonel, and colonel provide a better explanation of the pilot overrepresentation in the general officer ranks. Figure 7.10 graphically depicts the

Figure 7.9
Percentage of Line Officers Selected for Promotion to Major, Lt Col, and Colonel That Are Pilots, In-Primary-Zone, 1989–2003

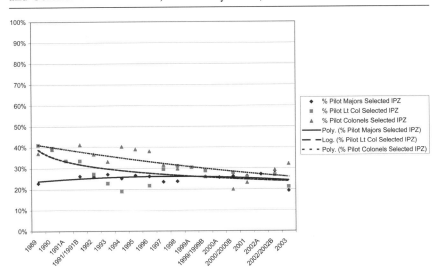

Figure 7.10
Percentage of Line Officers Selected for Promotion to Major, Lt Col, and Colonel That Are Pilots, Below-Primary-Zone, 1989–2003

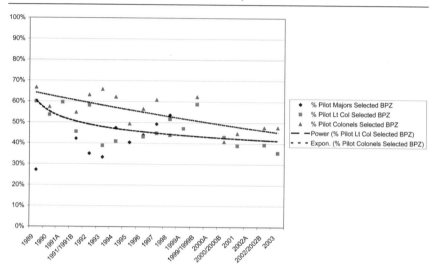

percentage of pilots selected below-primary-zone for major, lieutenant colonel, and colonel. Trendlines are added for lieutenant colonel and colonel.[15] These below-primary-zone trendlines for the percentage of pilots promoted to lieutenant colonel and colonel run approximately 20% higher than the in-primary-zone case. In addition, one can visualize the stair-step distillation of increasing percentages of rated officers from below-primary-zone lieutenant colonel to colonel, with the cream presumably continuing on to brigadier general.

Figure 7.11 looks specifically at line in-primary-zone and below-primary-zone promotion rates to colonel between 1989 and 2003. It depicts the results of a statistical test using difference of proportions to determine if there is a statistically significant difference between the promotion rates for pilots and those for all other line officers. If the promotion boards consider all line officers regardless of career field equally, and there is no skewing of "good" officers into any one field, one would expect the plotted result of the statistical test to fall in the box between the line along the 2 (critical value, positive tail, a = .025) and the line along the –2 (critical value, negative tail, a = .025) on the vertical axis. One would expect the results to fall within this box 95% of the time if there is no bias. If a result falls below the –2 line, that result indicates a bias in favor of the promotion rate for all other line officers. If a result is plotted above the 2 line, that result indicates a bias in favor of the promotion rate for pilots. In the in-primary-zone case, there is a statistically significant bias in favor of pilots in 8 of the 15 boards, with the other 7 showing no bias. In

Figure 7.11
Line Colonel In-Primary-Zone and Below-Primary-Zone Promotions,
1989–2003, Difference of Proportions

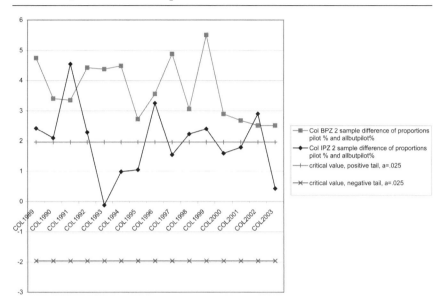

the below-primary-zone case, however, there is a clear, statistically significant bias in favor of pilots at every colonel promotion board between 1989 and 2003.[16] This is remarkable, but not unexpected. There is never a statistically significant bias in favor of non-pilot line officers.

IMPLICATIONS

Given the Air Force officer corps' traditional emphasis on flying and its historic tendency to limit command to pilots, the inclusion of flying and combat data as well as information on command experience in official biographies may not be surprising. After all, similar information is contained in officers' official records and used in promotion boards. However, the combined effect of this information together with the command restrictions on non-pilots is clear to see in Air Force officer promotions. There is a historic bias in favor of pilots, and although this bias appears to have diminished greatly in in-primary-zone promotions, it is still quite evident in below-promotion-zone promotions to field grade ranks. This process contributes to the overrepresentation of pilots among general officers. The below-primary-zone promotion system allows the profession to fast-track a small number of officers into command billets and/or billets that broaden their perspectives, make them more promotable, and line them up for further billets of increasing responsibility.

Pilots can broaden as majors, lieutenant colonels, and colonels into other line positions, but non-rated officers cannot broaden into cockpits or leadership positions in flying units at that level. Pilots are universally qualified within the profession, but other officers are not. Even at the general officer level, non-pilots cannot simply be given any position. They are restricted to appropriate positions. This of course requires more detailed planning and limits personnel options. Consequently, there is a limit to how many non-pilot general officers can serve in the Air Force, because non-pilots, and non-rated officers in particular, are inherently inflexible.

The percentage of non-pilot officers who are selected below-primary-zone for promotion to colonel may be an indication of what that limit for non-pilot general officers is believed to be (55% in 2003). Or at least this is perceived as an acceptable zone within which the profession can operate as it comes to grips with the growth of C4ISR officers, the decrease in pilots and navigators within its ranks, the shift of decision making out of the cockpit and into the C4ISR system, and the declining applicability of flying hours and traditional commands as proxies for leadership attributes. If the pilot heroic warrior reigns as the archetypical Air Force officer, it will be difficult for the officer corps, the Air Force at large, and society to comprehend the Air Force's claims for jurisdiction in space and cyberspace.

The Unnoticed Evolution of C4ISR Experience within the General Officer (GO) Ranks

Chapters 6 and 7 capture the struggle between the visionary and heroic warriors within the Air Force officer corps. The visionary warriors emphasized the importance of education, eased restrictions on command of flying units, and symbolically recognized the increasing importance of space and missiles by granting the space wings. The heroic warrior counter was a renewed emphasis on piloting and command, manifested in official biographies, official records, and promotions. However, beneath the rather public discussions on these issues, visionary warriors were making more subtle but nevertheless important inroads within the general officer (GO) ranks.

This chapter provides data and analysis on four trends that comprehensively demonstrate that the C4ISR experience base within the Air Force general officer corps has been steadily growing. These trends are reflected in (1) The increasing breadth of career fields represented in the general officer ranks; (2) The increasing percentages of general officers who have served one or more tours in C4ISR; (3) The increase in general officer missile and space badge wearing; and (4) The way that "hot stick" (skillful pilot) characteristics, which were previously based on flying skills, have evolved to include C4ISR aspects.

INCREASING BREADTH OF CAREER SPECIALTIES IN GO RANKS

The diversity of career fields being accepted into the inner corps of the profession as the percentage of non-rated general officers increased is captured in the *initial* and in the *apparent* Air Force (career field) Specialty Codes (AFSCs) of the line general officer samples. The data also provide information on the relative status of various career fields as measured by officers who have changed specialties during their careers. AFSCs are the career field classifications that are assigned to each officer. In addition, duty billets are categorized by AFSC requirement. An officer's AFSC determines which duty billets he is eligible to fill. This study uses the term *initial* AFSC to indicate the specialty that an officer appears to have been assigned upon entry into active, commissioned service. The term *apparent* AFSC is used to characterize an officer's specialty as viewed over his career prior to becoming a general officer.[1]

Looking at the samples, over the course of time the range of initial AFSCs has broadened considerably. Although the Air Force line general officer corps was close to 90% pilots in 1951, in the 1951 sample only about 65% of the line general officers had gone directly into pilot training and service with the Air Corps. Whereas all the graduates of the Aviation Cadet Program and many of the West Pointers had gone directly into pilot training, over a third of the line general officers served initially in non-flying billets. Furthermore, almost 25% of the line general officers initially served not only in non-flying billets but in Army billets outside of the Air Corps in, for example, the Coastal Artillery or Cavalry (see figure 8.1). Most of these officers then went to pilot training and transferred to the Air Corps, but some remained in their original specialties and branches and joined the Air Corps or Air Force in these non-rated capacities. Some of the officer pilots in the early Air Force general officer samples had actually left the Air Corps temporarily for career broadening tours in other Army branches before World War II.[2]

Figure 8.1
Line General Officer Initial AFSC by Percentage, Excluding Pilots

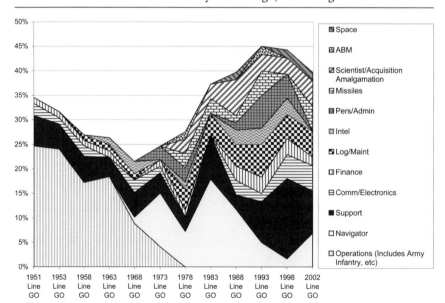

The other 10% of the line general officers in the sample (the non-pilots) initially served in the categories of communications/electronics, finance, and support. *Communications/electronics* officers provided the obvious and important functions of communications and radar links for command and control of a global Air Force, from the control tower at the local field to Air Force units scattered around the world. The term *finance* is somewhat deceptive because the category also includes statistics officers, who for example performed continual analyses of bombing missions during wartime in order to develop methods to increase bombing effectiveness and efficiency. In addition, early Air Force computer development occurred in both the communications/electronic and finance areas. Consequently, precursors to C4ISR were found in both fields. The term *support* is used in the general officer sampling as a catchall term for line career fields not specifically mentioned in the sampling.[3] Security police and civil engineers are examples of two types of support specialists that the Air Force required, and that, in these particular cases, had been provided to the Air Corps by other Army branches.

This diversity in initial AFSCs gave the Air Force general officer corps of 1951 much broader perspectives on warfare and concepts of profession than succeeding samples. The percentages of line general officers who had initially served in non-pilot billets steadily declined from the 1951 through the 1968 samples as the officers who had joined prior to World War II gradually retired. Then initial resurgence of non-pilot initial AFSCs comes primarily from general officers who initially served as navigators, which does not provide quite the same broadening effect as non-flying experience. By the 1993 sample, line general officers who had initially served as navigators were in such a decline that line general officers with initial tours in support exceeded initial navigators as the largest initial job group outside of pilots.

The trend in the samples from 1968 through 1993 is of increasing percentages of general officers who had served initially in non-pilot AFSCs. By the 1973 sample, the number of initial non-pilot career fields had risen to 6, and by 1978 some Air Force line general officers had initially served in 11 non-pilot career fields. The 1988 sample yielded the first general officer who had initially served in the space field. The percentage of general officers who had initially served in non-pilot billets peaked in the 1993 sample at 45%, but it was still approximately 40% in 2002. However, a major difference between the 1951 and 2002 samples is that although 35% to 40% of the general officers in each sample had initially served in non-pilot billets, most of those in the 1951 sample went on to become pilots, while most in the 2002 sample remained in non-pilot billets (see figure 8.2).

It is clear not only that the percentages of non-pilot officers generally increased across the samples but also that the diversity of *apparent* AFSCs among the non-rated general officers increased.[4] This indicates a widening of the inner core of the profession. Officers from career fields that once could only provide colonel technical specialists to advise general officers have become worthy in their own right to enter the inner core as general officers.

Figure 8.2
Line General Officer Apparent AFSC by Percentage, Excluding Pilots

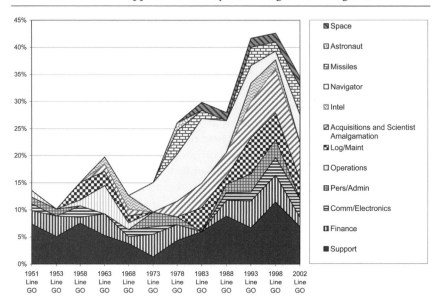

The data also indicate that a number of general officers in each sample have changed AFSCs during the course of their careers. This demonstrates that some career fields, such as pilot and space, are perceived to have status, since both have experienced net gains as officers have changed career fields. Some career fields are losers, and some show mixed results.

INCREASING EXPERIENCE IN C4ISR REGARDLESS OF CORE CAREER SPECIALTY

Officers can serve in C4ISR-type duties without being in C4ISR AFSCs. In fact, this accounts for the bulk of the general officer C4ISR experience.[5] Figure 8.3 provides a comparison of the curves for each of the three rank categories that I created to measure general officer C4ISR experience: at the ranks of lieutenant colonel and below, at the rank of colonel, and at the rank of general officer. The relationship between the curves appears to fall into two major divisions. From the 1951 through 1978 samples, the percentage of line general officer biographies listing some type of C4ISR tour as a general officer or colonel tends to equal or exceed the percentage for the lieutenant colonel and below category. However, the lieutenant colonel and below curve dramatically exceeds both colonel level and general officer level C4ISR tour experience in the 1983 through 1993 samples. This makes sense, in that the strategic air defense buildup in the 1950s and the later missile and space

Figure 8.3
**Line General Officer Comparison First C4ISR Tour as Lt Col and Below,
as Colonel, and as General Officer, by Percentage**

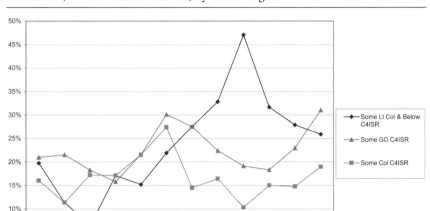

buildups that generated many more C4ISR billets below the rank of colonel should have a lag effect in the data. In addition, the Vietnam War required larger numbers of junior officers, who became generals a decade or two later, to serve as FACs and in CAOC-type jobs. The exposure to C4ISR while serving in junior ranks presumably has a bigger impact on an officer's perspectives and career than a C4ISR tour later in his career.

Up to this point, the line general officer C4ISR tour data has been pooled at each rank category without respect to whether an officer has had C4ISR experience in another rank category. Consequently, it is not clear whether many of the line general officers had one C4ISR tour or a few line general officers had multiple C4ISR tours at different ranks. Figure 8.4 clarifies this matter. It starts with the C4ISR tour data for the lieutenant colonel and below category. Then, at the colonel level, only general officers with biographical data indicating that their very first C4ISR tour occurred at the rank of colonel are added to the lieutenant colonel and below data. Similarly, at the general officer level, only general officers whose biographies indicate no C4ISR tours until the rank of general officer are added to the colonel level data. The effect is three lines showing the cumulative effect of adding these new officers with C4ISR tours at each level. The first and most obvious observation is that the lines do not overlap. Consequently, the same officers are not providing the C4ISR experience at each level. As the rank category increases, more new officers are added to the C4ISR experience base.

Figure 8.4
Line General Officer with One or More C4ISR Tours Coded in Ranks
of 2nd Lt to General versus General Officers with Apparent C4ISR AFSCs

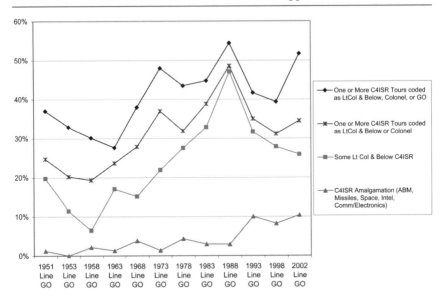

A second observation is that in terms of a rough order of magnitude, one-third to one-half of the general officers historically had at least one C4ISR tour in at least one rank category. A third observation is that the lieutenant colonel and below category has generally contributed the highest percentage of the cumulative total. Since CAOC experience accounts for the colonel and general officer level increases in the 2002 sample, it is reasonable to expect a lag, similar to the 1973–1988 Vietnam era hump in the lieutenant colonel and below category, in the post–2002 future, as officers who served as junior officers in CAOCs in the 1990s are promoted to general officer ranks. Finally, the bottom curve on the chart shows the percentage of total line general officers per sample with *apparent* C4ISR AFSCs.[6] In 2002, these officers comprised only 10% of the line general officers, but over half of the line general officers had served in some C4ISR capacity. Consequently, it is clear that the vast majority of general officers with at least one C4ISR duty tour are not career C4ISR officers.

Figures 8.5, 8.6, and 8.7 distinguish between 4-star and 1- to 3-star general officers with at least one C4ISR-type tour in the three rank categories of lieutenant colonel and below, colonel, and general officer.[7] Figures 8.5, 8.6, and 8.7 are each independent. The same general officer could be counted once in each rank category if that individual served one or more C4ISR tours in that particular rank category. I use the convention "some C4ISR" to distinguish this data from the data presented in figures 8.8 and 8.9, in which an officer is only counted one time and in the lowest rank category in which that officer served the first C4ISR-type tour.

In the lieutenant colonel and below case, it appears that the junior C4ISR tours do not become important at the 4-star level until the 1988 sample. The initial decrease in the percentage of line general officers with one or more C4ISR-type tours in the ranks of lieutenant colonel and below captures the departure of the general officers with extensive pre-World War II experience, which often included larger amounts of experience in billets not directly related to flying. The 1988 4-star spike is noteworthy, not only because of its quantity but also because of the diversity of C4ISR tours exhibited, that is, in space operations, missile operations, CAOC, FAC, and air defense. Of course, in the 1- to 3-star general officer samples, all types of C4ISR tours are represented at least once, and many continuously across all the samples. After all, very few 4-star general officers have C4ISR apparent AFSCs.

Figure 8.6 provides a comparison of the graphs for 4-star and 1- to 3-star general officers reporting one or more C4ISR tours in the rank of colonel without respect to whether the officer served in a C4ISR tour while in the lower officer ranks ("some C4ISR").

Figure 8.7 presents graphs of the percentages of 4-star and 1- to 3-star general officers reporting a general officer level C4ISR tour, regardless of C4ISR experience in the ranks of lieutenant colonel and below or colonel

Figure 8.5
**Four-Star versus 1- to 3-Star General Officers—Some Lt Col
and Below C4ISR**

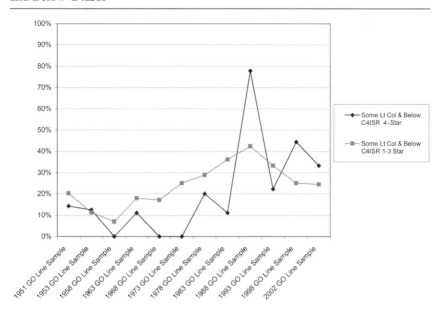

Figure 8.6
Four-Star versus 1- to 3-Star General Officers—Some Colonel C4ISR

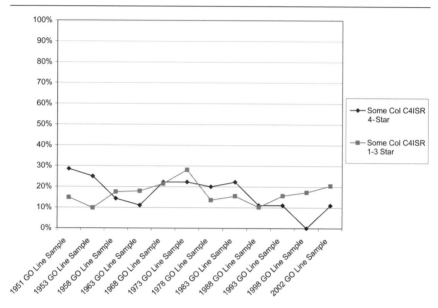

("some C4ISR"). The 4-star curve is quite erratic as usual, but it is notewor-thy that from the 1973 sample onward, the percentage of 4-star generals who have served a general officer C4ISR tour equals or exceeds the 1- to 3-star general officer percentage. The 1- to 3-star general officer curve is stable by comparison, but of course, the general officer level C4ISR jobs, which are typically not 4-star billets, must be filled. Since there is no prescribed path to reach general officer rank and there are no quotas with which to promote particular non-pilot line officers to general officer rank, any general officer might be selected to man the billets. In addition, some general officers might be assigned to general officer C4ISR billets to round out their experience and make them competitive with regard to further promotion: thus, C4ISR experience at the general officer level appears to be becoming more valued or more necessary.

From a qualitative perspective, no 4-star general officer served in a communications/electronics billet at the general officer level. This indicates that tours in communications/electronics appear to be seen by the profession as being more specialist-oriented, since out of all the samples across the three levels, there is only one 4-star report of a communications/electronics tour, and that occurred at the colonel level. On the other hand, at least one 1- to 3-star general officer reported serving in communications/electronics at each of the three rank categories in each sample. The Air Force Communications Service/ Command, which rated the status of a major command, was commanded only

Figure 8.7
Four-Star versus 1- to 3-Star General Officers—Some GO C4ISR

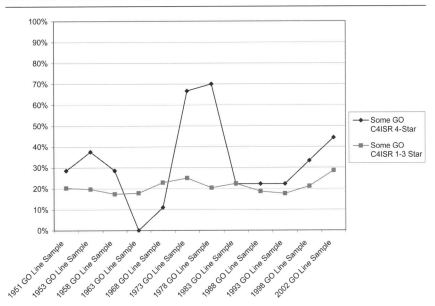

by major generals (2 stars); most major commands are commanded by 4-star general officers. We can see that communications and electronics have always been important to the Air Force, just not at the 4-star level.

Intelligence appears to have moved to a similar position across the samples. Whereas 4-star generals in the earlier samples often served in an intelligence-type billet at the general officer or lieutenant colonel and below level, none are included in the later samples. One or more 1- to 3-star general officers reported serving in intelligence-type positions at the general officer level in each sample as well as in all but one sample at the lieutenant colonel and below and colonel levels. Intelligence service does not appear to be a desired or required characteristic at the 4-star level, perhaps at least partly because as in the case of communications, there is no 4-star Air Force intelligence billet.[8]

Air battle managers were noticeably absent from the 4-star general officer samples at any level, and only two general officers from all the 1- to 3-star general officer samples reported being air battle managers at the colonel and lieutenant colonel and below levels. However, the lack of air battle manager tours at the general officer level may be misleading, in that many of the C4ISR categories such as air defense and CAOC are air battle manager functions, so many general officers perform air battle manager tasks and have performed them at lower ranks. However, they are not air battle managers. On the other hand, the fact that only two air battle managers show up across all of the samples, and these two had switched career fields by the time they made general officer rank, reflects the historical promotion problems for non-rated officers serving in flying-related fields. The functionality is required at all three rank category levels, but officers in the career field that provides that functionality from the rank of 2nd lieutenant onward are not typically promoted to the general officer ranks and are not used in the air battle manager functionality when promoted. This is a result of the profession's affinity for filling senior positions with responsibility over flying operations with pilots. Air battle managers appear to fall into the category of technical specialists that do not warrant general officer billets.

With respect to missile operations, the first general officer report of missile operator experience occurred in the 1953 sample at the colonel level, and the 1- to 3-star general officers reported at least one colonel level missile operations tour in every sample after 1953 except 1988. The first general officer level missile operations tour was reported in the 1958 1- to 3-star general officer level sample. However, the first 4-star general officer with general officer level service in missile operations was not seen until the 2002 sample. Of course, that same general in the 2002 sample also accounts for one of the two 4-star general officer reports of colonel level service in missile operations as well as one of the two reports of missile operations at the lieutenant colonel and below level.

The first report of space operations was in the 1968 sample at the general officer level in the 1- to 3-star group. The first 4-star general officer to report space operations experience at the general officer level followed in the 1978 sample, which is also when the first 1- to 3-star general officer reported serving in space operations at the lieutenant colonel and below level. Only one 4-star general officer ever reported a space operations tour in the lieutenant colonel and below ranks (1988 sample). The 1- to 3-star general officers first reported an officer who served a colonel level space operations tour in 1983, and continued reporting officers with colonel level experience through 2002. Four-star general officers did not report any colonel level space tours in any samples.

The juxtaposition of the almost 40 years between the first sample mentioning missile operations and the first 4-star general officer level missile operations report and the 10 years between the first space operations report and the first 4-star general officer level space operations report indicates that the importance of space operations was recognized more quickly and considered a more important experience for 4-star generals. Structural factors also played a role in the paths of missile and space operations. The Air Force integrated the strategic missile force into Strategic Air Command.[9] This of course meant that at some level, missile units would be amalgamated with flying units and at that level, if not before, missileers could no longer command. After all, the ICBM versions of unmanned bombers were not flown by pilots; they were simply launched.

The warning aspects of space operations tied functionally into air defense. As the justification for the Air Force officer corps' air defense jurisdiction waned in the face of the Soviet ICBM threat, the Air Force officer corps adjusted to provide warning against an ICBM attack. However, it was not in the Air Force officer corps' interest to publicly recognize this new jurisdiction and then have to compete to fill it. Instead, the Air Force officer corps sought to create the impression that minor modifications were being made to an existing jurisdiction.

Consequently, the Air Force was able to shift resources from the diminishing air defense jurisdiction into the new and expanding space operations jurisdiction under the guise of the same Aerospace Defense Command and NORAD structures, at least partly because of the overlapping functionality. The Air Force officer corps was simply increasing the altitude of air defense by changing the command's name from *Air* to *Aerospace* Defense Command. At the same time, by separating its space and missile activities into at least three parts, with ICBMs under Strategic Air Command, space and missile development and acquisitions under Air Force Systems Command, and space operations under Aerospace Defense Command (later Air Force Space Command), the Air Force officer corps also prevented the emergence of an integrated and potentially independent space and missile service.

The sample data capture the overall decline in the importance of air defense in the colonel and below ranks. As the active duty command and control aspects of air defense were consolidated in the 1980s and then those below the level of NORAD headquarters shifted to the Air National Guard in the 1990s, opportunities for colonel and below air defense positions disappeared. At the general officer level, at least one 1- to 3-star general officer reported an air defense tour in each sample, but 4-star reporting is more sporadic, and no air defense tours are reported for 7 out of the 12 samples.

After 1980, it is difficult to distinguish in the samples between general officer level space and air defense tours because of the overlap between NORAD and Air Force Space Command, with some biographies emphasizing NORAD or placing NORAD, which is air defense, first, and other biographies placing space first. The inclusion of the ICBM force under Air Force Space Command after Strategic Air Command was dissolved further complicates the distinctions between space, air defense, and missile operations. Although logical in many ways, the consolidation of space, missiles, and part of the remaining Air Force air defense activities into Air Force Space Command combines several aspects of C4ISR that could potentially seek independence from the Air Force and become an independent service with a functional monopoly on C4ISR-type issues if the Air Force were to remain tied to piloted flight as its prime raison d'être.

Although 1- to 3-star general officers reported Single Integrated Operational Plan (SIOP) tours at the lieutenant colonel and below, colonel, and general officer levels, the sampled 4-star general officers only reported SIOP experience in the general officer ranks, and only for the period of the 1973 through 1988 samples. Furthermore, this was typically included as part of the job description for commanding Strategic Air Command. Although there may have been some underreporting due to security concerns, it is interesting that so few general officers overall reported working in billets that developed the SIOP, since the SIOP after all governed the actions of all the bomber, tanker, and missile alert crews, and served as the basis for organizing and directing Strategic Air Command's combat forces for so long.

The 4-star general officer reporting of CAOC-type duty is very light at the lieutenant colonel and below and colonel levels, but heavier at the general officer level. More 1- to 3-star general officers reported CAOC experience at the lieutenant colonel and below level, reaching a peak of 9% in the 1983 sample. At the colonel level, 1- to 3-star general officers reported CAOC-type tours in two waves. The first lasted from 1958 through 1983, and the second started in 1998, jumping from the one or two officer level to five in 2002. At the general officer level, wartime CAOC service is a different story. It is valued at the 4-star rank, with 45% of the 4-star general officer 1973 sample and 30% of the 1978 sample reporting CAOC duty as general officers in Vietnam. This makes sense, since it is in the CAOC and its precursors that combat command is exercised.

The lack of any peacetime CAOC tours indicates that such roles were not valued or not really available in peacetime operations. However, the CAOC function was incredibly important during wartime. The same story is evident in the 1993 through 2002 samples, where one 4-star general and one 1- to 3-star general reported CAOC-type duty in the 1993 sample, and the number of 1- to 3-star generals reporting CAOC duty increased in each succeeding sample. No 4-star general officer reported CAOC duty in the 1998 sample, but two reported it in the 2002 sample. One can expect positive slopes in CAOC reporting in the future, since the Air Force began to stress the importance of the CAOC as a *weapons system* in the 1990s and because Desert Storm and successive Air Force operations in Southwest Asia and the Balkans have been run out of CAOCs. Consequently, there are both more opportunities for CAOC-type duty and more recognition of its importance.

The Forward Air Controller (FAC) factor is of particular note because of its relatively high level of reporting across the samples in terms of both number of samples and number of 4-star generals reporting FAC-type experience in at least one of the three levels. For example, at the lieutenant colonel and below level, 4-star generals reported one to four FAC-type tours per year in the 1978 through 2002 samples. The duration of the effect across six samples covers an almost 30-year period. The frequency with which colonel level FAC and liaison tours were reported tied tours with air defense as the most popular colonel level C4ISR-type tours for 4-star generals. Four-star general officers also reported FAC or liaison tours at the general officer level in three early samples, but there are no 1- to 3-star general officer reports of FAC-type duty at the general officer level.

Heroic warrior aspects are inherent in this particular C4ISR-type tour and might therefore explain its dominant position when looking at C4ISR experience in the Air Force 4-star general officer world. Serving as a FAC at the confluence of the tactical fighter and the command and control spheres certainly gave these officers a perspective on the complexity of air warfare far beyond that seen by their strictly fighter or bomber pilot peers. The officers were a vital part of the command and control system. It is remarkable that 44% of the 1998 4-star sample served as FACs at the lieutenant colonel and below level, since FAC aircraft accounted at any given time for only 10–25% of the total Air Force aircraft in theater during the Vietnam War.

The apparent importance afforded to this FAC experience in the 4-star ranks is further supported by the fact that the first post-Vietnam lieutenant colonel and below FACs appeared simultaneously in the 4-star and 1- to 3-star 1978 samples, which indicates that FAC experience was rewarded rather than being a hindrance to relatively quick promotion to 4-star rank. In addition, lieutenant colonel and below FAC experience in the 1- to 3-star general officers peaked earlier, at 24%, in the 1988 sample, but it did not peak for another 10 years at the 4-star level, so the percentage of 4-star FACs continued to increase as the selection pool decreased. The 1- to 3-star generals reported only two (1951 and 1958 samples) occurrences of colonel level FAC or liaison tours, which stands in marked contrast to the six reports by 4-star generals.

This is noteworthy because the colonel level FAC tours tend to be liaison duties or command over a FAC unit, not actually flying an aircraft on the front lines, coordinating targets while being shot at. Consequently, the colonel level FAC tours are less heroic warrior than the lieutenant colonel tours. However, they are still are considered worthwhile enough to have done and to include in biographies. The same holds true for the general officer level FAC-type tours.

When data only from those general officers whose first C4ISR tour occurred while in the rank of colonel are added to the overall lieutenant colonel and below C4ISR chart, the result is Figure 8.8. The dramatic peak created by the 1988 4-star general officer sample data for C4ISR tours in the rank of lieutenant colonel and below (figure 8.5) continues to dominate the graphs. Figure 8.8 also provides the curves for the initial Air Force Specialty Code C4ISR general officer amalgamation for 4-star and for 1- to 3-star general officers to show that the majority of the officers who have served one or more C4ISR tours in the ranks of colonel and below did not start their Air Force careers in C4ISR career fields. The growth in officers promoted to general officer who started out in C4ISR career fields has been primarily in the 1- to 3-star general officer ranks. Only two officers started their Air Force commissioned service in C4ISR career fields and were promoted all the way through 4-star general officer rank.

Figure 8.9 adds to figure 8.8 the data from general officers whose first C4ISR tour occurred in the general officer ranks and changes the comparison from *initial* AFSC to *apparent* AFSC. The 4-star 1988 peak is no longer the standout feature. In most of the 4-star samples, over half of the general officers have C4ISR experience. At the 1- to 3-star level, approximately one-third to one-half of the general officers have served a minimum of one C4ISR tour

Figure 8.8
Four-Star versus 1- to 3-Star General Officers—One or More C4ISR-Coded Tours per Individual Officer as Lt Col and Below or Colonel versus Initial C4ISR AFSC GOs

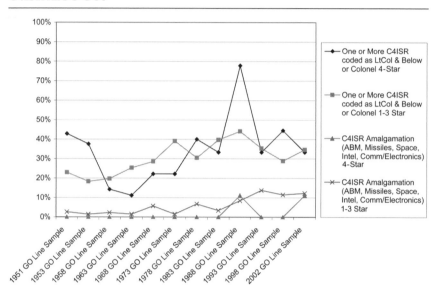

in the rank categories of lieutenant colonel and below, colonel, or general officer. Since 4-star general officers have become more C4ISR experienced over time, they may be looking for this experience when deciding which 3-star generals to promote to 4-star rank.

Figure 8.9 also provides the curves for the *apparent* Air Force Specialty Code C4ISR general officer amalgamation for 4-star and 1- to 3-star general officers. Although the overall trend in the 1- to 3-star curve is still positive, the overall values are lower than in the *initial* Air Force Specialty Code curve in figure 8.8, since many officers left the C4ISR fields during their careers. The same is true for the 4-star *apparent* AFSC curve. Of the two 4-star general officers who started their Air Force commissioned service in C4ISR career fields and were promoted all the way through 4-star general officer rank, only the one in the 2002 sample stayed in the C4ISR career field. It is clear that the largest part of the growth in general officer C4ISR experience comes from officers who do not have initial or apparent AFSCs that fall within the C4ISR amalgamation.

INCREASING MISSILE AND SPACE BADGE WEAR

The percentages of general officers who wear missile and space badges on their uniforms reinforce the growing importance of C4ISR as well as the fact

Figure 8.9
Four-Star versus 1- to 3-Star General Officers—One or More C4ISR-Coded
Tours per Individual Officer as Lt Col and Below, Colonel, or GO versus
Apparent C4ISR AFSC GOs

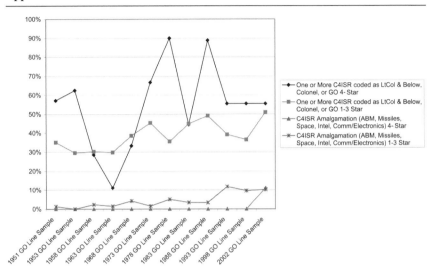

that most of the general officers with some C4ISR experience are not from C4ISR career fields. A short study of general officer badge wear indicates that badge wear has increased dramatically across the samples.[10] By the 1998 sample, over half of the line general officers were wearing one or more non-rated badges. Figure 8.10 allows multiple badge entries per individual officer. This inflates the overall percentage but provides more detail on the badges worn. The inflation generally increases with successive samples, indicating that not only the wearing of badges but also the wearing of multiple badges increased over time.

Wearing of the missile badge, which includes both the operations and support variants, and the space badge are of particular interest because of their C4SIR connection. The first missile badge appeared in the 1963 sample, and the first space badge was worn in the 1978 sample. By 2002, the number of space and missile badges per officer in the sample reaches almost 30%. The growth in popularity of wearing a missile or space badge is interesting, because these badges are being worn mostly by rated officers. Figure 8.11 provides a comparison between the percentages of missile badges and space badges worn and the percentage of line general officers with *apparent* space or missiles AFSCs. Although there were no general officers with apparent space or missile specialties until the 1978 sample, some general officers sported missile badges prior to 1978. In the 2002 sample, when there were close to 30% space and missile badges distributed over the sample, only 7% of the general officers in the sample had apparent space or missile career specialties.

Figure 8.10
Line General Officer Non-Rated Badge Wear by Percentage, Excluding Parachute Wings

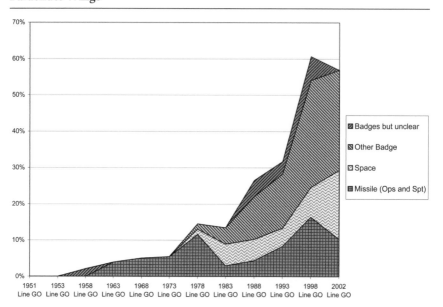

Figure 8.11
Line General Officer Missile (Operations or Support) Badge and/or Space Badge Wear by Percentage

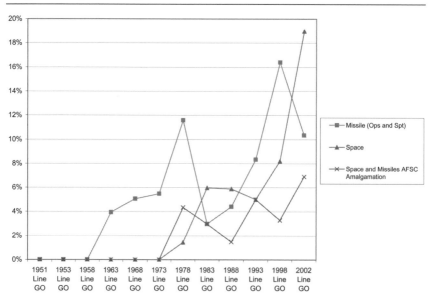

Consequently, there appears to be a sizable and growing segment of the general officer corps that is willing to or desires to appear to be associated with the space and missiles career fields. However, the cause of this growing association is not clear. The increased badge wear could indicate a desire for general officers to be or to have been connected to these C4ISR aspects of the Air Force officer corps' jurisdiction. It might also be the result of a purposeful funneling of up-and-coming officers through space and missile billets either for broadening experience or to bind a potentially rebellious arm to the service. Finally, it might reflect officer cross-training into acquisitions jobs that is masked by the space or missile badges. In any case, the 4-star general officers in the sample are not lagging behind in missile or space badge wear. Figure 8.12 shows 4-star general officer missile badge wear, which frequently exceeds the 1- to 3-star missile wear percentage. However, it also reflects the Strategic Air Command tradition of its 4-star commanders wearing a missile badge.

The case for space badge wear is not quite as compelling, although the 2002 sample data indicate the potential beginning of a trend toward increased space badge wear among 4-star general officers (see figure 8.13).

TRANSFORMATION OF THE "HOT STICK"

The final trend indicating increased C4ISR experience among general officers deals with the "hot stick," that is, being an extraordinary pilot, characteristic.

Figure 8.12
Four-Star versus 1- to 3-Star General Officers—Badges—Missiles (Operations and Support)

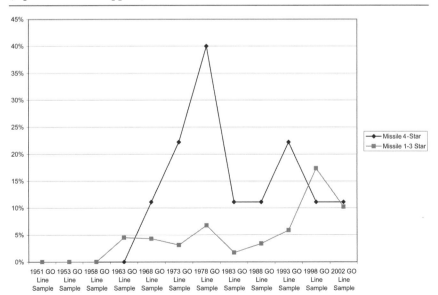

Figure 8.13
Four-Star versus 1- to 3-Star General Officers—Badges—Space

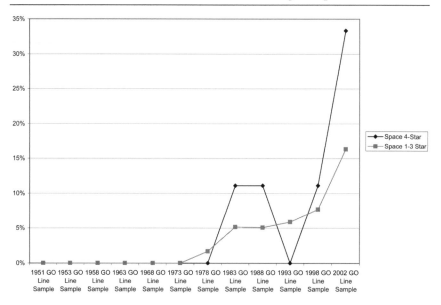

These data were captured by recording whether a general officer's biography refers to being an astronaut, a weapons school graduate, an ace, a member of an aerial demonstration team like the Thunderbirds, a recipient of an aviation trophy or holder of a flying record, or a test pilot. The percentage of general officers per sample reporting hot stick experience is presented in figure 8.14. The Vietnam War provides a distinct turning point with respect to the importance attached to general officer flying skills. This, however, masks a tension between the heroic warrior and visionary archetypes inherent in the hot stick category.

The Fighter Weapons School (FWS) subcategory, which includes officers who were graduates of a weapons school, instructors at a weapons school, or served as weapons and tactics officers, accounts for a large part of the hot stick category from the 1978 sample onward. From the heroic pilot warrior perspective, the FWS is a peacetime ace program. The FWS provides a way to recognize tactical hot sticks throughout the Air Force during peacetime, to teach them to become better tactical combat fliers, and to have them share the combination of their acquired knowledge and inherent flying skills with other aircrews. The FWS's emphasis on flying skills and decision making during free-flowing tactical engagements stands in stark contrast to the heavy scripting of missions flown by astronauts, modern test pilots, and aerial demonstration teams. Consequently, the FWS subcategory rivals acedom as a method for determining which pilots possess that special combination of inherent flying skill, nerve, intelligence, and luck—that *right stuff*. If the description is restricted to flying attributes, it

Figure 8.14
Line General Officer "Hot Sticks" by Percentage

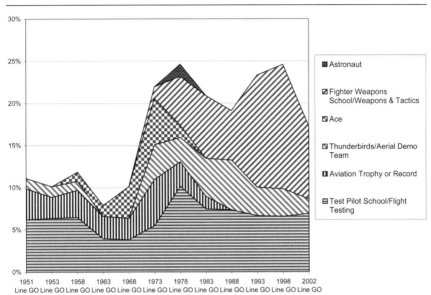

defines the heroic pilot warrior. However, since the FWS emphasizes the role of weapons and technology on tactics, it crossed into the visionary side when it integrated air battle managers in the mid-1980s, followed by other C4ISR officer specialties like intelligence and space, into its student body and faculty. Thus, the FWS has evolved from an emphasis on the heroic warrior fighter pilot to a visionary integration of C4ISR and tactical air operations.

Forward Air Controllers (FACs) form another piece of this complex discussion. FACs are not automatically hot sticks, since receiving a FAC assignment directly out of undergraduate pilot training during the Vietnam War was interpreted to mean that the officer's flying skills were not good enough to get an F-4. After all, an O-2 did not require much flying skill. However, the FAC job required tremendous organizational skill and a sharp mind. In addition, the job became not only the crossover link between the command and control world and the fighter pilot; it was also where all the action was. Consequently, some pilots volunteered for FAC duty. FACs can also serve on the ground, and navigators can also serve as FACs. Consequently, FACs demonstrate both heroic warrior and visionary characteristics and are treated as a separate but similar category to hot sticks. In the 1988 sample, there was in fact a higher percentage of general officers who listed FAC experience in their biographies than the total hot stick category (see figure 8.15).

With respect to differences between 4-star generals and 1- to 3-star general officers in the hot stick category, the interesting point is the number of 4-star

Figure 8.15
Line General Officer FACs by Percentage

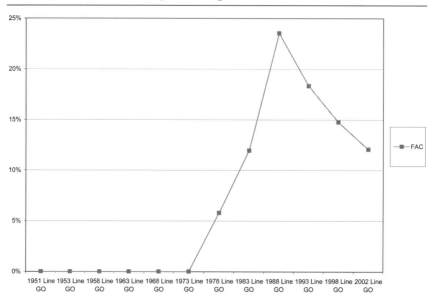

generals listing "hot stick"–type duties given the relative scarcity of such duties among the 1- to 3-star general officer samples (see figure 8.16). This would appear to indicate a preference for 4-star heroic pilot warrior-type generals, although not a big demand for such characteristics in the 1- to 3-star ranks.[11] Membership in the Thunderbirds or another aerial demonstration team and the FWS category remain represented by at least one general officer in the 4-star samples from 1978 onward. In fact, those two categories account for two-thirds of the 4-star peaks in the 1978 and 1993 samples. The situation with respect to FACs is somewhat similar to the hot stick data. Once again, at least one 4-star general in each sample from 1973 through 2002 reported serving as a FAC, and the 4-star general officer percentage of FACs exceeded the 1- to 3-star general percentage in every sample from 1978 through 2002, except in the 1988 sample, where the 1- to 3-star percentage exceeded the 4-star percentage by 2%. The 4-star general officer level appears to value the heroic pilot warrior image, although the inclusion of the FWS and FACs in this image means that associated visionary aspects are at least part of, if not the major emphasis.

IMPLICATIONS

C4ISR experience is valued and increasingly present in the Air Force general officer ranks. The increased C4ISR experience is coming from two sources. The first is a slow increase in the percentage of general officers who

Figure 8.16
Four-Star versus 1- to 3-Star General Officers—Hot Stick—Any Kind

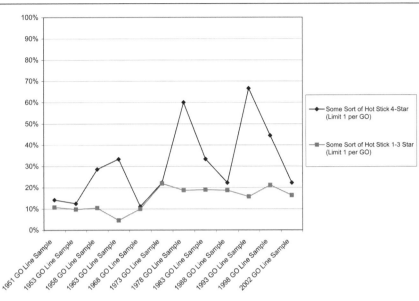

are career C4ISR officers. They comprised about 10% of the line general officers in the 2002 sample. The second source is experience as measured in C4ISR type tours by other officers, primarily pilots. Historically, one-third to one-half of the line general officers have served at least one C4ISR-type tour. A similar trend is evident in the numbers of general officers wearing space and missile badges in comparison to the number of general officers who are career space or missileer.

On the one hand, the Air Force officer corps has learned well the lessons of its own independence from the Army. Space, missiles, and C4ISR career fields in general have not been permitted to form their own corps under the leadership of officers who have spent their entire careers in these fields. Space, missiles, and the rest of C4ISR have been effectively bound to the Air Force officer corps. If placing a pilot over space, intelligence, or communications can be seen as the functional equivalent of the Army sending the old cavalry colonel to command the Air Corps, then the Air Force officer corps has successfully prevented the emergence of a competing profession. The Air Force officer corps has been able to do this for two reasons. The first, which has already been discussed at length, is the special status given to pilots and their domination of things remotely connected to flying. The second is that rated officers comprise the only career field that is consistently overmanned, and this creates surplus officers who can be placed in or over other fields. This concept will be further explored in chapter 9.

CHAPTER 9

How Many Pilot Officers Does the Air Force Need?

The issue of how many pilots the Air Force needs is important for a variety of reasons. In an airpower-based Air Force, it is important to have enough qualified pilots to adequately man the aircraft fleet, train new pilots, and conduct required testing. Undermanning would mean that the Air Force officer corps would not be able to efficiently meet its obligation to defend the nation. Worse, the officer corps might not be able to effectively defend the nation. However, overmanning increases costs, both in terms of higher expenditures for flying proficiency and higher flight pay and in terms of opportunity costs. Each redundant pilot in a non-pilot billet could be replaced by a more qualified officer with a higher level of expertise in the billet and a lower pay cost, since that officer would not require flight pay or bonuses. In addition, if excess pilots take supervisory and field grade positions in other career fields, they limit the career opportunities of non-pilot officers. Pilot overmanning could hamper the Air Force's exploitation of C4ISR. Consequently, the whole issue of how many pilots the Air Force needs is of importance not only to the Air Force officer corps but also to society and its representatives in Congress. This issue gains further relevancy because the Air Force has historically kept a somewhat hidden reserve of active-duty pilot officers in active-duty non-pilot billets. The Air Force's change from its fly for pay and currency system to a "gated" flying years flight pay system in the 1970s also touches on this issue and will be briefly examined in this chapter.

HOW MANY PILOT OFFICERS DOES THE AIR FORCE OFFICER CORPS NEED?

Although it would seem to be an elementary question, the answer is somewhat obscure. After all, it depends upon the Air Force officer corps' assessment of its needs. From roughly 1920 to 1940, the Air Force's predecessors were able to successfully hold the line that over 90% of the Air Service/Corps officers should be pilots. Then the requirements of the World War II buildup and of the Air Force's independence rendered the 90% line impossible to hold, at least below the general officer ranks. The Air Force currently gets by with less than 20% of its officers being pilots. Since pilots are still a critical part of the Air Force's ability to wage war, the officer corps would never want to be caught short of pilots. Therefore, it has a natural inclination to inflate its pilot requirement so that it can adequately maintain its airpower jurisdiction. On the other hand, if the number of aircraft is held fixed, but the number of pilots is allowed to climb, at some point there will be so many pilots competing for cockpit time that they will not all reasonably be able to maintain flying proficiency. Consequently, there must be some sort of equilibrium between the number of aircraft that the Air Force possesses and the number of pilots it requires.

Comparing the ratio of pilots to aircraft offers a way to assess Air Force pilot requirements, although this method runs the risk of codifying what the Air Force has been able to get, not what it needs. Figure 9.1 shows the ratio of total pilots on flying status to the active aircraft inventory per year, as well as the same ratio for the number of navigators on flying status and the active aircraft inventory. There is a correlation between the number of pilots and the number of aircraft at about 3.5 pilots per aircraft.

Figure 9.1
Ratios of All Officers, Pilots on Flying Status, and Navigators on Flying Status per Active Aircraft Inventory

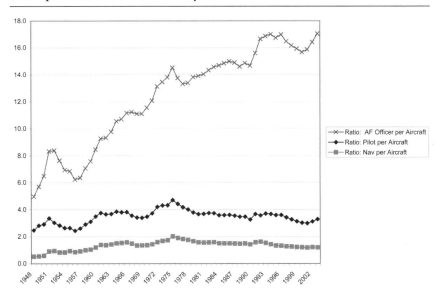

The Air Force does not use this ratio in any formal, public way, even though it conceivably could be used to good effect in justifying claims of pilot shortages. For example, in 1956, when the pilot to aircraft ratio was 2.4, the Air Force had roughly 22,800 aircraft. The Air Force officer corps could have argued that it needed an additional 22,800 pilots (41% of the total pilots on flying status in 1956) to bring the ratio up to 3.5. Of course, in 1975 when the ratio was 4.7, the Air Force had roughly 7,200 aircraft and would have had to fire 7,200 pilots to get down to the 3.5 ratio. The Air Force officer corps would certainly not be willing to let itself be caught short by approximately 41% of its pilot needs, but Congress and the American public would not want to needlessly pay flight pay and bonuses to one-third or one-quarter of the total number of pilots.

The Air Force officer corps does not rely on the ratio to justify the number of pilots it needs, partly because it is obviously a difficult target to maintain. The ratio changes with every new aircraft added to or removed from the inventory, and potentially would also vary with changes in doctrine and perhaps even tactics. In addition, both pilot and aircraft production are lengthy processes. Undergraduate pilot training takes approximately a year, followed by several months of further training before a pilot is qualified in a front-line aircraft. Furthermore, the Air Force's history can be characterized as a series of "anomalies" in reaction to external events such as the Korean War, the 1950s Cold War, Vietnam, the Vietnam drawdown, the post–Cold War interlude in the 1990s, and the post-9/11 world. The Air Force has never reached anything near steady-state operations.[1] The composition and size of the officer corps are the product of perpetual negotiations between society and the profession, manifested in Congress's role in the Air Force's budget as well as in the Air Force officer corps' personnel policies. Nevertheless, the Air Force officer corps of the 1980s, the 1990s, and the first decade of the twenty-first century seems to be closer to the 3.5:1 mark than ever in its history. And this despite the decline of the bomber force and the rise of fighters, which would have appeared to translate to a reduction in pilots per aircraft, since bombers typically require two pilots but fighters typically require only one.

In fact, the officer corps has a built-in bias toward having too many rather than too few pilots, as the rough maintenance of the 3.5 pilots per aircraft ratio inherently shows. Whereas the ratios of pilots and navigators per aircraft have remained in fairly narrow bands, the ratio of total Air Force officers per aircraft has tripled, going from approximately 5:1 in 1948 to roughly 17:1 in 2003. This reflects the officer corps' shift in focus away from an airplane-centric view of the world. While technology has led to a downsizing of direct aircraft support functions like maintenance and basic administrative functions, more officers are involved in activities not directly supporting flying operations. If technology brought manpower savings to flight operations, one would have expected the pilot per aircraft ratio to decrease. It remains constant, however, because the ratio includes the assumption that a certain number of pilots are not in flying billets. In fact, the ratio of pilots outside of flying billets is potentially rising if indeed technology does bring manpower savings to flight operations.

The system has been designed to make it easy to keep pilots in the officer corps. First, there is a longer service commitment for graduates of flying training than for officers simply commissioned or sent to technical training. Second, flight pay and bonuses provide economic incentives for remaining on active duty and in flying status. During wartime, stop-loss orders can keep pilots in, and in peacetime there is no personnel process in place to quickly dump pilots. In fact, the regular versus reserve system, which favored pilots for most of its history, meant that Reductions in Force (RIFs) would disproportionately eliminate non-pilot officers.[2] RIFs protected officers with regular commissions and dumped officers with reserve commissions. Consequently, the natural tendency to err on the safe side and overestimate pilot needs was magnified by the regular and promotion systems that benefited pilots over non-pilots. Consequently, the two big waves of former aviation cadets, regular boards, promotion boards, and successive draw-downs resulted in the creation of a pilot reserve within the active-duty Air Force officer corps.

FLIGHT PAY AND THE RESERVE PILOT BUFFER

As the World War II wave of pilots aged, this reserve buffer began to take on the appearance of a welfare system. Figure 9.2 indicates that the Air Force has historically maintained roughly 40%–50% of its pilots on flying status out on the flight line, that is, serving in flying units at wing level and below.[3] From 1957 to 1963, about one-third of the pilots on flying status were classified as "Rated Mobilization and Professional Resource." These pilots were scattered around in all sorts of staffs and jobs that were not directly connected to flying. However, they still flew whatever aircraft were available at their particular base in order to qualify for flight pay. If a major war were to break out, these pilots would be pulled out of their desk jobs and quickly brought up to speed in combat aircraft or at least in some sort of useful cargo or trainer aircraft in order to free full-time flying pilots to switch to combat aircraft.

However, as a pilot's front-line aircraft flying experience became more distant, this proposition became more questionable. As the Air Force quickly progressed through fighters in particular but also other aircraft types in the 1950s, World War II and even Korean War–vintage aircraft were first mothballed then declared totally obsolete. A group of pilots who had never flown the current generation of front-line aircraft was considerably less of an asset than a group of pilots who would be stepping back into aircraft that they had flown within the previous three years.

Congress was sensitive to the issues of paying flight pay to pilots who did not need to be flying, as well as paying flight pay to pilots who were no longer flying. Congress applied general pressure on the Air Force to minimize this cost and also at times set limits on the numbers of fliers that could receive flight pay. Although flight pay was initially tied to the flier's base pay and ratings, it

Figure 9.2
Percentages of Pilots Serving in Various Categories

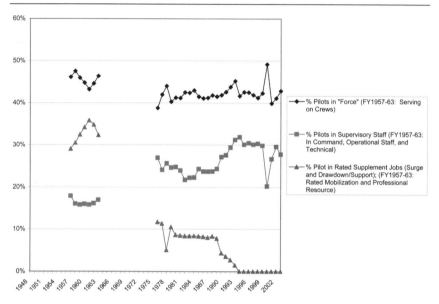

was separated into an independent pay scale in 1949. Until 1974, flight pay was based on the requirement that fliers fly a minimum of four hours a month to qualify for the proficiency pay, but over time, minor modifications were made concerning a flier's ability to carry hours forward or backward to cover several months of non-flying.[4]

The Air Force and its predecessors have always used some sort of flying board to review the records of pilots and navigators on flying status to determine when or if a flier should be taken off flying status, effectively ending that individual's flight pay. After the Korean War, the Air Force began running central flight status selection boards on a broad scale to limit the number of fliers drawing flight pay.[5] Although some fliers were grounded due to medical or other reasons, most rated officers grounded by the boards had spent larger amounts of their careers in non-flying jobs than those kept on flying status. Consequently, they were the easiest to sacrifice. These grounded fliers were kept in the Air Force officer corps, serving in non-flying positions. They effectively formed the deepest of deep reserves for potential wartime pilots and navigators. The annual USAF *Statistical Digests* tracked these officers as pilots not on flying status through 1966.

The flight status boards also determined whether those fliers kept on flight status would be placed in *excused* status or kept in active flying. Congress began authorizing the excused status in 1960 as part of the annual appropriations bill, in an attempt to trim some of the costs of proficiency flying.[6] Excused fliers were still paid flight pay but were excused from flying requirements. Excused fliers were generally older, with 15 or more years of service, although the loosely constructed decision points varied over time. Typically they had spent more time flying and had higher ratings than those fliers selected for grounding. Consequently, they were rewarded. Excused fliers were theoretically maintained on flying status because they might be used again as active fliers. This did happen during the Vietnam War, but as a general rule, excused status was granted automatically and maintained through retirement.

Fliers maintained on active flying status could be front-line, full-time fliers or fliers logging their four proficiency hours a month while serving in positions similar to their grounded and excused brethren. During the Vietnam War, many officers in the four-hour-a-month club were sent back to full-time flying positions. As the number of pilots in the Air Force continued to decline, it became more difficult for an officer to maintain flying status and totally avoid full-time cockpit duty after just one or two flying tours, although this had been common before the Vietnam War.

In some years, the categorization of fliers was a fairly automatic process, but in others records underwent more scrutiny, depending on perceived Air Force needs and Congressional limits or pressure. The Air Force viewed the central flying status selection board as critical "in shielding the Air Force from potential legislation which would threaten the welfare of the rated inventory."[7] The Air Force officer corps was caught between what it perceived to be required, but conflicting, responsibilities. On the one hand, the officer corps had to demonstrate to Congress that it was indeed judiciously using the excusal authority. The officer corps was not supposed to pad its requirements and have Congress continue to pay flight pay to officers who would most likely never fly again in front-line aircraft. On the other hand, the officer corps felt a need to convince young flying officers that the benefit would be there for them later, too. If they flew enough and earned their senior pilot or navigator rating at seven years and their command pilot or master navigator rating at 15 years, then they could be finished with flying at 15 but still garner flight pay until retiring.[8]

The *Air Force Times* reported in May 1966: "Without this incentive, AF [the Air Force] said, it could not hold able young men. They would not be interested if they saw the flight money ending when they left the cockpit and moved into more responsible command, staff, and technical jobs."[9] The assumption that rated officers, that is, primarily pilots, would be moving into "responsible command, staff and technical jobs" is telling, as is the apparent refusal to consider non-rated officers seriously for these jobs. It was somewhat perplexing that large numbers of officers who joined the Air Force simply for the joy of flying later wanted to be paid handsomely not to fly anymore. However, part of the explanation lay in the fact that pilots could easily transfer their flying skill to other organizations, for example, civilian airlines. It was a matter of which prism an officer used to define his profession and its expertise—flying or war. The *Air Force Times* reported on a 1967 Air Staff study on officer retention:

Young pilots are concerned about the return to the cockpit of many older pilots from R&D and other technical areas. The report says it appears that if a young officer sees nothing but cockpit duty ahead, he might just as well fly for the airlines "where the dissatisfiers [*sic*] are well controlled and his job is flying, per se, and not performing alert-duty."[10]

The Air Force officer corps' understanding of flight pay evolved over time from that of extra compensation for extremely dangerous work to that of a financial incentive to lure the best officer candidates into Air Force flying and then keep them in the Air Force officer corps to ensure a pool of pilots for wartime mobilization as well as a pool for senior leader selection. As the 1966 *Air Force Times* article summarized the evolution:

[The] Air Force's own view of flight pay has changed in recent years. It once stressed the dangers of flying and the fact that flying was AF's sole reason for being. As technology increased and ballistic missiles came in, a flight rating looked less like the sure ticket to the top in the Air Force. AF decided that remaining in a cockpit job could even become a penalty to career progression. Officials began to describe flight pay as an "incentive" to follow a rated career which might become an increasingly narrow one.[11]

The issue described here is less one of definitions for flight pay as much as one concerning the officer corps' realization that its expertise and jurisdiction were no longer only about flying. Furthermore, flight pay for excused fliers formed an integral part of the system limiting the progression of non-rated officers. The Air Force could not overman line flying units, since Congress controlled the manning, aircraft, and flying hours. So the surplus pilots, often in field grade ranks, were moved into non-rated jobs. Consequently, not only could non-pilots not command flying units, they also could not fill many of the top non-rated billets because these were being filled by fliers, often on excused status. Finally, if the prestige and promotions were not sufficient draws, rated officers were receiving incentive pay to stay in the Air Force and fill these command, staff, and technical positions, which obviously did not require flying currency, which non-rated officers might be more qualified to perform, and which non-rated officers were willing to perform without extra pay.

On the other hand, under the four-hours-per-month system, many of the pilot officers serving in other fields had actually developed expertise within those fields. For example, the Air Force often took an aviation cadet, service academy graduate, or other new 2nd lieutenant with experience or a degree in meteorology or communications, and sent him to pilot training. After graduation, he could spend most of his career forecasting weather or working in communications, but still fly for flight pay and earn his senior and command ratings. This officer might be periodically popped into pilot billets, but his career emphasis would be forecasting or electronics. However, as a pilot, he would be eligible for command over weather aircraft squadrons, or over the Air Force Communications Service. The Air Force could also take a junior officer, relatively fresh from pilot training, send him to get a degree in meteorology or electronics, and use him in the same way. In this system, senior officers serving in C4ISR specialties could be career-serving C4ISR specialists who also happened to have pilot wings.

In the gated system, tours either involve flying real front-line aircraft or are completely non-flying. The in-between world in which a pilot could be an intelligence, weather, or communications officer but still grab a few flying hours here and there on simple aircraft during the month is gone. As legislated in 1974, the first gate requires a minimum of 6 years of flying duty, including initial flight training, by an officer's 12th year of aviation service, in order to qualify for flight pay through the 18th year of service point. Aviation service typically begins with initial flight training. A total of 9 years of flying duty by the 18th year of aviation service ensures continuous flight pay through the 22nd year of service, and 11 years of flying duty by the 18th year of aviation service ensures flight pay through 25 years of service.[12] One can flip this around and state that if an officer front-loaded his flying career and served a bit more than the first 11 years on flying duty, he could theoretically receive flight pay for up to 14 years of not flying.

However, the theoretical limits do not match the common practice, even though the tendency has been to front-load the flying time. The officer corps has not typically retained officers who purposely fail to meet their gates. First of all, the officer corps wants flying squadron commanders, who are usually lieutenant colonels with roughly 15 to 20 years of service, selected from a pool in which all officers have met their gates and achieved senior and command pilot ratings on time, because these are indications of high experience levels in flying operations. Consequently, flying early and often ensures that an officer will not be caught short of flying hours when they become important. Second, the officer corps does not want to flood flying squadrons with field grade officers. It would potentially confuse the administrative structure of a squadron, where rank still plays a role, to have several officers with the same rank as the commander but having no real authority, or possibly having less authority than certain majors. It would also limit the promotion potential of the field grade officers serving in flying squadrons without being in positions of responsibility.[13]

Finally, there is the simple issue of time. The traditional career path calls for an academic year at Command and Staff College upon promotion to major, with a follow-on assignment to a staff job of some sort. This effectively cuts the seven years of potential non-flying time prior to meeting the third gate (11 years flying years required by 18 years of aviation service) down to four years if the officer serves only a two-year staff tour. The Goldwater-Nichols legislation on joint officers forces officers to serve a joint tour to remain competitive for promotion to general officer and, therefore, indirectly to colonel. If an officer does a second staff tour in order to have one tour for exposure on the Air Staff and one to meet the joint officer requirement, then the window is cut by another two to three years.[14] This leaves room for a one- to two-year tour in another specialty. Although an officer could trade staff jobs tours for more time in another specialty, this does not appear to be a frequent occurrence in company grade ranks. Consequently, it is not unusual for officers to gather 11 years of flying duty without much non-flying duty and spend many non-flying tours in the field grade and higher ranks. Early promotions also potentially cut into the non-flying window.

The end effect is that the officer corps front-loads the flying, thereby keeping most lieutenants and captains in the cockpit. More non-rated officers, in communications for example, must be available to work in the ever more complicated communications world, since pilots are unlikely to be able to squeak in more than one tour until they have met all their gates and ensured continuous flight pay through 25 years of aviation service.[15] At that point, the fliers typically are field grade officers, taking away staff opportunities for non-rated officers and not learning another aspect of the profession from the ground up.

In addition, when the law on the gated flight system was passed in 1974, the service obligation for pilot or navigator training was five years, which included flight training. A flier would face the decision on whether to stay in the Air Force or leave before having amassed enough flying duty to make the first gate and before he had reached the highest category of flight pay. The service obligations for flight training have increased, however, to the point where a flying officer now first faces the stay or leave decision after the officer has entered the maximum flight pay window and after the officer has easily met the 6 years of flying duty, is pretty close to, if not on, the 9 years of flying duty mark, and can easily see the 11 years of flying duty point. Furthermore, at nine years of service, the promotion board for the rank of major lies in the not too distant future. Consequently, the combined effect of the 1974 law and the increased service obligations for flying training is that the Air Force is now offering significant economic incentives to a group of officers whose past was largely flying but whose future consists primarily of non-flying duties.[16] This puts a squeeze on C4ISR and other non-pilot career fields, since officers in these fields must compete within their career fields as well as against pilots being paid bonuses to serve in non-flying jobs. Furthermore, unlike the situation in the previous system, these pilots who have met their gates do not have extensive experience outside of flying-related operations and staff positions.

The effects of the flight pay economic incentive show up in several spikes in the percentages of rated officers serving in non-rated billets (see figure 9.3). The end of the World War II rated wave led to a spike in the number of rated officers serving in non-rated billets in the early 1960s. The post-Vietnam drawdown, coupled with the Air Force's propensity to keep rated officers first, resulted in another spike of rated officers not serving in pilot or navigator billets in the mid-1970s. The post Cold War and Desert Storm drawdown created another such spike in the early 1990s. The graph also indicates another spike starting in 1999 and extending through 2003. The effect of each such spike was that rated officers took potentially promotable billets from non-rated

Figure 9.3
**Comparisons of Pilots and Navigators on Flying Status That Are Not
in Pilot or Navigator Billets**

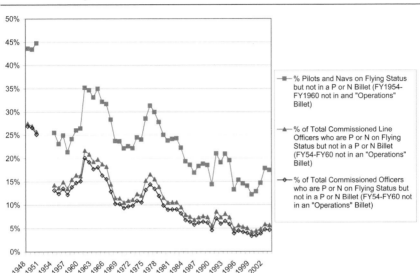

officers. This concurrently allowed rated officers, primarily pilots, to broaden
their portfolios and potentially increase their future promotion chances.

Non-rated officers did not have this possibility, since the officer corps did
not purposely seek a surplus of non-rated officers in any field. A non-pilot
officer could not command a flying unit legally until 1974, and since the law
changed, Air Force policy has restricted command of flying units to rated officers. Consequently, a rated officer, especially a pilot, was qualified for any position in the line. However, non-rated officers were limited to non-rated fields
and could not move into rated fields unless they applied for pilot, navigator,
or air battle management training and essentially started their career over in
the rated world.[17] The pilot, and now navigator and air battle manager, retention bonuses on top of flight pay indirectly perpetuate these conditions, since
the officers eligible for bonuses are also the officers with enough flying time
under their belts to be eligible for staff and other non-flying positions.[18]

Nevertheless, a big difference between the composition of the Air Force officer corps in the 1960s, the mid-1970s, and the late 1990s is that the total number of pilots and their percentage of the officer corps both declined. Equally
important, the numbers and percentages of pilots serving in non-rated billets
also declined. The billets coded for pilots and navigators are theoretically the
only jobs that require a pilot or navigator.[19] In 1951, the Air Force officer corps
had 13,800 more pilots and navigators on flying status than it had billets for.
If pilots and navigators no longer on flying status are included, the number of
pilots and navigators filling billets not requiring fliers jumped to 17,500. In

1961, the overage of fliers on flying status was 25,132. In percentage terms, that equated to 35% of pilots and navigators not serving in pilot and navigator billets, or 22% of line officers. Over one-fifth of the Air Force line officers were pilots and navigators on flying status serving in billets that did not require a pilot or navigator.

If pilots and navigators no longer on flying status are counted together with pilots and navigators on flying status in 1961, then 33,600 pilots and navigators in either grounded, excused, or active flying status were filling billets that did not require pilots or navigators. That equated to 29%—almost one-third of the line non-rated billets. The year 1999 saw by contrast the all-time low of 12% of the pilots and navigators on flying status not serving in pilot or navigator billets. These pilots and navigators comprised only 4% of the line officers. However, the percentages climbed again after 1999. In 2003, the difference between pilots and navigators on flying status and total pilot and navigator billets was 3,400, or 6% of the Air Force line officers. The Air Force officer corps does not seem inclined to bring these percentages lower; and the flight pay and bonus systems create a financial incentive aimed at retaining pilots long past their prime flying years. This, in turn, results in perhaps 15% on average of rated officers filling non-rated billets. This occurs more often than not in the field grade ranks. This provides the officer corps with a pool of pilot colonels with sufficient non-rated experience to justify filling non-rated-type general officer billets with pilots in over-proportional numbers.

It is interesting to note that for 2003 the Air Force reported that it was 430 pilots (3% of the pilot inventory) short of its requirement, but 550 navigators (13% of the navigator inventory) over its requirement. At the same time, its own data revealed that the officer corps had 3,400 more pilots and navigators on flying status (6% of the line officers) than pilot and navigator billets for them. Such discrepancies are partly explained by the Air Force's rather nebulous categorization of its requirements. For example, the Air Force days of excess rated officers appeared to conclude with the ending of the Rated Supplement job classification in 1994. However, Figures 9.2 and 9.4 indicate that the dramatic drop-off in the percentages of both pilot and navigator rated supplements from 1989 through 1994 is offset in each case by an equal percentage increase in pilots and navigators in supervisory staff.[20] Consequently, billets that were once coded as Rated Supplement appear to have been changed into Supervisory Staff pilot and navigator billets on an equal percentage basis. Former surplus billets became required staff jobs.

Figure 9.5 compares the numbers of pilots and navigators serving in pilot and navigator billets with the numbers of pilots and navigators on flying status not serving in pilot and navigator billets as well as with the numbers of officers in other amalgamated career groupings. The category of operations/combat billets, used from 1954 to 1960, contains the most officers since it holds pilots, navigators, and non-rated operators. The category of pilots and navigators in pilot/navigator billets is next most populated. The category of pilots-and-navigators-on-flying-status-but-not-in-pilot/navigator-billets was

Figure 9.4
Percentage of Navigators Serving in Various Categories

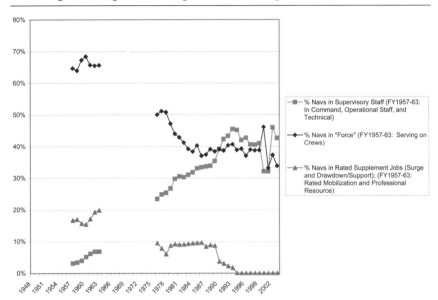

initially the second most populated category. That is, there were more pilots and navigators on flying status not serving in pilot and navigator billets than there were officers serving in any other career field or career field amalgamation in the officer corps.

Furthermore, this category does not contain the pilots and navigators removed from flight status primarily to placate Congress but still tracked by the Air Force as a reserve rated pool through 1966. These would add another 8,000 fliers serving in non-flying billets, depending on the year. In addition, the values for the pilots-and-navigators-on-flying-status-but-not-in-pilot/navigator-billets are artificially low for 1954–1960. [21] In any event, the pilots-and-navigators-on-flying-status-but-not-in-pilot/navigator-billets   category retained its second place position through 1967, when C4ISR passed it. The medical amalgamation did not clearly outman the pilots-and-navigators-on-flying-status-but-not-in-pilot/navigator-billets until 1979. At different times, every billet in any of the line amalgamations or specific non-rated career fields could have been completely manned by fliers on flight status.

As a further example, Figure 9.6 shows that almost 30% of the non-rated billets in 1961 were filled by pilots and navigators on flying status. If one assumed that every command/director billet was filled by one of these pilots or navigators, 17% of the remaining line officer billets would still have been filled by fliers on flying status in 1961. In 2003, fliers on flying status could fill all of the pilot/navigator billets, fill all of the command/director billets,

Figure 9.5
Selected Major Air Force Occupational Groupings

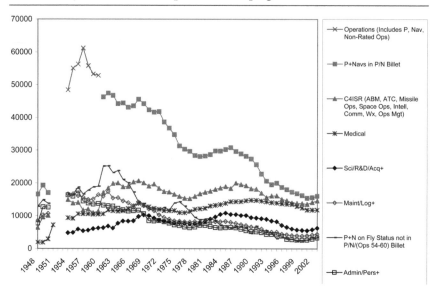

and still fill another 4% of the line officer billets. Furthermore, this 4% of the line officer billets translated to 14% of the pilots and navigators on flying status being surplus after filling all the pilot/navigator and command/director billets.

Consequently, it is not clear how the Air Force arrived at its statement that it was 3% (436 pilots) short of pilots but 13% (558 navigators) over its requirement for navigators in 2003.[22] If, as the Air Force says, navigators can indeed serve in rated staff billets and commands that ostensibly require pilots, one could argue that there is no shortage of pilots, and a small surplus of 122 rated navigators, which is 0.2% of line officers. Furthermore, if fliers on flying status could fill all the pilot/navigator and command/director billets and still fill another 4% of the line officer billets, it is hard to imagine what the other pilots would be needed for.

Figure 9.7 indicates that in the current gated flight pay system, the historical average for the number of general officer and colonel pilots that are actually in flying positions is roughly one-third.[23] The percentage of general officer and colonel navigators flying is traditionally much lower, historically below 10%.[24] Reaching the senior leadership of the officer corps has been historically predicated on flying (pilot) experience, but the majority of the general officer and colonel positions have no required flying duty. Flying wing commands are relatively rare compared to commands over non-flying units and the host of non-flying staff and other jobs at the general officer and colonel levels.

Figure 9.6
Pilots and Navigators on Flying Status That Are Not in Pilot, Navigator, or Command/Director Billets

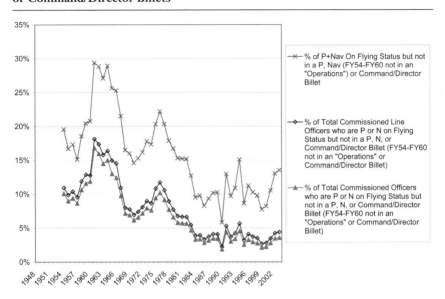

Figure 9.7
Percentages of Pilot and Navigator General Officers and Colonels Receiving Flight Pay and Actually Flying

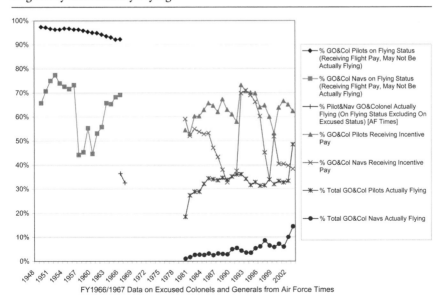

FY1966/1967 Data on Excused Colonels and Generals from Air Force Times

The final area of discussion in this section deals with two costs associated with keeping a huge pilot reserve within the officer corps. First was the issue of money. The four-hours-per-month proficiency flying system in place before the transition to the flying gate system between 1974 and 1977 was expensive. The Air Force had to maintain a fleet of relatively simple aircraft suitable for proficiency flying at all bases where flying was possible. The aircraft required maintenance support, as did the airfields and supporting infrastructure like air traffic control facilities.[25] There were also increased personnel costs to consider. The Senate Appropriations Committee reported in late 1975 that the "long-term goal" of the defense appropriations bill was:

To eliminate proficiency flying and achieve the associated economies not only in flying hours and maintenance costs, but the economies that would result from not taking time away from an individual's primary job duties for proficiency flying.[26]

The second issue concerns the role of the reserve forces. Besides losing the fliers for brief periods when they were proficiency flying, if the fliers really provided a reserve, calling out that reserve in mass would result in a large number of personnel holes in various Air Force organizations. Someone would conceivably need to back-fill the staff and non-rated positions so that the Air Force's war effort would smoothly continue as fliers were pulled back to aircraft. During the Vietnam War, the Air Force portrayed its pool of excused and proficiency fliers as a boon. Taking these fliers out of non-flying jobs and putting them back into active flying jobs minimized the call-ups of Air Force Reserve and Air National Guard pilots. In addition, using the excused and four-hours-a-month fliers reduced the need for active duty full-time fliers to serve multiple tours in Southeast Asia. However, the long-standing use of rated officers in non-rated billets meant that there was a shortage of non-rated officers to quickly fill billets vacated by rated officers.[27] Using Air Force Reserve or Air National Guard officers to fill these non-rated slots ran counter to the Air Force's claim that the excused and proficiency pilots eliminated the need to call up the real reserves.[28] However, in the post-Vietnam world, the military shifted its perspective on the reserve forces. The new emphasis was on drawing the reserves into battle as soon as possible, as a way to force Congress and the American people to decide early on to support a war or stop it before it became another Vietnam-style political morass. Consequently, in hindsight at least, the Air Force officer corps' portrayal of the excused and proficiency flier pool as a substitute for the real reserves appears misguided. Even at the time, the concept conflicted with the purpose of the Air Force Reserve and Air National Guard. In theory and in practice, the Air Force Reserve and in the Air National Guard have been activated in times of emergency to provide aircrews, maintainers, and aircraft.[29] Finally, maintaining a buffer of reserve pilots without aircraft for them to fly makes no sense, given the cost and time required to produce modern military aircraft.

IMPLICATIONS

The data are clear that the Air Force officer corps has increased its reliance on non-rated officers, at least up to the colonel level, to provide expertise and leadership in non-flying fields. This implies that as the officer corps continues to shed aircraft, the number of pilots that it actually needs will decrease. Simultaneously, the trend is that the ratio of non-rated officers to aircraft will continue to increase, which will make pilots an even smaller percentage of the officer corps. This will be complicated by issues such as how to classify people "flying" unmanned combat aerial vehicles, but such issues will not change the trends in a significant way.

What is not clear from the data is whether the officer corps can overcome its natural preference for having more pilots than it needs, especially at higher ranks. The implementation of the gated flight pay system eliminated the possibility of pilots gaining extensive experience in non-flying areas at junior ranks while still retaining flight pay and pilot status, and the flight pay and bonus systems continue to provide incentives for these pilots to stay in the Air Force and occupy senior non-flying positions. The end effect is a continued overrepresentation of pilots, who have become more flying focused than ever, in the general officer ranks. This in turn would seem to hamper the officer corps' exploitation of the space and cyberspace jurisdictions, since an overrepresentation of pilots means an underrepresentation of C4ISR officers. The Air Force officer corps' pilot buffer in the active duty force favors the heroic over the visionary warrior.

Conclusions and Implications

CONCLUSIONS

My theory of professions is a useful tool to explain my initial questions as to why the percentage of Air Force general officers who are pilots has been in a relatively steady decline from 1947 through 2003, and why pilots have remained over-proportionally represented in the general officer ranks. The answer to the first question lies in the Air Force officer corps' self-identification as a profession. A profession cannot exist without a jurisdiction, that is, without society's agreement that the profession provides a specific expert service that society needs and authorizes that profession to provide, either as a monopoly or as an oligopoly provider. A profession tries to defend and expand its dominance in its current jurisdictions, to compete with other professions to extend its current jurisdictions, and to create, find, and fill newly emerging jurisdictions. For the officer corps to remain competitive, its characteristics and composition must adapt or evolve. The answer to the second question lies in the Air Force officer corps' struggle for independence from the Army officer corps. During that struggle, the developing Air Force officer corps adopted several personnel policies that minimized meddling by the rest of the Army officer corps by emphasizing pilots and flying above all else within the Air Corps/Force. This in turn set the stage for an enduring struggle between the heroic and visionary warriors within the officer corps. The heroic warriors continued to emphasize piloting, and the visionary warriors expanded the officer corps' perspectives beyond flying to airpower, then space, and now cyberspace.

At the level of the interaction between professions, the history of the Air Force can be portrayed as follows. The predecessors to the Air Force officer corps developed an expertise in airpower, largely based on aircraft and flying.

They gained experience in World War I. After the war, they saw strategic bombing as the embodiment of airpower and worked to convince the public that strategic bombing was an emerging jurisdiction ripe for one or more professions to claim and occupy. Furthermore, the nation's survival depended on its ability to fill this new jurisdictional void, and since this new jurisdiction was independent of land and sea operations, the new jurisdiction should be monopolized by an independent Air Force. Consequently, the new profession of airman and the new jurisdiction of strategic bombing arose simultaneously and in entwined fashion. Events in World War II substantiated the claim, and the public accepted both the new jurisdiction and the independent Air Force's monopoly over it.

If there was going to be a new independent Air Force, it made sense to place most aircraft and aviation missions within the new Air Force. Bombers needed fighter escorts; fighters would defend the United States from enemy bombers, and so forth. The Air Force was given large parts in the jurisdictions of strategic air defense of the United States, tactical air, and strategic airlift. It was also responsible for training pilots and navigators for the Air Force and for accepting deliveries of aircraft for the Air Force and other services. This was conceptually easy for society and the services to follow. Each service had a medium of sorts. The Air Force had the air. The Army had a near monopoly in the jurisdiction of ground warfare. The Navy and Marine Corps had a combined near monopoly over the maritime warfare jurisdiction, including the conduct of amphibious landings and the waging of war on ground near large bodies of water. In addition, it made sense for the Navy and the Marines to keep carriers and aircraft under their own control to support their operations. Of course, any attempt to assign jurisdictions to professions creates tension at the borders of the jurisdictions, and this was indeed the case within the Department of Defense, which was established in 1947.

More importantly, however, new technologies were changing the nature of warfare and simultaneously affecting jurisdictions. For example, the unmanned bombers, long-range rockets, guided air-to-air missiles, and electronic warfare systems under development or in operational use at the end of World War II portended dramatic change in aerial warfare. For example, the ICBM would negate both strategic bombing and strategic defense against bombers. The threat of Soviet ICBMs hitting Air Force strategic bomber bases some 30 minutes after launch could not be logically countered by Air Force bombers flying 12-hour or longer missions to Soviet destinations. A new profession based on a monopoly jurisdiction over strategic bombing was destined for a rapid demise unless it could develop and broaden its jurisdictional basis. Consequently, the Air Force officer corps sought jurisdiction over the development of the unmanned competitors to the manned bomber, partially by broadening its definition of strategic bombing to include at least Air Force unmanned competitors. Without the strategic mission, the Air Force would be reduced to the tactical mission, which was by its very nature to support ground operations and plans. Airlift was not an Air Force monopoly, nor was it likely that it could be, and strategic airlift competed with civilian air transport. Without dominance over any jurisdiction, the future of the profession would eventually be called into question.

As the Air Force broadened its conception of strategic bombing to include medium-range surface-to-surface missiles and later ICBMs, the officer corps expanded beyond manned bombers, and indeed beyond manned flight itself. The Air Force officer corps also strove for dominance in missile warning and space surveillance, which morphed out of strategic air defense, as well as satellite launch and control. This in turn required ever more automated communications and command and control systems, with increasingly integrated intelligence and surveillance data. Command and control and communications systems became ever more automated, as did the gathering and processing of intelligence. These C4ISR functions became key supports for air operations and simultaneously reduced the role of the pilot in combat. Over time, however, command and control of air operations, together with counter-enemy command and control, began to become an expertise and a jurisdiction in its own right, a jurisdiction in which the Air Force officer corps claims a near monopoly.

Of course, the Air Force officer corps has not given up airplanes, but it has successfully prevented the creation of a medium-based space service, profession, and officer corps. This has been done by inundating the senior levels of space operations with pilot officers. In addition, there is a profession construct that logically bridges the gap between the Douhetian Air Force, focused on strategic bombing, and the post–World War II Air Force's relatively steady reductions in bombers, aircraft in general, and pilots, as well as the accompanying rise in C4ISR expertise and jurisdiction. That high-level construct is that "bloodless" or "clean" warfare is what the Air Force officer corps actually brings to the table. This abstract expertise is not tied to aircraft, or for that matter to missiles, rockets, or satellites. Although founded on aircraft, it quickly accommodated the ether of radar and electronic warfare, easily assimilated the A-bomb, later incorporated intercontinental ballistic missiles, played a role in the development of information warfare, and now advocates for effects-based operations.

The Air Force has been historically led by men pursuing the vision of bloodless, or clean, war. This is what sets the officer corps of the Air Force apart from those of the Army, Navy, and Marine Corps. The Army is stuck on the ground, be it in trenches, maneuver warfare, or low-intensity conflicts. Combat occurs between groups of people at relatively close quarters. Enemy soldiers, non-combatants, and terrain pose obstacles to reaching goals, which are defined in terms of controlling territory and people over time. The Navy and Marine Corps have the littoral and the blue ocean. Battle is waged by large groups of men, from and against other ships or shore installations. Naval forces can blockade an enemy, control sea-space for specific periods of time, or attack from the sea. Once the Marines are deployed, however, they largely face the same conditions as the Army. The Air Force, on the other hand, has always offered the promise of a cleaner, less bloody war. The Air Force slips past the old ways of war and with "surgical strikes" suppresses or destroys the enemy's command and control over its forces and population, its lines of communications, and its general ability to wage war. Ideally, this could be done without resorting to the bloody traditional forms of warfare, and although it is historically conceived with respect to aircraft, its implementation does not require aircraft.

The Air Force cannot give up its domination of the jurisdiction over the long-range, precision strike—the ability to attack anywhere at any time, within hours, or potentially minutes, of a decision to attack. It is the abstraction of the Air Force's core historical justification for existence, the modern evolution of the old strategic bombing. Whether conducting daylight "precision" bombing over Europe in World War II, firing laser-guided or GPS-guided missiles in Iraq, or using ICBMs to counter-force target potential enemy forces; accuracy has always been an Air Force hallmark. The Air Force has been pursuing precision munitions since its inception.

At the strategic level, conventional precision munitions offer the possibility of being able to attack a nuclear-armed enemy and destroy large parts of its nuclear capabilities while retaining all of one's own. Consequently, preponderance in long-range conventional precision capability could potentially make a nuclear stalemate meaningless. At the tactical level, precision supports the general clean/bloodless concept, since it brings a victorious end to the ground war faster, thereby minimizing casualties. In addition, precision weapons minimize collateral damage and civilian casualties, thereby enhancing claims of legitimacy. The Air Force also uses precision to gain leverage in its competition with the Army, Navy, and Marine Corps in the shared jurisdiction of tactical warfare. Finally, the growth in emphasis on precision weapons contributes to the blurring of strategic and tactical perspectives in the Air Force officer corps, since precision shifts the expertise away from a basis in airframes to one in weapons.

This in turn requires the technology to achieve ever more accurate weapons as well as the intelligence to aim them at the right places at the correct times. This combination of intelligence and technology also opens the door to information operations and effects-based operations. The Air Force officer corps cannot let another profession develop an expertise in information attack or effects-based attack independent of Air Force airplanes, missiles, or C4ISR. Air Force C4ISR is what makes the kinetic, electronic, computer, or information attack possible—in terms of not only targeting but also mission planning, execution, and feedback. Without it, the Air Force would have very limited claims in any jurisdiction, and without jurisdiction, a profession is not a profession.

IMPLICATIONS

A major implication of this trend, however, is that there will be a continued reduction in the importance of manned piloting within the Air Force officer corps on the one hand, but a need to develop combat commanders, staffs, and future Air Force leaders in this less pilot-dominant world on the other. This will be a difficult task for the officer corps, since it has had great difficulty overcoming its pilot-centric focus and the perceived connection between flying and leadership skills. If flying is no longer the proxy for leadership, what will the officer corps use to assess what Carl von Clausewitz called "military genius"? Furthermore, the Air Force officer corps continues to pay homage to an antiquated concept of command that no longer has a direct connection to leadership and decision making in combat. Squadrons, groups, and wings do not fly in massed formation into combat anymore. The CAOC and the command and control system are where the real decisions are made, but flying hours, combat hours, and traditional command are still the yardsticks for promotions.

The Air Force officer corps has added cyberspace to its Mission Statement, but it has not defined cyberspace or decided which officers "do" cyberspace. As the Air Force officer corps begins to work through these issues, it will also have to create a cyberspace officer career path. A review of current C4ISR career paths could reveal existing untapped synergies. For example, the Air Force currently has intelligence officers working in signals intelligence; electronic warfare officers, who form a branch of various navigator specialties; and ABM electronic support measures operators. These three career fields work overlapping aspects of the detection, identification, and exploitation of electronic signals. They conceivably could be cross-fed to widen these officers' C4ISR experiences and perspectives. The same could be done with various aspects of the communications, ABMs, intelligence, and space career fields.

Such a review would also potentially reexamine the officer corps' tendency to downgrade officer positions in C4ISR to enlisted positions. If cyberspace is the main game, then that is where decision makers with military genius are required. Perhaps Air Force personnel deciding what type of bomb should be dropped where and when on the battlefield should be officers instead of enlisted terminal attack controllers. The same may be true for ABMs controlling UCAVs, as well as computer operators deciding where, when, and how to launch computer attacks. Finally, the promotion bias in favor of pilots and the surplus pilot buffer must be eliminated if the Air Force officer corps intends to embrace cyberspace officers and to fully exploit cyberspace.

Although these ideas sound visionary and perhaps even revolutionary and anti-heroic warrior, their essence dates back at least to the Army Air Forces. The visionary Hap Arnold predicted major changes in the composition of the officer corps when he told his staff late in World War II:

The pilot will not always be the key to airpower. For the present, yes. For the immediate future, yes. But even now mechanical gadgets are fast encroaching on the pilot's domain. We are entering the era of the guided missile.

Someday, perhaps in our time, the man holding my job will meet here with a staff of scientists, and they will wear no pilot's wings on their chests. That insignia will cease to be the yardstick of Air Force achievement. That's something for you to think about.[1]

To complete the circle and return to the conversation contained in the introduction, the next time somebody is introduced as an Air Force officer, don't ask if he is a pilot or what she flies. Instead, ask what he does in the medical field or which C4ISR specialty she serves in!

Appendix:
General Officer Samples

BASIC METHODOLOGY

Since there is no readily accessible database on Air Force general officer characteristics available, I created one. My intent was to create this database to span the time frame from 1948 through 2003. Since it was difficult to find accurate lists of all Air Force generals on a yearly basis and the total number of general officers is quite large, on the order of over 300 a year with considerable year-to-year duplication, I decided to draw periodic samples to analyze the long-term trends of various characteristics of the general officer pool. I used the Air Force section of *Pentagon (DoD) Phone Book* editions to generate the samples. Only the USAF section was usable, since most editions did not label officers in the Office of the Secretary of Defense or in the Joint Staff by service. Although my original intent was to run in five-year increments from 1948 through 2003, the phone books did not list officer names with staff positions until 1951 and returned to the no-name practice after 2002. Consequently, I ran at five-year intervals from 1953 to 1998, and added 1951 and 2002 as the bookends. I also decided to include major command (MAJCOM) commanders to pick up a larger set of the four-star Air Force general population, much of which resides outside the Washington, DC, area. This pseudo-random sampling yielded an average of 86 Air Force general officers per sample. Although they are not truly random, the samples are consistent and the skewing is not done by me but by whoever in the USAF decided which names to place in the *Pentagon Phone Book*. The phone book obviously emphasizes the DC area and positions on the Air Staff. However, this is the brain of the Air Force, and, consequently, the best cross-section of Air Force general officers. Although this sampling misses all of the operational wing commanders scattered around the globe, many should cycle through Washington sooner or later. In any event, this technique appeared to be the best available option and the Air Staff should be the most interesting case for analyzing pilot and non-rated generals. The Air Force Web site provided biographies for most of the general officers in the samples. The biographies were then coded and loaded for analysis.

INDICATORS OF THE SAMPLING VALIDITY

The samples are large enough to provide meaningful data on the population of Air Force general officers. If measured in terms of the individual samples as a percentage of the total Air Force general officer population in the sample year, the average participation across all 12 samples is 25%. The 1951 sample, with 34% of the total Air Force general officers included, has the highest participation. The 1968 and 1973 samples, each with 21% of the total Air Force general officers included, have the lowest. In terms of total numbers, the 1958 sample has the most participants at 105, and the 2002 sample the lowest at 67. The average number of participants is 86 across all the samples.

The sampling method, using the *Pentagon Phone Book*, captures an over-proportional number of non-line general officers because they are overrepresented at Air Force Headquarters. Figure A.1 provides a comparison of the composition of the general officer samples to the composition of the total Air Force general officer population. The data show that the percentage of pilots and the percentage of non-rated (not pilot or navigator) line officers from the total general officers in the sample are both underrepresentative, while the percentage of navigators in the samples is relatively close to the percentage of navigators in the total general officer population.

However, a comparison of the composition of the line general officers in the samples to the composition of the total Air Force line general officer population yields figure A.2. This chart, which contains information on the line general officer population from FY1950 through FY1980, shows a closer alignment of the sample and population data for pilot and non-rated (not pilot or navigator) line general officers.[1] Furthermore, the absolute value of the difference in the percentage of pilots from the line general officers in the sample and in the population over the period of the 1951 through 1978 samples varies from 0% to 6%. However, the absolute value of the difference in the percentage of pilots from total Air Force general officers in the sample and in the population over the period of the 1951 through 1978 samples varies from 3% to 16%.

Consequently, the sample data is much more representative of the line officer population than the total officer population. The same is true for non-rated line officers (not pilot or navigator). The absolute value of the difference in the percentage of non-rated (not pilot or navigator) line general officers from line general officers in the sample and in the population over the period of the 1951 through 1978 samples varies from 0% to 6%. However, the absolute

Figure A.1
Comparison of Sample Compositions to Total General Officers

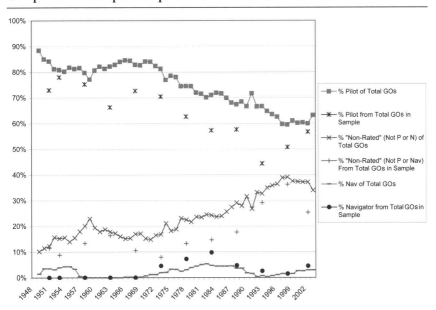

Figure A.2
Comparison of Sample Compositions to Line General Officers

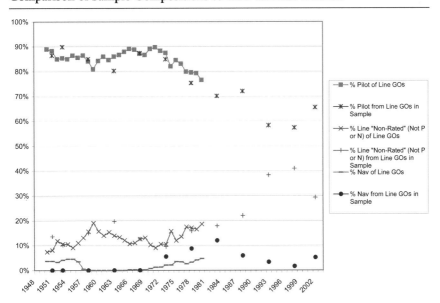

value of the difference in the percentage of non-rated (not pilot or navigator) line general officers from total Air Force general officers in the sample and in the population over the period of the 1951 through 1978 samples varies from 1% to 9%. Consequently, the overrepresentation of non-line officers forces an underrepresentation of primarily pilot general officers, followed by non-rated (not pilot or navigator) line general officers. The small number of navigators in the general officer samples and populations means that it is difficult to get a big difference between the percentage of navigators from the line and total Air Force general officer samples and populations. The absolute value of the difference in the percentage of navigators from line general officers in the sample and in the population over the period of the 1951 through 1978 samples varies from 0% to 5%. However, the absolute value of the difference in the percentage of navigators from total Air Force general officers in the sample and in the population over the period of the 1951 through 1978 samples varies from 0% to 4%. Consequently, I feel confident using the sample data in the case of line general officers.

GENERAL OFFICER (GO) BIOGRAPHY SAMPLE CODING PROCEDURE

List all officers identified as general officers in the "summer" editions of the Pentagon phone books for 1951, 1953, 1958, 1963, 1968, 1973, 1978, 1983, 1988, 1993, 1998, and 2002.

Search Air Force online general officer biographic database for biographies of each GO identified. If no biography is available, search Google and Air Force Office of History biographic references for biographic material. If none is available, check for reasonable typographical errors. If there is still no biographic information, discard as typographic or administrative error.

Add the three and four-star major command (MAJCOM) commanders from *Air Force Magazine* for the same time periods. If *Air Force Magazine* lists MAJCOM commander changes in the summer, choose the spring (i.e., the previous) commander. Get biographies from Air Force online general officer biographic database.

Except where noted otherwise, the intent is to code information from the biographies based on the officer's experience in the ranks of 2nd lieutenant through colonel, not as a general. If no information on dates of rank is contained in the biography, the default is to assume the officer becomes a colonel at 20 years of commissioned service and a brigadier general at 25 years of commissioned service.

The phone books are being used to generate names for the sample. Consequently, biographies of officers contained in the phone book will be used, even if the biography makes clear that the officer had moved on to a different position or retired by the time of the phone book edition. Not all the biographies are updated; so there is no way to tell with regard to many of them.

- *Name:* Last, first, middle initial
- *Rank:* Current rank as listed in phone book or *Air Force Magazine* at time of sample (may be referred to in biography as *temporary rank*)
- *"Component":* [USAFR, ANG, Medical, JAG, Chaplain, Line]
  - Purpose: To weed out all but line officers; if a GO is not line, no further coding except for current job
  - USAFR—reserve serving in USAF Reserve billet/capacity, even if on extended active duty
    - Intent is to weed out those serving as top USAFR leadership, not those officers with a non-regular commission serving extended active duty (EAD) in USAF positions with no connection to USAF Reserves.
  - ANG—Air National Guard member
    - Intent is to weed out those serving as top ANG leadership, not those officers with a non-regular commission serving EAD in USAF positions with no connection to ANG.
  - Medical—Medical/Dental/Doctor/Nurse/Biomedical Services/Veterinarian, etc.
  - JAG—serving in Judge Advocate Corps, i.e., lawyer serving as a lawyer
  - Chaplain—chaplain
  - Line—Not falling into the above categories
- *Flying Hours :* [none, small, medium, large]
  - None—no flying hours listed in biography
  - Small—under 1,000 flying hours listed in biography
  - Medium—between 1,000 and 2,500 flying hours listed in biography
  - Large—over 2,500 flying hours listed in biography
- *Combat Hours/Sorties:* [Yes Small, Yes Medium, Yes Large, No]
  - Small—< 40 sorties or < 100 hrs
  - Medium—40–150 sorties or 100–250 hrs
  - Large—> 150 sorties or > 250 hrs
  - No—none listed in biography
- *"Hot Stick":* [FWS, T-Bird, TPS, Trophy, Astro, Ace, ACTS, Not] (Multiple entries possible)
  - FWS—Fighter Weapons School or any weapons school (graduate or faculty), also if reference to *weapons and tactics* officer; after 1986 not necessarily a flyer
  - T-Bird—Thunderbird pilot, maintenance, or squadron commander, or other aerial demonstration team
  - TPS—Test Pilot School graduate or faculty, also count vague references to flight testing, which might include experimental airplanes (labeled X-something) and IOT&E (Initial Operational Test and Evaluation)
  - Trophy—set aviation records, win aviation trophies in conjunction with personal flying ability; count crew trophies

- Astro—Astronaut rating of some sort; reference to astronaut program; selection to astronaut program also counts
- Ace—shot down five airplanes or more, or labeled as ace
- ACTS—attended or graduated from Air Corps Tactical School
- Not—no "Hot Stick" categories listed in biography

- *Not a "Hot Stick"*: [POW, FAC, Not] (Multiple entries possible)

  - POW—Prisoner of War
  - FAC—Forward Air Controller (FAC)
  - Not—No not a "Hot Stick" categories listed

- *Squadron Command*: [Yes FB, Yes FF, Yes FT, Yes FO, Yes O, Yes T, Yes MS, Yes OTH, No] Code first squadron command position chronologically

  - Yes FB—Flying Bomber Squadron Command
  - Yes FF—Flying Fighter Squadron Command; could be labeled as "TFS" (tactical fighter squadron) or "FIS" (fighter interceptor squadron)
  - Yes FT—Flying Training Squadron Command
  - Yes FO—Flying Other Squadron Command (e.g., tankers, reconnaissance, airlift, etc.)
  - Yes O—Operations Squadron Command, non-flying but still operational, such as missiles, space, weapons controlling, etc.
  - Yes T—Training Squadron Command, non-flying but still a training squadron; could be labeled "TTS" (technical training squadron)
  - Yes MS—Maintenance or Support Squadron Command; could be labeled as "FMS" (field maintenance squadron), "EMS" (equipment maintenance squadron), "AGS" (aircraft generation squadron), "CRS" (component repair squadron)
  - Yes OTH—Any other non-flying squadron command
  - No—No squadron command listed

- *Group Comand*: [Yes FB, Yes FF, Yes FT, Yes FO, Yes O, Yes T, Yes MS, Yes OTH, No] Code first group command position chronologically
  - Yes FB—Flying Bomber Group Command
  - Yes FF—Flying Fighter Group Command
  - Yes FT—Flying Training Group Command
  - Yes FO—Flying Other Group Command
  - Yes O—Operations Group Command, non-flying but still operational, such as missiles, space, weapons controlling, etc.
  - Yes T—Training Group Command, non-flying but still a training group
  - Yes MS—Maintenance or Support Group Command
  - Yes OTH—Any other non-flying group command; include *operations groups*
  - No—No group command listed

- *Wing Command:* [Yes FB, Yes FF, Yes FT, Yes FO, Yes O, Yes T, Yes MS, Yes OTH, No] Code first wing command position chronologically

  - Yes FB—Flying Bomber Wing Command
  - Yes FF—Flying Fighter Wing Command
  - Yes FT—Flying Training Wing Command
  - Yes FO—Flying Other Wing Command
  - Yes O—Operations Wing Command, non-flying but still operational, such as missiles, space, weapons controlling, etc.
  - Yes T—Training Wing Command, non-flying but still a training wing
  - Yes MS—Maintenance or Support Wing Command
  - Yes OTH—Any other non-flying wing command
  - No—No wing command listed

- *Center Command:* [Yes + rank, No] (Multiple entries possible)

  - Yes + rank (Lt Col, Col); if states commanded center or equivalent but no rank, then say "yes"
  - No—No reference to command of a center below general officer rank

- *Program Director/Director Program Office:* [Yes + rank, No] (Multiple entries possible)

  - Yes + rank—(Lt Col, Col); if says in program, program director, program office, etc., must have to do with acquisitions or SPO (system program office)
  - No—No reference to specific acquisitions programs or SPO or program office prior to becoming general officer rank

- *Initial AFSC:* [P, N, ABM, Missiles, Space, ATC, Ops, Log/Maint, ACQ, Intel, Comm/Electronics, Personnel/Admin, Finance, Scientist, Support]

  - Initial Air Force Specialty Code, i.e., occupational specialty. Casual status jobs (up to a year at times) while awaiting training slots do not count. Initial jobs typically require some kind of training and typically last at least a year.
  - P—Pilot
  - N—Navigator Nav/EWO (electronic warfare officer)/WSO (weapons system officer)/Bombardier, etc.
  - ABM—Air Battle Manager
  - Missiles—Missile operations or maintenance
  - Space—Space, only count operator or maintenance tours, not space acquisitions
  - ATC—Air Traffic Control
  - Ops—general operations, including Army tours in infantry, artillery, etc.
  - Log/Maint—Logistics/Maintenance
  - ACQ—Acquisitions
  - Intel—Intelligence
  - Comm/Electronics—Communications, Electronics, and Computers
  - Personnel/Admin—Personnel, Administration, etc.

- Finance—Finance, Comptroller, Statistics
- Scientist—Research and Development work as scientist, not program manager
- Support—everything else

- *Apparent AFSC:* [P, N, ABM, Missiles, Space, ATC, Log/Maint, ACQ, Intel, Comm/Electronics, Personnel/Admin, Finance, Scientist, Support]
  - (In the following rank order, only one choice allowed)
  - P—Pilot, any pilot wings or has flown as pilot
  - N—Navigator, any navigator wings or has flown as Nav/EWO/WSO/Bombardier, etc.
  - ABM—Air Battle Manager, any version of ABM wings/badge or multiple tours as ABM
  - Missiles—Missiles, any version of missile badge or tours in missile ops or maintenance
  - Space—Space, only count operator or maintenance tours, not space acquisitions
  - ATC—Air Traffic Control, any version of ATC badge or multiple tours in ATC
  - Ops—general operations, includes multiple Army tours in infantry, artillery, etc.
  - Log/Maint—Logistics/Maintenance, any version of maint/log badges or multiple tours in log/maint (broadly defined)
  - ACQ—Acquisitions, any version of acquisitions badge or multiple tours in acquisitions
  - Intel—Intelligence, any version of intelligence badge or multiple tours in intelligence
  - Comm/Electronics—Communications, Electronics, and Computers, any version of communications, or electronics badge, or multiple tours in communications, electronics, or computers
  - Personnel/Admin—Personnel and Administration, etc., any version of personnel or administration badge or multiple tours in personnel/admin (broadly defined)
  - Finance—Finance, Comptroller, and Statistics, any version of finance/comptroller badge or multiple tours in finance, comptroller, or statistics
  - Scientist—Research and Development work as scientist, not program manager
  - Support—everything else

- *Badges:* [Parachutist, Missile Ops, Missile, Space, Other Badges, No Pic, No Badges, Badges but unclear] (Multiple entries possible; can be from text of biography or photograph)
  - Intent: Since only wings required to be worn, look to see who wears/how many officers wear other occupational badges and perhaps which badges
  - Parachutist—Parachute wings
  - Missile Ops—Missile ops badge merged into "Missile," below
  - Missile—Missile badge
  - Space—Space badge
  - Other Badges—other badges

- No Pic—no picture, picture does not show badge area, and no references to badges in text
- No Badges
- Badges but unclear

- *Lt Col and Below C4ISR:* [Air Defense, FAC, CAOC, SIOP, ABM, Intel, Missile Ops, Space Ops, Comm/Electronics, No] Credit first tour chronologically in C4ISR at rank of 2nd lieutenant through lieutenant colonel. Intent is to capture tours in operations, maintenance, and staff, but not in acquisitions.

  - Air Defense—Tour as an ABM, or in any non-acquisitions position on staff or in command with North American Aerospace Defense (NORAD) Command, or an Air Defense Region. Also count air-defense-related C4ISR staff positions that are not clearly acquisitions. Flying as an interceptor pilot or command of a fighter intercept squadron does not count.
  - FAC—Forward Air Controller. Credit tours as airborne, ground, or fast FACs; Air Liaison Officer tours with ground units; ground/surface unit liaison tours; and command over FAC or close air support units.
  - CAOC—Combined Air Operations Center. Tour as commander or staff member in any tactically oriented air operations center. Examples include Tactical Air Control Center (TACC), Tanker/Airlift Control Center, Airlift Control Center, CAOC, etc. Also count pilots and navigators of AWACS or JSTARS units; and tactical-type C4ISR staff positions that are not clearly in acquisitions.
  - SIOP—Single Integrated Operations Plan. Tours mentioning staff work with the SIOP or Joint Strategic Target Planning Staff.
  - ABM—Air Battle Manager. Tour as an ABM, weapons controller, weapons director, intercept controller, or surveillance officer, or in an air control squadron, etc.
  - Intel—Tour as an intelligence officer or in an intelligence unit. Serving in an *operations and intelligence* staff division does not count. Flying as a reconnaissance pilot and command of a reconnaissance squadron do not count.
  - Missile Ops—Tour in a missile operations, missile maintenance, or missile staff position that is not clearly acquisitions.
  - Space Ops—Tour in a space operations, maintenance, or staff position that is not clearly acquisitions.
  - Comm/Electronics—Tour in communications, electronics, or command and control systems in operations, maintenance, or staff positions that are not clearly acquisitions.
  - No—No C4ISR tours between ranks of 2nd lieutenant and colonel in biography

- *Colonel C4ISR:* [Air Defense, FAC, CAOC, SIOP, ABM, Intel, Missile Ops, Space Ops, Comm/Electronics, No] Credit first tour chronologically in C4ISR at rank of colonel. Intent is to capture tours in operations, maintenance, and staff, but not in acquisitions.

  - Air Defense—Tour as an ABM, or in any non-acquisitions position on staff or in command with North American Aerospace Defense (NORAD) Command, or an Air Defense Region. Also count air-defense-related C4ISR staff positions that are not clearly acquisitions. Flying as an interceptor pilot and command of a fighter intercept squadron do not count.

- FAC—Forward Air Controller. Credit tours as airborne, ground, or fast FACs; Air Liaison Officer tours with ground units; ground/surface unit liaison tours; and command over FAC or close air support units.
- CAOC—Combined Air Operations Center. Tour as commander or staff member in any tactically oriented air operations center. Examples include Tactical Air Control Center (TACC), Tanker/Airlift Control Center, Airlift Control Center, CAOC, etc. Also count pilots and navigators of AWACS or JSTARS units; and tactical-type C4ISR staff positions that are not clearly in acquisitions.
- SIOP—Single Integrated Operations Plan. Tours mentioning staff work with the SIOP or Joint Strategic Target Planning Staff.
- ABM—Air Battle Manager. Tour as an ABM, weapons controller, weapons director, intercept controller, or surveillance officer, or in an air control squadron, etc.
- Intel—Tour as an intelligence officer or in an intelligence unit. Serving in an *operations and intelligence* staff division does not count. Flying as a reconnaissance pilot and command of a reconnaissance squadron do not count.
- Missile Ops—Tour in a missile operations, missile maintenance, or missile staff position that is not clearly acquisitions.
- Space Ops—Tour in a space operations, maintenance, or staff position that is not clearly acquisitions.
- Comm/Electronics—Tour in communications, electronics, or command and control systems in operations, maintenance, or staff positions that are not clearly acquisitions.
- No—No C4ISR tours as a colonel mentioned in biography

- *GO C4ISR:* [Air Defense, FAC, CAOC, SIOP, ABM, Intel, Missile Ops, Space Ops, Comm/Electronics, No] Credit first tour chronologically in C4ISR at rank of general officer (GO). Intent is to capture tours in operations, maintenance, and staff, but not in acquisitions.

  - Air Defense—Tour as an ABM, or in any non-acquisitions position on staff or in command with North American Aerospace Defense (NORAD) Command, or an Air Defense Region. Also count air-defense C4ISR staff positions that are not clearly acquisitions. Flying as an interceptor pilot and command of a fighter intercept squadron do not count.
  - FAC—Forward Air Controller. Credit tours as airborne, ground, or fast FACs; Air Liaison Officer tours with ground units; ground/surface unit liaison tours; and command over FAC or close air support units.
  - CAOC—Combined Air Operations Center. Tour as commander or staff member in any tactically oriented air operations center. Examples include Tactical Air Control Center (TACC), Tanker/Airlift Control Center, Airlift Control Center, CAOC, etc. Also count pilots and navigators of AWACS or JSTARS units; and tactical-type C4ISR staff positions that are not clearly in acquisitions.

- SIOP—Single Integrated Operations Plan. Tours mentioning staff work with the SIOP or Joint Strategic Target Planning Staff.
- ABM—Air Battle Manager. Tour as an ABM, weapons controller, weapons director, intercept controller, or surveillance officer, or in an air control squadron, etc.
- Intel—Tour as an intelligence officer or in an intelligence unit. Serving in an *operations and intelligence* staff division does not count. Flying as a reconnaissance pilot and command of a reconnaissance squadron do not count.
- Missile Ops—Tour in a missile operations, missile maintenance, or missile staff position that is not clearly acquisitions.
- Space Ops—Tour in a space operations, maintenance, or staff position that is not clearly acquisitions.
- Comm/Electronics—Tour in communications, electronics, or command and control systems in operations, maintenance, or staff positions that are not clearly acquisitions.
- No—No C4ISR tours as a general officer mentioned in biography

Notes

INTRODUCTION

1. Bureaucratic politics models indicate that once a group has political power in an organization, it will not relinquish this power. The group will fight to keep itself in control, and attempts to change the organization internally will fail unless the change can be shown to be in the controlling group's interest. The group "pilots" self-identifies as both a group and as the group in power. "Wings," flight suits, leather jackets, flight pay and pilot bonuses, better promotion rates, real and glass ceilings limiting opportunities for command for non-pilots, and a general cultural emphasis on flying as the bedrock of the Air Force all indicate both a strong group self-identity and a clear pilot-dominated organizational culture as well as the successful implementation of structural features preserving the group and its power within the institution. There are many barriers to entry into the pilot group. Since 1965, one must be an officer. That means that one must be a U.S. citizen, meet not only regular commissioning physical standards but flying standards as well, and normally complete Officer Training School (OTS), or Reserve Officers' Training Corps (ROTC) or United States Air Force Academy (USAFA) pre-commissioning training. Entry via the Aviation Cadet Program is discussed in more detail in chapter 5. In addition, the Air Force has performed additional screening of pilot candidates prior to or during OTS and ROTC. Traditionally (until 1993), Air Force Academy graduates physically qualified to fly have been given pilot training slots. After successfully completing these hurdles, the officer must successfully complete the approximately one-year long Undergraduate Pilot Training (UPT) program to earn pilot wings and status. Although restrictions on female pilots have gradually eased over the last 25 years, United States Air Force (USAF) pilots are typically white males. Leaving aside the issues of race, gender, and ethnicity representation in U.S. colleges in general, the USAF does not appear to overtly discriminate in favor of white males. Anecdotally, prior to 1993 the primary difference between those going to UPT or not from a USAFA class was whether the cadet needed glasses or

not. The discrimination on the basis of visual acuity is interesting from the point of view that it is largely an initial barrier to group entry. Once the individual begins pilot training, that officer will remain on flying status even if required to wear glasses or contact lenses later. Culturally, however, wearing glasses has been a source of embarrassment for many pilots. They would only wear the glasses when they really needed to read or see something, usually with a quip about how bad it is to need glasses, and of course, they would quickly take their glasses off again as soon as possible. Furthermore, since glasses interfere with wearing night vision goggles, the Air Force has subsidized contact lenses and laser surgery for pilots and some navigators, while simultaneously barring candidates who wear contacts or have had laser surgery from UPT and Undergraduate Navigator Training.

2. Although I question the exclusion of enlisted personnel from the profession and it is clear that there is a blurring between some civilian and military positions, I leave that for future books.

3. Despite this concrete interest, work on issues of profession tends to fall outside of the major fault lines of academic study. Political scientists and public policy experts tend to concentrate on government and political processes and favor bureaucratic politics models. Studies from this perspective tend to emphasize the military as a bureaucracy engaged in political struggle or look at the effects of organizational culture on political power within military organizations. Business schools tend to ignore the military, since the military is heavily regulated and not run for profit. Professions often have their own professional schools (e.g., medical schools, law schools, and seminaries), but their emphasis is passing on professional knowledge, not analyzing the profession itself. Consequently, sociologists, some political scientists, and a few practitioners work between the cracks on issues of profession. However, many works deal with definitions of profession, often to justify the consideration of a particular line of work as a profession.

4. Visionary warfare includes aircraft without pilots on board, the use of space and space-based assets, surface-based missiles, computer and information warfare, and the concept of effects-based operations.

CHAPTER 1

1. Samuel P. Huntington, *The Soldier and the State: The Theory and Politics of Civil-Military Relations* (Cambridge, MA: Belnap Press, 1985), 7.
2. Huntington 8.
3. Huntington 11.
4. Huntington 9.
5. Huntington 11.
6. Morris Janowitz, *The Professional Soldier: A Social and Political Portrait* (New York: Free Press, 1960), 367, 217–225.
7. Janowitz 21.
8. Janowitz 164.
9. Janowitz 21.
10. Janowitz 21.
11. Janowitz 161.
12. Counting coups was a Native American tradition in which a warrior would demonstrate bravery in battle by physically touching a worthy opponent in battle.

Each touch was a coup, so a warrior with many coups demonstrated his bravery many times.

13. Janowitz 228.

14. The percentage of Air Force general officers who are pilots has declined from over 90% to about 60% over the course of the independent Air Force's history.

15. Andrew Abbott, *The System of Professions: An Essay on the Division of Expert Labor* (Chicago: University of Chicago Press, 1988), 3.

16. Abbott 59.

17. When discussing technology's affect on jurisdiction, Abbott writes: "New technological jurisdictions are therefore usually absorbed by existing professions with their strong organizations. Yet not always. The technology of airplanes revolutionized the tasks of war. Yet the air arm of the American military became separate from the Army only after an internal battle of several decades; and it lost a similar fight with the Navy." See Abbott 92. Also see Abbot 344, note 13.

18. The speed at which each service has discarded the common battle dress uniform under the guise of post-9/11 operational requirements is an indication of a potential services retrenchment against "jointness."

19. Abbott 8.

20. Abbott 5.

21. Abbott 30.

22. Abbott 48.

23. For example, the Air Force's use of enlisted weapons controllers to perform the same job as junior officers and the entire Aviation Cadet Program are two examples that indicate that the distinction between officers and non-commissioned officers is quite gray.

24. Abbott 84.

CHAPTER 2

1. Gen Abrams was speaking at a hearing before the Committee on Armed Services, House of Representatives, 93rd Congress; quoted in William W. Momyer, General, USAF, Ret., *Air Power in Three Wars (WWII, Korea, Vietnam)* (Washington, DC: Department of the Air Force), 274–275 (italics added).

2. Although bombers from World War II on were equipped with high frequency (HF or shortwave) radios, which theoretically provide global communications, HF frequencies are affected by atmospheric conditions and very noisy. Consequently, they were not used for extensive decision-making discussions.

3. The phrase *centralized control, but decentralized execution* has been a long-standing tenet in the U.S. Air Force. The phrase represents an attempt to reach a practical compromise between the visionary and heroic warriors. The heroic warrior is willing to bow to centralized control, if centralized control is does not delve too deeply in the details of executing the mission. The post–Vietnam Air Force leadership traditionally emphasized the decentralized execution piece, despite the expansion of centralization into the execution phase brought about by C4ISR.

4. In a similar vein, in a multi-crewmember aircraft, it is often the case that the aircraft commander, a pilot, is junior in rank to other officers on the crew, but nevertheless still is the commander over all onboard during flight operations. In multi-ship operations, it is also possible that a wingman is senior in rank to the flight lead, but

once again, the position, not the rank, determines who is in charge. Rank becomes meaningless in the air, and this then has certain repercussions on the ground, which will be discussed in later chapters.

5. Air Defense Command (ADC) remained the organizational command of the Air Force contribution to NORAD, but it was subordinated for a time to the U.S. joint Continental Air Defense Command (CONAD), which was formed in 1954 as the umbrella for all American services' contributions to NORAD. CONAD and its successors also provided the option for the United States to act unilaterally if necessary. Eventually, since the Air Force provided the vast majority of people and systems, ADC became *Aerospace* Defense Command (ADCOM) and replaced CONAD as the American contribution to NORAD and a U.S. specified command. In this capacity, Army SAM units were placed under ADCOM, which was still an Air Force Major Command, commanded by an Air Force general. The commander of NORAD has typically, but not always, been the "multiple-hatted." That is, he has been the commander of the Air Force Aerospace Defense Command, which evolved into Air Force Space Command, the commander of U.S. Space Command (in existence since 1985), and the commander of NORAD. The DEW Line is a string of radar stations stretching from northwest Alaska to the east coast of Greenland, which formed the outer surveillance perimeter for warning of an impending Soviet bomber attack.

6. Western Electric Company Inc., *The SAGE Direction Center, SAGE Air Defense System* [USAF Contract No. AF 33 (600) 29307], August 15, 1958, 3.

7. Secretary of the Air Force, Office of Information, *Fact Sheet (79–12): F-106 Delta Dart* (Washington, DC: Secretary of the Air Force, 1979), 1.

8. The Bomarc surface-to-air missile was also capable of carrying a nuclear warhead.

9. From this perspective, the accidental shootdown of two Army Black Hawk helicopters over Iraq in April 1994 by a flight of two Air Force F-15s under control of a U.S. AWACS was a particularly significant event. The Air Force aircraft were enforcing the No-Fly-Zone over northern Iraq. The F-15 flight lead was a captain; his wingman was both a lieutenant colonel and the squadron commander on the ground. The F-15s detected the helicopters with their radars, but the AWACS systems only intermittently detected the helicopters. The F-15 flight advised AWACS of their contacts and ran an intercept to visually identify the unknown contacts. The F-15 flight visually identified the helicopters as Hinds and shot them down. The Air Force court-martialed the Senior Director on AWACS, a captain who was in charge of the air battle managers controlling the F-15s and all other aircraft in the area of operations, and other AWACS personnel accepted administrative punishments in lieu of courts-martial. The AWACS Senior Director was acquitted—a visual identification trumps any other type of information on unknown aircraft. The pilots, at least initially, were not punished in any way; their annual evaluations did not mention the incident and their records appeared to recommend further advancement. Although it could be argued that the Air Force indicated the dramatically increased role and responsibility of the command and control system by court-martialing the Senior Director and not the pilots, it appeared to ignore the tremendous implication that the man in the loop, the final sanity check, the pilot's eye was no more infallible than the rest of the people and equipment in the command and control system. Scott A. Snook provides a very detailed and different analysis in his *Friendly Fire: The Accidental Shootdown of U.S. Black Hawks over Northern Iraq* (Princeton, NJ: Princeton University Press, 2000).

10. A part of Aerospace Defense Command (ADC) had already evolved into providing warning of an inbound missile attack. In addition, as the interceptor aircraft numbers in ADC shrank, ADC became more involved in space, for example, tracking satellites. Consequently, ADC shed its aircraft and transitioned to Air Force Space Command in the early 1980s.

11. The Navy continued to use Link-4, as the data-link system was known, and even developed a two-way capability. The Navy's continued reliance on the system stemmed in part from the fact that a naval battle group is always in an air defense mode against aircraft and air-to-surface missiles. The advent of ICBMs did not have the same diminishing effect on air defenses for naval battle groups, since it would be difficult for an attacker to continually update an ICBM's navigation and targeting system as the battle group moved about. Consequently, long-range bombers with cruise missiles remained a bigger threat to naval forces under way than ICBMs. Furthermore, in the late 1980s, the Air Force led the introduction of the new Joint Tactical Information Distribution System (JTIDS) data-link system. The system was first fielded on command and control platforms, with a gradual spread to air-to-air fighters. JTIDS is not one-way and directive from the command and control center to the fighters like the earlier air-defense Link-4. Instead, JTIDS shares information in a pool. Fighters can transmit data on their own aircraft location and targets that they have acquired with their own systems. Consequently, the pilots have more situational awareness with respect to where friendly aircraft are, and where unknown or hostile aircraft are with respect to their own fighter. This emboldens the heroic warrior to make the claim that the information is provided for his tactical decisions and that he should make engagement decisions based on this information and not be directed by air battle managers. On the other hand, the visionary points out that the air battle manager and the entire command and control system now have much more accurate information on both friendly aircraft and others, and still have the big situational awareness picture far beyond that which surrounds the individual fighter's JTIDS scopes. In addition, the command and control system has intelligence feeds and other information that is not on JTIDS, further increasing the command and control system's awareness of the larger battle space. JTIDS is not tied into the fighter's autopilot controls. The air battle manager can send commands over JTIDS, but the pilot receives the commands, interprets them, and flies the aircraft. The impact of JTIDS on the heroic warrior versus visionary archetype discussion is unclear, because JTIDS is relatively new. It is generations above the old F-106 data-link, and few pilots in service today have had any experience with the F-106 anyway. Some air battle managers have experience with the Navy's use of Link-4, but JTIDs is dramatically different. Finally, the Air Force officer corps' apparent acceptance of the concept of the unmanned combat air vehicle (UCAV) could take this discussion in many different directions. For example, Soviet data-link-equipped interceptors and Navy F-14s have both been used as "mini-AWACS," controlling other, less capable fighters at the outer reaches of an air-defense-oriented command and control system. One might do something similar, de facto making a fighter pilot, or more likely a fighter weapons system operator, part of the command and control system controlling (through some mechanism) a flight of JTIDS-equipped UCAVs that thereby extend the entire command and control system.

12. NATO provided some AWACS aircraft after 9/11, and U.S. Navy and Marine aircraft also flew combat air patrols. In addition, a large part of the strategic air defense

provided by the "Air Force" is actually provided by Air National Guard and Air Force Reserve units.

13. General Momyer identifies the highest-level control system within the World War II JOC as the Tactical Air Control Center (TACC; Momyer 258). This gets confusing because the term JOC was used in World War II and in Korea but briefly replaced by the term Air Operations Center (AOC) in Vietnam before the term TACC became the term for the air commander's operational headquarters for planning, directing, and controlling air operations. By Vietnam, coordination between the ground and air units for close air support occurred in the Air Support Operations Center (ASOC), later renamed the Direct Air Support Center (DASC), which was usually located with ground unit headquarters and subordinated to the TACC.

14. Momyer 156.

15. Momyer 250. The "Farm Gate" special operations counterinsurgency air unit was not deployed to Vietnam until October 1961, and it was primarily involved in training, not taking on combat tasks until late 1962.

16. Momyer 254. The TADC in Korea is the functional equivalent to a CRC or CRP in Vietnam.

17. Momyer 178–179, 218–219, 282–283; Carl Berger, ed., *The United States Air Force in Southeast Asia, 1961–1973* (Washington, DC: Office of Air Force History [GPO], 1977), 151, 156–157.

18. Momyer 159.

19. Momyer 159. Momyer's point is also interesting in that the general assessment of the Air Force office corps in the 1980s was that what Momyer calls "positive control," or GCI (Ground-Controlled Intercept), was the Achilles heel of the Soviet air forces because Soviet pilots obviously lacked flying skill and initiative, living in a world where everything was controlled by intercept officers on the ground. Consequently, American pilots, flying the F-15 with a much more capable radar than the F-4, would rely on their initiative and their wonderful aircraft and its onboard systems to defeat any future airborne adversaries in battle. "Positive control" was a sign of weakness, something that the Air Force had outgrown.

20. The package commander is often assigned by aircraft call sign, leaving it to the unit to determine who it will be. The person, usually a pilot, has no official authority on the ground, but he coordinates some level of mission planning among the participating units, by secure phones if the aircraft in the raid package are based at different bases. In the air, his primary responsibility is the decision to cancel the raid or to shift the attack to the secondary target set. If, for example, the supporting electronic warfare aircraft do not arrive, that may be a reason to cancel; if weather obscures the primary target set, he may shift the raid to the secondary set. He has no more information, and not necessarily any more experience or rank, than the other pilots in the raid package, but assigning this responsibility to one person reduces the uncertainty and chaos when beyond radio range of the command and control system. Since the aircraft are coming from different units and perhaps bases, and rank has no meaning in the air, somebody has to be given the responsibility. If the duty was not assigned to one person, the raid packages might plow ahead on suicide missions or break down.

21. Momyer 203.

22. Momyer 269–270.

23. Momyer 265–266, 276–277.

24. "Part II, Command and Control Report," *Gulf War Air Power Survey, Volume 1, Planning and Command and Control* (Washington, DC: GPO, 1993), 74.

25. In the Navy, the basic fighting unit is traditionally the ship. The ship is both a home and a mobile fortress. It is subdivided into different departments, responsible for particular aspects of the ship. Officers begin their careers in these departments, moving up to become department heads, with intermittent staff duties, and eventually become skippers of ships. Ships can be joined together into task forces or battle groups with the ensuing large staffs, forming a bigger pyramid of command, but the ship with its internal pyramid remains the basic unit.

26. Furthermore, the Air Force tends to stovepipe its officers' careers. Unlike Army officers, for example, who balance command tours with tours in battalion, brigade, and higher-level staffs, Air Force C4ISR officers stay in the C4ISR system. Air Force pilots fly and often concurrently serve in administrative positions in the squadron, wing, and higher-level staffs, but they are less frequently found in the C4ISR system except in senior positions or in operations or planning sections. Consequently, there is minimal experience overlap between the flying squadron and the C4ISR command lines.

27. The Joint Staff defines command as follows: "*Command:* The authority that a commander in the Armed Forces lawfully exercises over subordinates by virtue of rank or assignment. Command includes the authority and responsibility for effectively using available resources and for planning the employment of, organizing, directing, coordinating, and controlling military forces for the accomplishment of assigned missions. It also includes responsibility for health, welfare, morale, and discipline of assigned personnel." See Department of Defense, *Dictionary of Military and Associated Terms,* Joint Publication 1–02, April 12, 2001, 79. *Control* currently exists in two variations: operational control and tactical control. Operational control occurs when a combatant commander transfers his command authority over a particular unit or force to a lower-level commander. Operational control over a particular unit means that a commander can train, make plans for, and use that particular unit, and even integrate it into a bigger force, but he cannot divide or reorganize the unit's subunits or interfere with the unit's internal organization, administration, logistics, training, and discipline. Tactical control over a unit or force is further limited, but like operational control, can be delegated from the combatant commander on down. See Department of Defense 310.

CHAPTER 3

1. Carl Builder touched on this phenomenon in his two books on military and Air Force organizational culture, *The Masks of War* (1989) and *The Icarus Syndrome* (1994). Builder described an obsession with technology inextricably tied to manned flight, that is, piloting. In fact, Builder questioned whether Air Force pilots are really tied to the institution of the USAF and its claim to be a decisive instrument in warfare, or just tied to flying: "One could speculate that, if the machines were, somehow, moved en masse to another institution, the loyalty would be to the airplanes (or missiles). . . . The prospect of combat is not the essential draw; it is simply the justification for having and flying these splendid machines." See Carl H. Builder, *The Masks of War: American Military Styles in Strategy and Analysis* (Baltimore: Johns Hopkins University Press, 1989), 23. However, Builder did not have it quite right. Builder's emphasis on organizational culture overlooked the key role that the sense of professional responsibility plays within the officer corps. "The prospect of combat" has skyrocketed since 1991 with Desert Storm and the ensuing no-fly-zone patrols, which did not end until

Operation Iraqi Freedom, no-fly-zone enforcement in the Balkans, the air campaign against Serbia, and the ongoing operations in Afghanistan and Iraq. Heroic and visionary Air Force officers remain firmly committed to their "splendid machines," but there is no doubt in any officer's mind that the profession is about war.

2. In this book, I do not restrict the term Forward Aircraft Controller or FAC to its typical connotation. In the Air Force, it typically refers to an officer, usually a pilot, who acts as a man-on-the-scene coordinator between Army or Marine units on the ground and aircraft providing close air support for the ground troops. The FAC may be on the ground or airborne, and he specifically directs the supporting aircraft as they attack the targets that he assigns them. However, there are other officer positions such as the air liaison officers and some members of tactical air control parties and also enlisted positions that perform the same work or do some of the work under a ground controller's supervision. For example, in the Air Force there are enlisted terminal attack controllers, enlisted special operations combat controllers, and enlisted radio operators maintainers and drivers (ROMADs). In addition to the Air Force mix, the other military services have a similar mix of enlisted and officer positions, which frequently also include the mission of requesting and controlling artillery support. Consequently, I frequently use the term FAC in the broader sense of all these positions that directly assign targets, mark targets with lasers, and control aircraft performing close air support. Joint Terminal Attack Controllers (JTACs) fall under my definition of FAC.

3. The process can be likened to programming or getting used to a new cell phone, although the consequences of mistakes can be more severe. For example, a District of Columbia Air National Guard F-16 (stationed at Andrews Air Force Base, Maryland) inadvertently strafed a public school near a gunnery range in New Jersey on the evening of November 3, 2004. The accident report faulted both the pilot and the software design, since pulling the trigger in some modes lets the pilot use the targeting laser to verify his position in relation to the target, and this was what the pilot was trying to do. However, since the pilot had already selected the air-to-ground gun mode and armed ready, pulling the trigger fired the gun. See Donna De La Cruz, "Report Blames Pilot in School Strafing," *Air Force Times*, January 3, 2005: 20.

4. General Momyer reports that "Almost all of these kills [USAF victories during the Korean War] were without the benefit of on-board radar even though the F-86 had a forward ranging radar. Most of the pilots used a fixed sight setting and got their kills from the 6 o'clock position with the six fifty caliber machine guns. Most of the fighter kills in World War II were also from the 6 o'clock position." See General William W. Momyer, USAF, Ret., *Air Power in Three Wars (WWII, Korea, Vietnam)* (Washington, DC: Department of the Air Force, 1978), 115, footnote.

5. During the Vietnam War, however, the use of beyond-visual-range air-to-air missiles was limited by the Rules of Engagement (ROE) and the related need to identify targets before shooting. This frequently required pilots to visually identify enemy aircraft, which of course negated the advantages of beyond-visual-range-capable missiles. In addition, radar bombing was limited to targets with good radar returns, which are limited in a guerrilla insurgency in agrarian areas. Radar bombing depended on the radar operator's ability to discriminate between various radar returns, and the delivery of gravity ("dumb") bombs was no more accurate when aiming at a radar return than when aiming at a visually acquired ground target. By Desert Storm, the combination of technology (new identification systems and AWACS radar coverage), lessons learned from Vietnam, and experience gained from years of combat exercises led to Rules of Engagement that minimized situations requiring visual identification of

airborne targets and maximized opportunities for beyond-visual-range air-to-air missile shots. Technology in the form of better airborne computers and algorithms in fighters and attack aircraft led to increased bombing accuracy for "dumb" bombs, and of course, the precision guided munitions (PGMs) epitomized the great technological strides in weaponry between 1973 and 1991.

6. Perhaps the most exotic of these weapons was the AIR-2A Genie, an unguided, nuclear-armed air-intercept rocket carried primarily by the F-106. The AIR-2A was designed for use against Soviet bombers attacking North America. The pilot would fly into range of the bomber formation, point his nose where he generally wanted the AIR-2A to go, and fire.

7. Although there might not appear to be any obvious command and control system involvement, B-52s in Southeast Asia were routinely controlled by special ground radar sites, which set the bombers' course, altitude, speed, and bomb drop when B-52s were bombing close to American ground forces.

8. "VB" stands for vertical bomb; "Azon" stands for Azimuth Only. The bomb could only be steered left or right (azimuth), but not up or down (range). The VB-1 was a 1,000-lb. bomb with a tail assembly containing radio-controlled rudders that made it possible to "fly" the bomb into the target. The VB-1 carried a flare in its tail, which the bombardier used as a reference point in steering the bomb toward the target. See "VB-1 Azon Guided Bomb," *US Air Force Museum Weapons Gallery*, Wright-Patterson AFB, Ohio, November 7, 2005, http://www.wpafb.af.mil/museum/arm/arm34.htm.

9. Circle Error Probable (CEP) refers to the radius in which 50% of the ordnance can be expected to fall.

10. "Razon" stands for Range and Azimuth Only. This bomb had range and azimuth controlling surfaces. The 19th Bombardment Group had to overcome several problems in its use of the Razon. Razons were used for the first time on August 23, 1950. Three B-29s attacked the Pyongyang railway bridge with 15 Razon bombs, but only one of the bombs stayed under control and registered a hit. The bombers apparently flew over the area for 40 minutes—an amazingly long time—as they tried to acquire the target, make a bomb run, release a Razon, and try to steer it to the bridge. One B-29 was hit by North Korean AAA. Subsequent groupings of missions yielded statistics of roughly 30%, and later 60%, of the released Razon bombs being controllable. Of course, not all controlled bombs actually hit their targets, since there was obviously an art to steering the bomb, with no references except a flare, falling three or more miles below. Since it often took multiple hits to destroy bridge segments, the USAF tried a further development, the 12,000-lb. VB-13 Tarzon. The Tarzon, also known as the ASM-1, was used in Korea to destroy bridges between December 1950 and April 1951, when it was withdrawn because of safety concerns and a low success rate. See "Razon-Tarzon," Wright-Patterson AFB, Ohio, November 7, 2005 http://www.ascho.wpafb.af.mil/korea/tarzonRazon.htm; Albert Simpson and Robert Futrell, "Interdiction—Razon Attacks," in *United States Air Force Operations in the Korean Conflict, 25 June–November 1950, USAF Historical Study No. 71—USAF Museum*, July 1, 1952, Wright-Patterson AFB, Ohio, November 7, 2005 http://www.wpafb.af.mil/museum/history/korea/no71–55.htm; and "VB-3 Razon Guided Bomb," *US Air Force Museum Weapons Gallery*, Wright-Patterson AFB, Ohio, November 7, 2005 http://www.wpafb.af.mil/museum/arm/arm35.htm.

11. Bill Gunston, ed., *The Encyclopedia of World Air Power* (New York: Crescent Books, 1981), 369.

12. Gunston 368; Editors of *Air Force Magazine, The Almanac of Airpower* (New York: Simon & Schuster), 196.

13. Gunston 372; Editors of *Air Force Magazine* 83–84.

14. Fighter radars project a small but normally steerable cone of coverage forward from the nose of the aircraft. In air-to-air modes, the radar is typically scanned in an overlapping raster pattern something like a LED "2." The pilot or weapons system operator sets the pattern, direction, and processing range of the radar scan. The radar only "sees" targets that reflect sufficient radar energy back to the antenna and meet other parameters. Consequently, aircraft to the sides and rear of a fighter are not "seen" by its radar. Aircraft that are too far away or are facing in certain directions may not reflect enough energy to be projected on the scope, and aircraft that are flying at an altitude of 30,000 feet when the radar is looking lower or higher do not get hit by the main radar beam and hence are invisible to the radar. In addition, setting the radar to scan the entire gamut of possibilities from 50,000 feet in altitude down the surface and from 60° left of the fighter's nose to 60° right of the nose would take such a long time that an enemy aircraft could be beyond the processing range when first hit by the main beam but be in firing position before being hit again. Finally, in most fighter systems through the 1980s, locking on to one target with the radar left the pilot "blind" with respect to all other radar targets. Although fighters working in pairs can split the search and condense it in terms of altitude or azimuth because of known enemy tactics, radar-equipped fighters are in many ways still looking for the proverbial needle in the haystack while searching for enemy aircraft. In Vietnam for example, an F-4 might be able to detect aircraft at 30 or so nautical miles, depending on a variety of conditions. However, detecting an aircraft at 30 nautical miles is not the same as identifying the aircraft at 30 nautical miles, and even if an aircraft could be identified at 30 miles, the AIM-7's tactical range was closer to 10 miles. Locking on to the target too early left the fighter blind to other radar returns; so there was no point in locking on to aircraft that were well beyond missile range. It only served to alert them that they were being tracked.

15. In Vietnam, the Rules of Engagement did not permit beyond-visual-range engagements, at least until the 1972 air campaign, partly because the command and control radar networked coverage contained many holes, into which both friendly and enemy aircraft could disappear. See Momyer 158. Consequently, in order to prevent fratricide, in the majority of fighter engagements during the war, the fighters had to visually identify the target before firing missiles or guns at it. The requirement for visual identification kept the responsibility and decision making for air-to-air engagements with the pilot. However, it negated the superior range, the all-aspect nature, and the beyond-visual-range capability of the AIM-7/F-4 combination over the Mig-21's short-range, rear-aspect only, visual range Atoll missiles. In addition, it yielded the initiative to the enemy aircraft in any engagement, since the American fighters had to get close enough to visually identify the enemy aircraft, while trying to maintain the ability to fire weapons as soon as the identification was made. However, during the identification they could conceivably get too close to the Mig to fire the AIM-7, which required a minimum range to arm the missile, and the F-4 did not have an internal gun until the F-4E model. Meanwhile, the Migs were under ground-controlled intercept (GCI) control, which had a comprehensive radar picture of the airspace over North Vietnam. The North Vietnamese command and control system could keep the Migs from being surprised by American fighters, determine the Migs' targets, and direct

them on the intercepts. Consequently, the Migs were frequently able to fly up, shoot, and run, before the American aircraft could react and counterattack. The combination of the Rules of Engagement and the spotty command and control system coverage limited the effectiveness of the Air Force's use of semi-active radar missiles over Southeast Asia. These issues were not factors in Desert Storm, however. In addition, the development of the Track-While-Scan modes in certain fighter fire-control computers permits a pilot to lock onto an aircraft without becoming blind. The radar can continue to scan and detect other targets while locked on to one. Furthermore, the Advanced Medium Range Air-to-Air Missile (AMRAAM) now gives certain fighters the capability to simultaneously attack multiple air targets at beyond-visual ranges. It should also be pointed out that the requirement for a visual identification was not really an issue in Korea or World War II, because the primary air-to-air weapon was the gun. Its effective range was within visual range; so all targets were de facto visually identified.

16. Early versions of air-to-air infrared missiles could only be fired from the rear of the target, since the seekers were not extremely sensitive. From the 1980s onward, many infrared guided air-to-air missiles can also be fired from the front or side of a target, making them all-aspect missiles. They typically have a longer range in the front, since the target is coming to meet the missile, but they are still short-range, that is, within-visual-range, missiles.

17. In the Air Force, the F-4 was initially manned by two pilots, with the front-seater being the aircraft commander and the rear-seater the "guy in back" (GIB). However, the increasing demand for pilots during Vietnam and a general unwillingness of pilots to perform the GIB's duty of running the radar and weapons control system resulted in the move to man the back seats with weapons system operators (navigator specialty). The transition actually lasted several years. See "Pilots to Leave F-4 Rear Seats," *Air Force Times*, November 18, 1970: 8. Nevertheless, two of the Air Force's three Vietnam War aces were actually weapons system operators.

18. On the other hand, Navy aviators achieved most of their kills in Vietnam with the AIM-9 Sidewinder missile. Gen Momyer attributes the difference to the fact that the Navy routinely worked in areas where they were attacked by Mig-17s, which were less capable than Mig-21s and forced to close in to gun range to shoot down U.S. aircraft. Consequently, the engagements were at very close range, and as the Navy F-4s did not have guns, their short-range weapon was the Sidewinder. See Momyer 157.

19. Editors of *Air Force Magazine* 195. Hap Arnold was involved in the development of "the Bug."

20. The *Gulf War Air Power Survey* makes the case that using PGMs to attack individual tanks in Iraqi Republican Guard and Army units would have been too time-consuming and expensive. Furthermore, massive bombardment or carpet bombing of ground units with dumb bombs creates a psychological atmosphere of terror or panic, which can lead to the breakdown of morale and discipline in some units. See "Weapons, Tactics and Training," in *Gulf War Air Power Survey Volume IV* (Washington, DC: GPO, 1993), 261–266.

21. Brigadier General David A. Deptula, USAF, *Effects-Based Operations: Change in the Nature of War* (Arlington, VA: Aerospace Education Foundation [Air Force Association], 2001), 8. Of course, the Azon case indicated the possibility of attacking multiple targets per raid late in World War II.

CHAPTER 4

1. Headquarters United States Air Force, Comptroller, Director of Statistical Services, *United States Air Force Statistical Digest 1947* (Washington, DC: HQ USAF, 1948), ix.

2. Separate squadrons included in the list of combat units were strategic weather reconnaissance, air rescue, liaison, aerial resupply, tow target, and MATS long-range or "strategic" air transport. Headquarters United States Air Force, DCS Comptroller, D Statistical Services, Operations Statistics Division, *United States Air Force Statistical Digest Fiscal Year 1951* (Washington, DC: HQ US Air Force), 91.

3. The Air Force has always had a relatively unchallenged monopoly over the jurisdiction of providing the aircraft for large-scale airborne operations, which is another seam issue. The numbers and size of aircraft required for such operations would be prohibitive for the Army and seen as needless duplication by the public.

4. For example, in fiscal year (FY) 1957, the USAF shipped 62,154 military dependents outbound from the continental United States to overseas destinations. A total of 31,909 went via the Military Sea Transportation Service, 14,173 went via MATS, and 16,072 went via commercial air. See Headquarters United States Air Force, Comptroller of the Air Force, Directorate of Statistical Services, *United States Air Force Statistical Digest Fiscal Year 1957* (Washington, DC: HQ US Air Force), 204.

5. Headquarters United States Air Force, Deputy Chief of Staff Comptroller, Directorate of Statistical Services, *United States Air Force Statistical Digest Fiscal Year 1952* (Washington, DC: HQ US Air Force), 84.

6. Headquarters United States Air Force, Comptroller of the Air Force, Directorate of Statistical Services, *United States Air Force Statistical Digest Fiscal Year 1957*, 3.

7. Headquarters United States Air Force, Comptroller of the Air Force, Directorate of Statistical Services, *United States Air Force Statistical Digest Fiscal Year 1958* (Washington, DC: HQ US Air Force), 3; Headquarters United States Air Force, Comptroller of the Air Force, Directorate of Statistical Services, *United States Air Force Statistical Digest Fiscal Year 1959* (Washington, DC: HQ US Air Force), 3.

8. Paradoxically, the replacements for the EC-121, the E-3 Airborne Warning and Control System (AWACS) aircraft squadrons that were forming in the late 1970s, were not included in the combat and support unit table in the USAF *Statistical Digest* series.

9. The FAC flying squadrons are captured under the category "Other" in the reintroduced USAF *Statistical Digest* series.

10. Headquarters United States Air Force, Comptroller of the Air Force, Directorate of Data Automation, Data Services Center, *United States Air Force Statistical Digest Fiscal Year 1966* (Washington, DC: HQ US Air Force), 1, 3.

11. Headquarters United States Air Force, Comptroller of the Air Force, Directorate of Data Automation, Data Services Center, *United States Air Force Statistical Digest Fiscal Year 1967* (Washington, DC: HQ US Air Force), 1, 3.

12. Comptroller of the Air Force, Directorate of Cost and Management Analysis, *United States Air Force Summary 1981* (Washington, DC: HQ USAF), FOR 11; Comptroller of the Air Force, Directorate of Cost and Management Analysis, *USAF Summary 1982* (Washington, DC: HQ USAF, 1982), 3–11. Although the table is continued through the USAF *Summary* series of the 1980s and the reintroduced USAF *Statistical Digest* in the 1990s, the table is no longer the lead chapter of the publication. Instead of being the major part of a relatively small but nevertheless important lead

chapter, from 1981 on the table is buried in a back section. The lead chapter and the emphasis of the USAF *Summary* series and the later USAF *Statistical Digest* versions concern financial and budget issues.

13. Headquarters United States Air Force, Comptroller of the Air Force, Directorate of Cost, Economics and Field Support Division, *United States Air Force Summary 1986* (Washington, DC: HQ USAF, 1986), D-2A.

14. "Air Operations Centers (formerly Tactical Air Control Centers)" and "Air Control Squadrons (including Air Control and Reporting Centers and Control and Reporting Elements)."

15. For example, the USAF *Statistical Digest* volumes in the early to mid-1990s contain a listing for the MX Peacekeeper ICBM, and the FY1998 issue contains procurement information on "Global Positioning (SPACE), Defense Support Program (SPACE), and Medium Launch Vehicle (SPACE)." See Assistant Secretary of the Air Force (Financial Management and Comptroller of the Air Force), Deputy Assistant Secretary (Cost and Economics), *United States Air Force Statistical Digest Fiscal Year 1993* (Washington, DC: Assistant Secretary of the Air Force, 1994), E-103; and Assistant Secretary of the Air Force (Financial Management and Comptroller of the Air Force), Deputy Assistant Secretary (Cost and Economics), *United States Air Force Statistical Digest Fiscal Year 1998* (Washington, DC: Assistant Secretary of the Air Force, 1999), 94.

16. The USAF *Statistical Digest* changed its reporting format in FY1997, dropping ICBM squadrons completely and dropping the distinction between strategic and tactical airlift.

17. Fighter/attack includes fighters, which also includes fighter-interceptors, and attack aircraft. Attack aircraft include single-seat A-7s and A-10s, which look like "fighters," but also the AC-130 gunship, which is a four-engine cargo aircraft modified to fire heavy weapons at targets on the ground. However, its relatively small numbers have only a minor impact on the Tactical amalgamation, which is simply fighter/attack aircraft. C4ISR aircraft include reconnaissance, electronic warfare, and observer (FAC), as well as communications, liaison, and utility aircraft. The communications, liaison, and utility aircraft are included with observer aircraft because the same types of aircraft are included under the various category headings in different years and it is difficult to break out the individual aircraft or missions in most years. The USAF *Statistical Digest* series does not include a separate category for command and control aircraft. At times they have been lumped under their basic aircraft types. For example, airborne early warning and control EC-121s were included without specific reference in the C-121 total, and SAC's EC-135 command and control aircraft were hidden under the C-135 total under cargo aircraft. The same occurs with special operations aircraft like the EC-130. Consequently, the cargo totals are at times inflated to the detriment of the C4ISR numbers. After FY1996, command and control aircraft and special operations aircraft were generally tallied under reconnaissance.

18. See for example, Richard I. Wolf, *The United States Air Force Basic Documents on Roles and Missions* (Washington, DC: Office of Air Force History, 1987).

19. Navy SLBMs form the third leg of the nuclear triad.

20. For example, F-15E bomb loads and ranges are loosely comparable to those of the B-29 or B-47, which the B-52 replaced. An F-15E can carry up to 24,500 lb. of ordnance and has a ferry range of 3,500 miles with conformal fuel tanks. A B-29 could carry 20,000 lb. of bombs with a range of 3,250; and a B-47 could carry 22,000 lb. of bombs with a range of 3,600. See Editors of *Air Force Magazine*, *The Almanac of Airpower* (New York: Simon & Schuster, 1989), 72, 185–186.

21. The USAF *Statistical Digest*'s counting methods exaggerate this effect, since aircraft like the RC-135, EC-135, AC-130, and EC-130, which had cargo-carrying equivalents, were all lumped under cargo, resulting in artificially low numbers or no numbers for C4ISR aircraft categories. In fact, for FY1973–FY1975, the tanker category briefly disappeared, because KC-135s were included under cargo aircraft.

22. Incidentally, this shift and its perceived or implied permanence affect all officers serving today, since a lieutenant serving in 1972 would hit the 35 years of service retirement mark for a general officer in 2007.

23. For most of its history, the USAF *Statistical Digest* series does not break pilot or navigator billets out of the combined category.

24. The C4ISR career field billet amalgamation includes the air battle manager (ABM); air traffic control (ATC); missile operations; space operations; intelligence; communications, electronics, and computers; weather; and operations management career field billets.

25. The medical career billet amalgamation includes the medical professional (which includes physicians and surgeons), nurse, medical services (which includes health services administrators), veterinary, and biomedical sciences (which includes veterinarians after FY1979, psychologists, and other medical-related fields) career field billets.

CHAPTER 5

1. Aviation Service Act, Pub. L. 63–143, 63rd Cong., Ch. 186, July 18, 1914, Stat. 38–514, pp. 514–515.

2. The Aviation Section was "charged with the duty of operating or supervising the operation of all military air craft, including balloons and aeroplanes, all appliances pertaining to said craft; and signaling apparatus of any kind when installed on said aircraft; also with the duty of training officers and enlisted men in matters pertaining to military aviation." See Aviation Service Act, Pub. L. 63–143, p. 514.

3. Aviation Service Act, Pub. L. 63–143, p. 515.

4. Officer aviation students were paid bonuses and were to be paid 125% of their pay, junior military aviators were advanced one rank up to the rank of captain and additionally paid 150% of the new rank's rate, and military aviators were also advanced one rank up to the rank of captain and paid 175% of that new rate. Enlisted aviators and aviation mechanicians were paid 150% of their rate. A widow, or a designated beneficiary, was to be paid one year's pay upon the death of an aviation officer or enlisted man due to an aviation accident in which the military member was not at fault. See Aviation Service Act, Pub. L. 63–143, pp. 514–516.

5. The pay scales of aviation officers, junior military aviators, and military aviators remained at 125%, 150%, and 175% respectively, and junior military aviators and military aviators on flying status were advanced one rank up to the rank of major. See .National Defense Act, Pub. L. 64–85, 64th Cong., Ch. 134, June 3, 1916, Stat. 39–166, pp. 174–176.

6. National Defense Act Amendment, Pub. L. 66–242, 66th Cong., Ch. 227, June 4, 1920, Stat. 41–759, p. 768.

7. Vance O. Mitchell, *Air Force Officers Personnel Policy Development 1944–1974* (Washington, DC: Air Force History and Museums Program [GPO], 1996), 353.

8. National Defense Act Amendment, Pub. L. 66–242, 1920, p. 769.

9. National Defense Act Amendment [Public—No. 446—69th Cong], [H.R. 10827], July 2, 1926 (Washington, DC: GPO), p. 2.

10. National Defense Act Amendment, Public—No. 446, 1926, p. 2.

11. U.S. Senate, Committee on Military Affairs, *The Army Air Service Hearing on H.R. 10827*, 69th Cong., 1st sess., May 10, 1926 (Washington, DC: GPO, 1926), 8.

12. National Defense Act Amendment, Public—No. 446, 1926, p. 3.

13. U.S. Senate, *The Army Air Service Hearing on H.R. 10827*, 16.

14. U.S. Senate, *The Army Air Service Hearing on H.R. 10827*, 15.

15. When asked about how pilots disqualified due to age are counted, Major General Patrick replied, "No, sir; they are not retired for disability. They are still regarded as flying officers within the provisions of the law, Senator Reed. They are not disrated, nor are they retired or taken out of the corps at all. They still fulfill the definition of a flying officer." With respect to flight pay, Major General Patrick then went on to explain that some of these officers might still get flight pay as observers even though disqualified by age for pilot duties. "It has been thought that in future wars the man who commands air troops in the air would not necessarily pilot his own machine; in fact, he probably would not. He would give his entire attention to commanding the air force and would be flown by some one else. So there is a chance there for them to use the knowledge they have acquired in a proper fashion in commanding air troops in the air, although they themselves do not pilot the machines in which they ride." This is a remarkably prescient description of the future air battle manager career field—although it actually became part of the definition of the command pilot rating for many years. See U.S. Senate, *The Army Air Service Hearing on H.R. 10827*, 10.

16. Major General J. E. Fechet, *Annual Report, Chief of the Air Corps, Report to the Army Adjutant General*, August 22, 1930, 5.

17. See Attachments 1 and 2 to Major General Robert T. Ginsburgh (Chief Office of Air Force History), letter to Lt General Charles B. Westover, December 9, 1971, Office of Air Force History, Anacostia Annex (USN), DC. The letter concerns the connection between Westover's father's accident in September 1938 and the establishment of command pilot and senior pilot ratings. Similar wording is also to be found in Attachment 4, Office of the Chief of the Air Corps, War Department, Air Corps Circular 50–11, Training, November 21, 1939, p. 2.

18. According to a 1943 aviation cadet recruiting brochure, "Mechanical aptitude, unusually quick reflexes, perfect physical coordination, and the ability to make rapid decisions are desirable in the applicant who wishes to become a pilot. A knowledge of mathematics and some experience in the field of applied sciences are useful." Furthermore, concerning the pilot, "His is the spectacular role," but the training is "grueling" and the longest (36 weeks) of all aircrew members. On the other hand, the navigator "is the man behind the man at the controls, and his instructions enable the pilot to guide the ship directly to its objective." The navigator course is a mere 33 weeks long. "A definite mathematical bent is essential, and it is desirable that pre-Cadet training should have included a sound fundamental ground work in mathematics." In fact, "Those interested in pursuing their mathematics studies still further, will find an excellent opportunity for doing so in the navigation schools of the U.S. Army Air Forces." A bombardier, however, takes only 27 weeks to train. His duty "is performed in a matter of seconds—but the most important seconds of the flight. At the crucial moment, when the bomber reaches its objective, the bombardier takes over from the pilot. Upon his skill in landing his bombs on the target depends the success of the

entire mission." See Army Air Forces, *Aviation Cadet Training* (Washington DC: U.S. Army Recruiting Publicity Bureau, May 25, 1943), 15–17.

19. Mitchell 353.

20. National Defense Act Amendment, Public—No. 446, 1926, p. 1. During a Senate committee hearing on the bill, Major General Patrick, Chief of the Air Service, U.S. Army, stated that without Senator Bingham's proposed amendment to require the Chief of the Air Service/Corps to be a flying officer, a supply officer without any flying experience could at that time theoretically become the Chief. The interchange between Senator Bingham and Major General Patrick is revealing: "Senator Bingham. You do not think that the head of the Air Service ought ever to be a nonflying officer, any more than you would have a chief of the Cavalry a man who was afraid to ride a horse? General Patrick. I do not." See U.S. Senate, *The Army Air Service Hearing on H.R. 10827*, 12. In addition to Senator Bingham's inference that non-pilots were somehow afraid to ride in aircraft, the senator's choice of the cavalry for the analogy is quite strange, yet prophetic. In 1926, the Army still had a cavalry branch, and this branch was a much sought-after assignment, yet a totally anachronistic branch of service. "Cavalry" regiments continue in Army service, but without the requirement for horsemanship as the cavalry mounts shifted to vehicles and later also helicopters. In tradition and belief, the Air Force officer corps has not abandoned the pilot requirement for the Chief of Staff position, although it is not a Title 10 requirement.

21. The 1925 edition of the U.S. Code specified that Army "vacancies in grades below that of brigadier general shall be filled by the promotion of officers in the order in which they stand on the promotion list, without regard to the branches in which they are commissioned." See Volume 44, Part 1 of the United States Statutes at Large (Washington, DC: GPO, 1926), Title 10, Army §552.

22. National Defense Act Amendment, Public—No. 446, 1926, p. 4.

23. U.S. Senate, *The Army Air Service Hearing on H.R. 10827*, 27, 7.

24. National Defense Act Amendment, Pub. L. 76–795, 76th Cong., Ch. 742, October 4, 1940, Stat. 54–963; Army Air Forces, Army Regulation No. 95–60, "Aeronautical Ratings; Flying Officers; Command of Flying Units" (Washington, DC: War Department), August 20, 1942 [cites the October 4, 1940, Act, Stat. 54–963], p. 2.

25. Army Air Forces, Army Regulation No. 95–60, 1942 [cites the July 2, 1942, Act; Bull. 30, War Dept., 1942], p. 2.

26. "Flying units shall in all cases be commanded by flying officers who have received aeronautical ratings as pilots of service types of aircraft and who are commissioned in the Air Corps, or qualified permanent general officers of the line who have received aeronautical ratings as pilots of service types of aircraft." See National Defense Act Amendment, Pub. L. 76–795, 1940; and Army Air Forces, Army Regulation No. 95–60, 1942, p. 2.

27. Army Air Forces, Army Regulation No. 95–60, 1942, p. 2.

28. "All units or activities having aircraft organically assigned thereto or having authority to issue flying operations orders will be commanded only by flying officers on duty with the Army Air Forces who have received an aeronautical rating as Command Pilot, Senior Pilot, Pilot, Senior Balloon Pilot, or Balloon Pilot." See War Department, Headquarters Army Air Forces, *AAF Regulation No. 55–1*, "Operations, Flying Units—Command," Washington, DC, August 4, 1943. The regulation also continued existing exceptions allowing senior service pilots, service pilots, and glider pilots, who of course were still pilots, to command specific flying units. Service pilots, who had a lower-level rating in terms of aircraft horsepower and hours required, were

permitted to command air transport, liaison aircraft, and glider units. Glider pilots were restricted to commanding units that contained only glider aircraft. The exceptions for senior service pilots, service pilots, and glider pilots are interesting from the point of view that the regulation does not impose similar restrictions on senior balloon pilots and balloon pilots. Theoretically, an old balloon pilot could command bombers units of any size, whereas a senior service pilot, who had heavier-than-air flying time in the thousands of hours, could not. Of course, there were more senior service pilots and service pilots than the odd few senior balloon and balloon pilots. Nevertheless, in all cases, the prerequisite for command of flying units was still the possession of a pilot rating.

29. By June 2, 1918, volunteer medical screening boards had examined 38,777 men and disqualified 18,004 from entering flying training. The qualified cadets attended an eight-week ground school at one of several civilian universities. Those that passed ground school went on to primary flight training, which lasted another eight weeks. Graduates of primary flight training were awarded Reserve Military Aviator wings and an officer's commission and sent to advanced flying training. See Major General William L. Kenley, USA, *Annual Report of the Director of Military Aeronautics, U.S. Army to the Secretary of War, 1918* (Washington: GPO, 1918), 8.

30. 10 USC 293 1925.

31. 10 USC 297 1925; 10 USC 299 1925.

32. *Reorganization of the Army Air Service: Hearing before the Committee on Military Affairs United States Senate, Sixty-ninth Congress, First Session on S. 2614, A Bill to Increase the Efficiency of the Air Service of the United States Army, February 5, 1926* (Washington, DC: GPO, 1926), 18.

33. National Defense Act Amendment, Public—No. 446, 1926, p. 2.

34. *Reorganization of the Army Air Service*, 16–17. General Patrick also made an interesting comment on flight pay. When asked about incentives to get more qualified enlisted men to become pilots, General Patrick replied: "The only incentive would be—and I expect that applies to all of us—the higher pay. If they thought they would get higher pay, it might." Money, not an inherent interest in the joy and excitement of flying, is the primary motivation for undergoing pilot training.

35. *Reorganization of the Army Air Service*, 17.

36. Enlisted men served as pilots and observers, although, in 1942, enlisted pilot positions appear to have been limited to students in pilot training and the liaison pilot rating (the lowest pilot rating with restrictions on aircraft horsepower and assignments). Enlisted men also served as "bombardiers, navigators, and observers when assigned to combat crews in lieu of officers." See War Department, Headquarters Army Air Forces, *AAF Regulation No. 35–29*, "Personnel, Military: Flying Status of Enlisted Men," Washington, DC, July 20, 1942. By December 1943, the Army Air Forces had occupational specialties for enlisted airplane pilot, enlisted glider pilot, enlisted liaison pilot-mechanic, enlisted service pilot, and enlisted bombardier. See War Department, Headquarters Army Air Forces, *AAF Regulation No. 35–46*, "Personnel, Military: Use of Military Occupational Specialties for AAF Enlisted Personnel," Washington, DC, December 11, 1943, 2. Enlisted pilot opportunities had increased, but observer opportunities had shrunk, most likely because of the increasingly technical nature of navigation and other observer duties.

37. War Department, Headquarters Army Air Forces, *AAF Regulation No. 35–3*, "Personnel, Military: Eligibility for Appointment as Flight Officers in the Army of the United States," Washington, DC, January 21, 1943.

38. "In no case will a flight officer be recommended for commissioning unless he possesses such qualities of leadership, integrity, and professional ability as to make him especially desirable as a commissioned officer in the Army Air Forces." See War Department, Headquarters Army Air Forces, *AAF Regulation No. 35–8*, "Personnel, Military: System for Selecting Flight Officers to be Commissioned as Second Lieutenants in the Army of the United States," Washington, DC, November 12, 1942.

39. Cadets were to be judged on "qualities of leadership, judgment, responsibility, military bearing, initiative, self-confidence, force of character, alertness, comprehension, cooperativeness, and attention to duty." In addition, cadets were to be given a final examination stressing "the duties and responsibilities of officers" one month prior to graduation from their advanced flying course. The scores from the various ratings of the officer's estimated professional proficiency, given in each of the various courses, as well as the officer's Aviation Cadet Mental Qualifying Examination (later the "Mental Alertness Score" from the Psychological Classification Test Battery) and final examination were combined in a formula that gave the most weight to ratings from flying courses. The Commanding General of Flying Training Command set a minimum composite score. Cadets above the minimum became second lieutenants. Those scoring below became flight officers. See War Department, Headquarters Army Air Forces, *AAF Regulation No. 35–9*, "Personnel, Military: System for Selecting Aviation Cadets to be Commissioned as Second Lieutenants in the Army of the United States," Washington, DC, November 12, 1942.

40. The Air Force reported a few warrant officer pilots on flying status through 1949 and some warrant officer observers on flying status through 1952 in the annual *Statistical Digest* series.

41. General Curtis LeMay, for example, was one of these college-educated former aviation cadets and already a general officer when he led the fire bombing campaign against Japan as commander of the 20th Air Force. After the war, he served as the commander of Strategic Air Command from 1948 through 1957, then as the Air Force Vice Chief of Staff until 1961, when he became Chief of Staff of the Air Force; he served in this capacity until January 1965.

42. The Air Force played all sorts of games with its statistical classifications to try to minimize this fact. For example, at times, it created categories for some college, less than two years of college, more than two years, more than three years, and even four years but no degree, to show that officers were indeed college educated, if not college graduates. The USAF *Statistical Digest* also dropped reporting on general officer education levels after its first year of reporting in FY1951, but continued to report levels for the other ranks through FY1957. In FY1951, colonels and lieutenant colonels both included higher percentages of officers with bachelor's or higher degrees than general officers.

43. Of course, during World War II, the length of service academy and ROTC commissioning programs was cut; commissioned officers from these periods and programs did not necessarily have bachelor's degrees either. Furthermore, many of the former aviation cadets who were promoted through the system to general officer rank had bachelor's degrees.

44. The FY1960 and FY1961 portions of the graph are based on a low population, with the ensuing problem of potentially wild percentage swings from year to year. For example, there were altogether 11 UPT fatalities per year in FY1960 and FY1961; so a single death would affect the graph by 9%, and if the category of one fatality was changed, the losing category would decrease by 9% and the gaining category

would increase by 9%. Total UPT fatalities were well above 20 per year from FY1949 through FY1957, peaking in FY1953 at 66 fatalities. From FY1958 through FY1960 there was a gradual decrease in UPT fatalities from 18 to 11.

45. A caveat with regard to the aviation cadet program was that aviation cadets were formally enlisted in the Air Force and faced the prospect of serving an enlisted tour if they failed pilot or navigator training and were still physically qualified for military service.

CHAPTER 6

1. In order to prepare pilot officers for more senior positions, and because pilots were seen as the only officers who routinely faced responsibility (for their aircraft and crew) and decision making under stressful conditions (flying the aircraft), pilots were the preferred, if not required, candidates for all billets of responsibility and decision making.

2. The Air Force Academy admitted 306 cadets into its first class in 1955; 207 graduated in 1959.

3. The Air Force Academy's engineering emphasis, which is similar to that of the other American service academies, is another area of deviation from Huntington's concept that the undergraduate degree should be broad and in the liberal arts, with professional knowledge being added later.

4. Air Force Academy graduates have never achieved the overrepresentational dominancy of the Air Force general officer ranks once maintained by their West Point brethren. In fact, wings tend to trump rings. The Air Force's emphasis on pilot wings has resulted in AFROTC, Air Force Academy (AFA), and OTS graduates filling the Air Force's general officer ranks in rough proportion to their contribution to the officer corps, with AFROTC and AFA graduates slightly overrepresented and OTS graduates underrepresented.

5. To give an example of a typical report on promotions, the *Air Force Times* reported in the mid-1960s: "Among the BG selectees … fifteen hold bachelors degrees, three masters degrees, one is a Ph.D., another a dentist and 14 are not college graduates. Six others are Academy graduates, and one is an Academy graduate with an M.A. Most are pilots (35), one is double-rated as a pilot-navigator, another is a navigator and three are non-rated." See Nick Sivulich, "Forty Colonels, 15 BGs Named for Promotions," *Air Force Times*, August 18, 1966: 1, 10. "That education was a significant factor in the selection is demonstrated by the fact that 20 percent of those eligibles holding master's degrees and PhDs were named for advancement. Only eight percent of those with 'some college' and seven percent of those with no college were picked. Among secondary zone [below-the-zone, i.e., those chosen early for promotion] selectees, 86 of the 101 selectees are college grads. Forty-nine hold masters; two are PhDs. Only two have no college. Thirteen have 'some college.'" See "745 Named Temporary Colonels," *Air Force Times*, October 7, 1970: 1, 26.

6. This "requirement" led to a generally acknowledged "square-filling" exercise, as company-grade officers struggled in their off-duty time to get any sort of master's degree in any field from any college before hitting the promotion board for major. The Air Force decided in 1988 to stop unit commanders from taking off-duty civilian education into consideration for promotion recommendations. However, civilian education was still listed in the officers' records at the central promotion board. The

policy was reversed in 1995. Unit commanders were allowed to take civilian education into account (since many were doing it anyway), and it stayed in the promotion records. See Andrew Compart, "Officer System Will Undergo Major Changes," *Air Force Times*, March 27, 1995: 3. In 1995, the Air Force removed all references to off-duty civilian education from officer promotion records for promotion to captain and major, but retained such references for promotion to lieutenant colonel and colonel. The justification was that not all junior officers had the same opportunity to earn off-duty degrees, while lieutenant colonels, colonels, and general officers "require the maturity and exposure provided by advanced studies." There was some question as to whether the real driving factor behind the masking of degrees was that larger numbers of pilots were being deployed more frequently and for longer periods than before—and consequently were unable to earn master's degrees—which would put them at a disadvantage in comparison with their non-rated colleagues facing the same promotion board. See Bryant Jordan, "Promotion-Folder Change: Advanced Degrees Lose Luster for Captains, Majors," *Air Force Times*, January 15, 1996: 10. By 1999, it was clear that the promotion boards were not just using master's degrees and completion of professional military education (PME) courses as tie breakers but using them as promotion criteria. Officers with "definite promote" recommendations, which were limited to a small percentage of the officers being considered for promotion, were not being promoted, because they either did not have advanced degrees or had not completed the normal level of PME for their rank. See Bryant Jordan, "Education No Longer Make-or-Break Criterion for Promotion: Ops Tempo Prevented Officers from Getting Degrees and PME," *Air Force Times*, September 6, 1999: 10. In February 2005, the Air Force finally eliminated all references to off-duty civilian education from officer promotion records for all grades, ostensibly because the boards gave too much weight to having, or not having, a master's degree and not enough to whether the degree was useful to the officer or to the Air Force. See Rod Hafemeister, "A New Degree of Anonymity: Civilian Education to Be Hidden from Promotion Boards," *Air Force Times*, February 14, 2005: 13. However, the Air Force quickly reversed that policy, announcing in April 2006 that officer civilian education would once again be part of the promotion records, starting in January 2008. Apparently too many officers stopped pursuing academic degrees in their off-duty time, and those that did pursue degrees wanted credit for it. See Rod Hafemeister, "Officers: Your Civilian Education Is Showing," *Air Force Times*, May 1, 2006: 10. Square-filling prevails.

7. There are of course exceptions to this generalization. Nurses without graduate degrees, for example, fall under the officers with bachelor degree category, and officers with PhDs serving at the Air Force Academy, for example, are usually still line officers of company or field grade rank.

8. Vance O. Mitchell, *Air Force Officers Personnel Policy Development 1944–1974* (Washington, DC: Air Force History and Museums Program [GPO], 1996), 345–346.

9. Mitchell 347–348.

10. Mitchell 347–348.

11. Command of Flying Units, Pub. L 93–525, December 18, 1974, Stat 88–3906.

12. The act itself amends the code "by repealing section 8577 (relating to the command of flying units of the Air Force) and by striking out the corresponding item in the analysis of chapter 845." Command of Flying Units, Pub. L 93–525.

13. "Navigators Near Command Role," *Air Force Times*, September 25, 1974: 4.

14. In fact, the confusion over who exactly would be allowed to become commanders of flying units under the act became an issue of debate among some members of Congress. This delayed the passage of what the Air Force had ostensibly considered a non-contentious bill. Although the bill was quickly passed by the Senate, it ran into some opposition in the House Armed Service Committee. During discussions on the bill, Representative Bill Nichols (D-AL), who was the sole dissenting vote in the subcommittee, stated, "If I were an infantry lieutenant, I would want the company to be commanded by an infantry officer rather than a quartermaster." Representative Samuel Stratton (D-NY), Chairman of the House Armed Services Subcommittee that initially passed the bill, reported that the purpose of the bill was to "improve the morale of the navs, and make them think they aren't second class citizens." Representative Otis Pike (D-NY) initially opposed the bill: "I just don't like the idea of non-pilots commanding flying units. . . . By removing the restriction, aren't we saying that anybody who has any kind of aviation rating can command an aviation squadron?" When Representative Stratton mentioned further that the Navy had removed similar barriers to non-pilot command over naval aviation units, Representative Pike retorted that "the way to attack the problem would be to remove that right from the Navy rather than give it to the Air Force." See George Foster, "Foes Slow Command Navigator Bill," *Air Force Times*, October 16, 1974: 3. However, only one representative voted against the measure in the full House vote. Representative H. R Gross (R-IA) was concerned that simply repealing the paragraph would open up command of Air Force flying units to non-flying officers. Representative Stratton once again represented the Air Force position that only navigators, and not non-rated officers, would be used for command of flying units. Furthermore, Representative Stratton urged his colleagues to support the bill: "If we do not have enough confidence in our top officers in the Air Force to allow them to make the selection of commanders for subordinate units, then we are going to be in for real trouble. We ought to leave that kind of decision up to them." See "Legislative Actions: Nav-Command Bill Passes House," *Air Force Times*, December 25, 1974: 2. It is not clear why exactly the Air Force did not restrict the new measure to just navigators. Perhaps visionaries saw this as just the beginning of things to come.

15. "Navigators Near Command Role," 4.

16. Navigator command over single-seat fighter units was automatically excluded, just as the Air Force was on the verge of starting to shift its primary frontline fighter from the two-seat (one pilot; one weapons system operator/"navigator") F-4 to the single-seat F-15. Navigators would be limited largely to command of big plane units flying cargo, bomber, and some C4ISR aircraft, which further lost prestige by virtue of the possibility of navigator command.

17. "Navigators in Command: Long Road Ahead," *Air Force Times*, January 29, 1975: 5.

18. "Navigator to Head Combat Flying Unit," *Air Force Times*, February 12, 1975: 2.

19. "10 Navs Head Flight Units," *Air Force Times*, September 10, 1975: 24.

20. The independent Air Force continued its predecessors' tradition of three levels of pilot ratings. The first level was the basic pilot wings. The second level, senior pilot, was represented by a star centered at the top of the pilot wings. The highest level, command pilot, was indicated by a wreath around the star centered at the top of the pilot wings. The Air Force did not permit the senior observer/navigator rating and wings until 1953, matching the long-standing senior pilot rating with a requirement

for seven years of flying and 2,000 flight hours. However, the issue of the navigator equivalent to the command pilot with 15 years of flying and 3,000 flight hours was not resolved until 1959, with the decision to call such navigators master navigators. See Mitchell 349.

21. See for example, "New 'Kill' Policy Set for Pilots," *Air Force Times,* November 30, 1966: 15; "No Credit Given 'Kills' on Ground," *Air Force Times,* January 4, 1967: 11; John Allen, "Stake Your Claim: Shavetail Commands F-4," *Air Force Times,* September 11, 1968: 11.

22. F-4 pilot Captain Steve Ritchie began his description of his fifth kill, which made him an ace, as follows: "After Chuck [the WSO] picked them up on radar, we made a hard turn to meet them head on. The 'bandits' were very high, approximately 4,000 feet above us as we climbed. I turned as hard as I could and I squeezed off two missiles." Ritchie and "Chuck" DeBellevue were alerted to the "bandits'" general location by the command and control system. The first two missiles missed, as did a third, but the fourth hit the Mig. See Secretary of the Air Force, Officer of Information, "First Air Force Ace in Southeast Asia," *Air Force Fact Sheet 73–7, AF Aces/ 1918–1972* (Washington, DC: Secretary of the Air Force, May 1973), 19. A head-on attack required the use of semi-active radar guided missiles and constant WSO involvement.

23. As General Thomas White, Air Force Chief of Staff, told the American Fighter Aces Association at their inaugural gathering in 1960, "As a young boy dreaming of becoming an airman—if I had a choice between becoming chief of staff of the Air Force or becoming a fighter Ace, I would have chosen to become a fighter Ace." Secretary of the Air Force, Officer of Information, "Tribute to an Ace," *Air Force Fact Sheet 73–7, AF Aces/ 1918–1972* (Washington, DC: Secretary of the Air Force, May 1973), 20.

24. "Retirement-Eligible Losses" (see figure 6.6) refers to officers who appear to have reached their potential retirement age and left the Air Force through retirement, separation (without retirement benefits), or death. I selected 39 years of age and older as the cutoff, since 20 years of service is the minimum for retirement, and an aviation cadet with one year or less of college would reach that point at age 39. Consequently, 39 would be the earliest possible beginning of the retirement window for most officers, with the majority hitting retirement eligibility by the age of 42. There are huge economic disincentives to leaving the Air Force short of 20 years of active duty service, so by the age of 39 most stay in at least until qualifying for a pension.

25. "10 Navs Head Flight Units," 24.

26. Lee Ewing, "Some Career Ideas OKd, 12 Killed," *Air Force Times,* August 13, 1975: 4. Italics added.

27. Mitchell 343–344.

28. Richard B. Frank, *Downfall: The End of the Imperial Japanese Empire* (New York: Random House, 1999), 186.

29. Only pilots can be *aircraft* commanders in the Air Force. An aircraft is after all an airplane, fraught with danger, where the lieutenant or captain with one hand on the wheel or stick, the other on the throttles, and his feet on the rudders commands *everything.* Even a large aircraft with a large crew like the E-3 AWACS is not viewed as a flying ship with a flight section, a navigation section, a radar section, a communications section, and an air battle management section, each subordinated to a field-grade mission commander. Instead it is viewed as an aircraft with a flight deck and a mission crew compartment, all under the command of the pilot aircraft commander who bears responsibility for all things that remotely have to do with the aircraft and the flight.

This includes mission planning through debriefing, and even extends to command of the life rafts if the plane were to make an emergency ditching.

30. George Wilson, "Leaders Heed the AWACS Lesson: Ways Are Sought to Avoid an Exodus of Overtaxed Crews," *Air Force Times*, January, 1998: 7. General Ralston (USAF) was serving as Vice Chairman of the Joint Chiefs of Staff in 1998 but was Air Force Deputy Chief of Staff for Plans and Operations in 1994–1995. It was in that capacity that he took steps to improve conditions for AWACS crews.

31. Wilson, "Leaders Heed the AWACS Lesson," 7.

32. Command of an operations group is a colonel-level position over the flying squadrons. The rating status issue took considerable time to work its way through the system. After it had been discussed for years, the Air Force's most senior general officers agreed to the change in February 1998. The *Air Force Times* speculated that it would be implemented in October 1998, but it was not implemented for another year. See Bryant Jordan, "Air-Battle Managers Will Be Rated: New Status for Career Field May Begin in October," *Air Force Times*, May 25, 1998: 4.

33. National Defense Act Amendment, Pub. L. 76–795. Ch. 742. October 4, 1940. Stat. 54–963, p. 963.

34. Jennifer Palmer, "Air-Battle Managers Get Rated Status: Move Means Incentive Pay, Better Career Opportunities," *Air Force Times*, October 18, 1999: 35.

35. Gordon Trowbridge, "New Retention Bonus Brings Navigators, ABMs Out in Droves," *Air Force Times*, November 18, 2002: 22. Gordon Trowbridge, "Aviator Bonuses Tell Nonpilots They Count, Too: Officers: First-Time Perk a Big Step toward Recognition," *Air Force Times*, August 19, 2002: 24.

36. Rated officers were not enthralled with the plethora of non-rated badges. In 1969, General McConnell, Air Force Chief of Staff, provided specific guidance to the Uniform Board that restricted the creation of new non-rated career-field badges. Specialties requiring badges were broken down into four categories: (1) functional badges for non-line officers and Air Force Academy permanent professors; (2) flying functions that "require specific training, qualification and actual participation in flights of air and space vehicles," that is, wings; (3) emergency and law enforcement; and (4) other badges that do not fit into the above categories, like the missile and weapons controller badges. However, category 4 was "closed." The *Air Force Times* interpreted this to mean that the "AF apparently is saying these badges slipped into the inventory without really being justified but that won't happen again." See "Job Specialty Name Tags OK'd … But," *Air Force Times*, January 8, 1969: 3.

37. Similar cultural overtones are present in the evolution of the decisions on which Air Force personnel can wear leather jackets as part of their uniform and whether missile launch officers can wear flight suits.

CHAPTER 7

1. See the appendix for further information on general officer sampling.

2. Since the flying hour requirements for the command pilot and master navigator ratings have varied somewhat over time, the sample data was coded using categories of less than 1,000 flying hours, 1,000 to 2,500 flying hours, and over 2,500 flying hours. No general officers in the sample reported having less than 1,000 total flying hours, and only the occasional general officer admitted to having between 1,000 and 2,500 total flying hours. The supermajority of general officers that reported total flying time

had well over 2,500 total flying hours. No 4-star general officer in the sample listed a total number of hours within the 1,000 to 2,500 hour category.

3. The Air Force has varied its criteria for what constitutes a combat, combat support, or essentially peacetime mission flown in the theater of operations. It is typically the aircraft commander's call as to how to log the sortie and the flying hours. Furthermore, it is possible that some officers are saving space and simply conveying the message that they flew in "combat," without breaking down the hours or sorties into combat and combat support.

4. In fact, the Air Force added a commander's badge to the uniform in 2002, making it immediately apparent to all whether an officer has served as a commander at the squadron level or higher. The commander's badge is worn on the opposite side of the chest from the wings (and ribbons), so a balanced officer sports both.

5. Although it was clear by the Vietnam War that combat command above the flight level was migrating to the command and control system, the Air Force officer corps preferred to treat this development as a wartime aberration. Peacetime training did not require an extensive and invasive command and control system dictating training sorties. Training was best handled at the local squadron level, and the squadron, group, and wing structure was a time-tested and proven organizational entity. In addition, it was obviously easy enough to piece together a tactical Combined Air Operations Center (CAOC) with accompanying C4ISR, since it had been done in World War II, Korea, and Vietnam. Consequently, there was also no need to waste too many resources organizing, building, and training such structures in peacetime. After all, why trap a bunch of pilots, who would obviously be necessary to run the operations centers, in non-flying, dead-end jobs in the gated flight pay world? Even air defense operations centers were not given command over flying assets in peacetime, and a structure without assets is an empty shell. Furthermore, command experience was valued, and more straightforward, in the other services. In order to compete for its share of senior joint jobs and in order for its officers to have credibility in them, it was important for the Air Force officer corps to be able to define structural equivalents. For example, squadrons are typically commanded by lieutenant colonels and have some quantifiable level of staff, personnel, and equipment. Consequently, they are seen as battalion equivalents, even though squadrons vary dramatically in terms of people and equipment and do not actually serve as a fighting unit. If the Air Force was to use the CAOC, in its current configuration, as a fighting level of command, the Air Force would have no level of apparent combat command below the mid-general officer level. Although this is true, it would make competition for joint jobs difficult because there would be no apparent functional level equivalent to companies, battalions, brigades, or divisions, or ships for that matter. In addition, there is no real career path that prepares officers for CAOC command, and the CAOC has no standard level of assets assigned to it. Although the Air Force officer corps could think of its combat CAOC C4ISR structure along the lines of task forces, it does not. Whereas Army units and Navy ships contain internal C4ISR systems that can theoretically take on the responsibility for units subordinated to them, the Air Force officer corps historically separates by functionality. Fighters are in one wing, bombers in another, AWACS in a third, communications in a fourth, intelligence in a fifth, and CAOCs for tactical operations are put together on an ad hoc basis. The Air Force officer corps has experimented with composite wings to match peacetime structures with the way it fights. The composite wing, made up of several types of aircraft, provides a basis for building strike packages or other tactical flying functions out of one wing. Such a wing may even have a radar

unit attached, but it makes no attempt to provide CAOC C4ISR functions. At best, a composite wing provides a force to implement a CAOC's plan. However, composite wings are expensive since they lose the economies of scale associated with a wing using only one type of aircraft. Consequently, the Air Force officer corps developed the current system of building air expeditionary packages from various wings and pieces of wings, and rotating them through deployments. These do not provide internal CAOC C4ISR functions, either. Outside of air defense, there has been limited professional interest in quality permanent CAOC C4ISR structures, which would be the basis for creating task forces. In the absence of something better, the vestigial wing, group, squadron organizational structure remains.

This is not to say that the Air Force officer corps was oblivious to its need for CAOC C4ISR structures. It was clear that unit-level flying training had limitations in terms of numbers of aircraft available per day, airspaces that were considered big in the 1940s but completely within a fighter's radar coverage in the 1980s, and a lack of training opportunities against other types of aircraft. The Air Force officer corps sought to address these problems and the equally important decline in combat experience among its younger pilots by instituting Red Flag in 1975 and a host of other "Flag" training exercises. Red Flag brought together different types of aircraft from different units to fight mock air wars over an extensive instrumented range. The Red Flag staff simulated a CAOC with an extensive C4ISR system, generated air tasking orders, provided the opportunity for the fliers from the different units to mission plan together, used AWACS or the ground-based range command and control system to monitor and control the air battle, and then debriefed the entire thing. This cycle would be repeated one to two times a day for a two-week session with a single group of participants. Red Flag essentially trained aircrews to work within a CAOC C4ISR system without developing the CAOC C4ISR system itself or training personnel to man such a system. In the mid-1990s, with lessons from Desert Storm and its aftermath as well as from the Balkans operations, the Air Force officer corps placed a new emphasis on the CAOC C4ISR system. However, the officer corps still sees command as existing primarily within the squadron, group, and wing structure.

6. There is an obvious degree of subjectivity here, but it is possible that when comparing two officers for a specific job, an officer without command experience but with Joint or Air Staff experience might nudge out an officer with non-flying command but not Washington time.

7. However, since the data are only for an officer's first wing command, some officers may have commanded a second, or even third, time at the wing level, and a later wing command may have been over a flying wing.

8. This section specifically addresses the promotion system, but there was also a historical bias favoring pilots in the awarding of regular commissions. For example, in 1940, over 97% of the Air Corps officers with regular commissions were pilots. Officers with reserve commissions selected for augmentation in the limited number of regular commissions were presumed to be the best and the ones that the officer corps wanted to keep for careers in the Army Air Corps. In short, they were pilots. This presumption continued within the independent Air Force. Despite a decision in 1947 to end the practice of tendering regular officer commissions at the ratio of 70% for rated officers and 30% for non-rated officers, rated officers continued to be rewarded. See Vance O. Mitchell, *Air Force Officers Personnel Policy Development 1944– 1974* (Washington, DC: Air Force History and Museums Program [GPO]), 1996, 353. In FY1951, 56% of the Air Force officers with regular commissions were pilots,

although the percentage of total officers who were pilots had already fallen to 44%. In 1952, when only 303 regular officer commissions were extended, 90% went to rated officers, and in 1958, when a massive augmentation practically doubled the size of the regular officer component, rated officers still garnered over 70% of the regular officer commissions. See Mitchell 341. The status differentiation between having a reserve commission and being expressly selected for and rewarded with one of the limited number of regular commissions had obvious implications as a sorting tool for use by promotion boards—an Air Force professional board had already indicated a desire to keep (and promote) the officer with the regular commission. Furthermore, since an officer with a regular commission was able to serve beyond 20 years of active duty tenure, he was conceivably a better investment for assignments like attendance at intermediate and senior service schools than a reservist facing termination at 20 years. Attending the schools, however, also increased an officer's promotion chances, thereby continuing the inequities.

The complicated system of regular and reserve commissions is not addressed in this book. The system has changed over time, to the point that all officers serving on active duty start with regular commissions beginning in FY2006, which will effectively end the dual system of commissions. Previously, however, the number of regular commissions was limited, and the Air Force established allocations based on officers' rated status as a tool to manage the projected future proportions of pilots, navigators, and non-rated officers. The Air Force consistently maintained that active duty officers with regular commissions were not given an advantage or an allocation of field grade promotions. However, they tended to be promoted at higher rates because they were better than their peers, as evidenced by their previous selection for regular status over generally the same peers. In the earlier years, pilots tended to be awarded regular status earlier than non-rated officers. This allowed a natural selection of sorts to take place, as the better pilots in a given year group were presumably already regular in status, and many non-rated officers had already left the service before the bulk of the non-rated officers were considered. Later, this was changed, in an effort to indicate to non-rated officers whether they were career material before they ended their initial service obligations. Rated officers had more time because they had longer service commitments. Regular officers were essentially guaranteed a career. Whereas officers on active duty with reserve commissions had two opportunities for promotion to temporary rank before being separated, officers with regular commissions had two temporary and two regular opportunities, which traditionally came later, to be selected for promotion. In addition, officers with regular commissions were not liable for involuntary separation before being eligible for retirement if there was a reduction in force levels. Until the 1990s, regular commissions were automatically granted to service academy graduates, the majority of whom became pilots in the Air Force, and sometimes to outstanding ROTC and OTS graduates upon graduation. The majority of the regular commissions, however, were awarded by promotion-type boards, at various intervals during an officer's career. As the military moved away from the two-track system of commissions, some of the intermediate steps involved granting regular commissions to all officers promoted to major, and eliminating the granting of regular status to academy and other officer training graduates. See, for example, Lee Ewing, "Regulars 'Generally Better' Jones on Records of Officers," *Air Force Times*, March 1, 1976: 3; George Foster, "Promotion Edge in RegAF Denied," *Air Force Times*, January 21, 1970: 1; and Ed Gates, "2469 Will Receive Selection for RegAF," *Air Force Times*, May 8, 1968: 1.

9. The Air Force officer corps has traditionally provided little statistical information on general officer promotion boards beyond lists of those who were selected for promotion.

10. Officers are also considered after-primary-zone, that is, they can be selected for promotion later than their peers. However, the percentages of officers who are promoted in this way are quite small, roughly the size of the below-primary-zone numbers, but without the same future prospects.

11. George Foster, "6472 New Majors, 5829 Go Up on First Try," *Air Force Times*, June 18, 1969: 4.

12. Officers are not eligible for selection to attend Command and Staff College until promoted to major; so this was not a distinguishable factor. Most officers were sent to Squadron Officer School, so this also should not have been a factor in decision making, and both rated and non-rated officers could equally sign up and take courses for a master's degree. However, as pilots began to be deployed more to police no-fly zones and participate in operations in Southwest Asia and in the Balkans, the Air Force decided to mask an officer's graduate education level. This was done because deployed officers had a harder time earning master's degrees, which might put pilots at a disadvantage in promotion boards. This had not been an issue previously, when, for example, members of other specific career fields like air battle managers had very high deployment rates in the 1980s. For more details Air Force policies with respect to graduate degrees, see note 6 in chapter 6.

13. For example, navigator selection rates were pulling rated rates below pilot selection rates most of the time from 1989 through 1996 as well as in the 2002B and 2003A promotion boards. However, navigator selection rates actually equaled or exceeded pilot selection rates from 1997 through the 2002A promotion board. In fact, from 1997 through the 2002A board, the curves are tightly together, with minimal dispersion; indicating very close selection rates for each officer category.

14. Trendlines selected by best fit using R^2 values. $R^2 = 0.5436$ for the colonel's, 0.4885 for the lieutenant colonel's, and 0.099 for the major's trendline.

15. The trendline for pilot officers selected below-primary-zone to major is omitted, since the last below-primary-zone promotion board for majors occurred in 1998. The trendline would be misleading, since it would extrapolate the clearly upward trend visible in 1998 through to 2003. However, this trend for below-primary-zone promotion to major starkly contrasted with the prevailing trend toward increasing percentages of non-pilot officers in the profession.

Trendlines selected by best fit using R^2 values. $R^2 = 0.4677$ for the colonel's, 0.3951 for the lieutenant colonel's, and 0.7308 for the major's trendline.

16. Using difference of proportions for pilots versus all other line officers, below-primary-zone, two-tailed test, $\alpha = 0.05$, $t = 2$.

CHAPTER 8

1. Following the Air Force's system of tracking of rated officers, once an officer is a pilot, he remains classified as a pilot regardless of what other jobs he performs. For further details on the Air Force general officer biography sampling and coding, see the appendix.

2. For example, in the 1951 sample, Major General Robert M. Lee reported serving such a tour with the cavalry.

3. The categories used in the general officer sampling are as follows: Support, Scientist/Acquisition, Finance, Intelligence, Communications/Electronics, Personnel/Administration, Logistics/Maintenance, Operations, Space, Missiles, Air Battle Manager, Navigator, and Pilot.

4. It is not clear why in 2002 the percentage of non-pilot general officers and the number of AFSCs represented at the GO level decreased. It could reflect a random fluctuation, or a resurgence of the heroic warrior archetype in the aftermath of 9/11. However, since the Pentagon removed names from its phonebook in 2003, the sampling method used for the rest of the samples cannot be repeated after 2002. See the appendix.

5. In this section, C4ISR tours include not only tours in Air Battle Management (ABM), Air Traffic Control (ATC), Space Operations, Missile Operations, Intelligence, Weather, Communications-Electronics, Computers, and Operations Management but also tours in air defense sector staffs and headquarters, in Single Integrated Operational Plan (SIOP) staffs, in Combined Air Operations Centers (CAOCs), and as Forward Air Controllers (FACs). Consequently, these data should not be confused with career broadening, since, for example, a pilot flying as a FAC or serving in operations or plans on a staff is not career broadening out of the standard pilot track and into another career field but is nevertheless gaining C4ISR experience.

6. The C4ISR Air Force Specialty Code amalgamation includes the air battle manager, missiles, space, intelligence, and communications/electronics career fields.

7. The 4-star general officer curves are extremely sensitive to minor differences between samples because of the small sample sizes involved, that is, 7–10 persons per sample.

8. In addition, the Air Force has not done well in competing for senior joint intelligence billets. The Air Force's preference for rated officers in the general officer ranks has limited the opportunities for Air Force career intelligence officers, which means the Air Force intelligence officers are at a disadvantage when competing against intelligence officers from the other services. In addition, the other services are reluctant to give senior joint intelligence billets to officers who are not career intelligence officers. Consequently, the Air Force loses out all around. In January 2007, the Air Force Chief of Staff, General Moseley, reported that he had tasked LTG Deptula, a fighter pilot by experience, to draw up plans to restructure the Air Force's intelligence community, which also would create more general officer billets in intelligence to address the problems. See T. Michael Moseley, "Transforming Air Force Intelligence, Surveillance, Reconnaissance," *CSAF's Vector*, January 29, 2007.

9. Space Command took responsibility for the Air Force ICBM fleet on July 1, 1993.

10. There are several caveats that must be kept in mind when studying Air Force officer badge wear. First, with respect to the general officer samples, the primary method for identifying non-rated badge wear is the officer's picture. However, in the 1951 through 1968 samples, the majority of the general officer biographies do not contain photographs. Even in the 1973 sample, 36% of the sampled biographies do not contain photographs. Although the trend from the 1973 sample through 2002 is a steady increase in the percentage of biographies with photographs, reaching 100% in 2002, the 1993 sample is an anomaly, with 42% of the biographies not having photographs. Furthermore, the photographs may not capture missile operations and missile badges, which are worn on the pocket and often below the photograph's crop line. Another caveat is that most of the career field specialty badges were not part of the

original Air Force uniforms and were introduced over time from the 1950s onward. Consequently, an officer in an earlier sample may have performed duty that later might have qualified him to wear a particular specialty badge. In addition, Air Force regulations limit the number of wings and badges that can be worn and prioritize the wearing of aeronautical-type ratings and badges. Non-rated badges are optional, but wings are mandatory wear. A pilot must wear the pilot wings, and if the officer has earned parachute "wings," they must also be worn, which precludes the wearing of any other occupational specialty badges except the missile variants that are worn on the pocket. Consequently, there are many reasons why the samples may undercount badge wear.

Furthermore, the qualification requirements for a particular badge may be misleading. For example, although a space or missile badge seems to imply experience in space or missile operations, an officer can qualify for these badges by working in acquisitions on space or missile systems. Since there is an acquisitions career field badge, this aspect is particularly interesting and peculiar, because the qualifications seem specifically designed to allow rated officers to add space or missile ornamentation to their uniforms. After all, an acquisitions officer who buys aircraft is not awarded pilot wings. There also appears to be a connection to the Strategic Air Command bomber and missile unit amalgamations. Obviously only a pilot could command, but since he was also responsible for a missile unit, he earned a "pocket rocket" (a missile badge on his pocket) that also might somehow ameliorate relations with his missileer subordinates. Of course, the pilot commander would not typically have earned the missile *operations* badge, which required sitting alert in missile silos. I do not include parachute wings, because they typically do not indicate any job functionality. Instead, they have been called an Air Force Academy fraternity pin because of the high number of cadets who earn jump wings while at the Academy.

11. Take aces, for example. The 1958 and 1963 1- to 3-star general officer samples list one ace each, and the 1968 and 1973 1- to 3-star general officer samples list two aces each. At the 4-star general level, the 1968 and 1978 samples each list one ace, and the 1973 sample lists two. Consequently, half of the general officer aces in the 1973 sample are 4-star generals. These were aces from Korea or World War II; the Vietnam aces were too junior. There have not been any Air Force aces since the Vietnam War, and two of the three Air Force aces from Vietnam were not pilots but F-4 "backseater" weapons systems operators.

CHAPTER 9

1. For example, figure 9.1 capture the lags between decisions to change the number of pilots or aircraft and their implementation. The initial increase in the ratio of pilots per aircraft is the result of the independent Air Force's initial buildup of pilots in 1949 combined with the elimination of excess aircraft beginning in 1950. The Korean War necessitated a recall to active duty of pilots and an increase in pilot training that initially outpaced aircraft production. This resulted in the ratio peaking in 1951 at 3.4 pilots per aircraft, followed by a decline through 1956 where the ratio bottomed out at 2.4 pilots per aircraft. Both pilots and aircraft continued, however, to increase in numbers through the Korean War and into the Cold War, with the number of aircraft peaking in 1956 and the number of pilots peaking in 1957. After that, although both pilot and aircraft numbers were in decline, the number of aircraft decreased faster

than the number of pilots, resulting in an increasing ratio of pilots to aircraft from 1956 through 1961. The ratio hovered around 3.8 pilots per aircraft through 1966 then dropped through the hardest years of the Vietnam War as the number of pilots declined faster than the number of aircraft. By 1970, the ratio was again on an upswing, peaking in 1975 at 4.7 pilots per aircraft as the Air Force dumped aircraft faster than pilots in the post-Vietnam drawdown. The ratio dropped until 1980, from which point on it leveled out at roughly 3.5–3.7 through 1995, except for a blip in 1990 as pilots began to leave faster in the post–Cold War world before Desert Storm. Overall this period reflected both the Carter/Reagan "buildup," which had the effect of leveling both the number of pilots and the number of aircraft through the end of the Cold War, and the initial post–Cold War drawdown in which aircraft and pilots were cut in the same orders of magnitude. From 1996 to 2000, the number of pilots decreased faster than the number of aircraft, resulting in the ratio decreasing to 3.0. The ratio remained constant in 2001, but began a new increase in 2002 as the Global War on Terrorism began. The Air Force quickly issued a stop-loss order preventing rated and other officers from leaving the Air Force. Presumably, many officers would have stayed in without a stop-loss order, out of a sense of duty or patriotism, and perhaps because of 9/11's negative impact on air travel and airline hiring.

2. For example, in the post-Vietnam drawdown, the Air Force held a Reduction in Force (RIF) board in November 1974 that reviewed 20,295 reserve officers and selected 1,133 for involuntary separation. Of those officers, 32 were non-line, 337 (31% of line officers separated) were pilots, 53 (5% of line officers separated) were navigators, and 711 (65% of line officers separated) were non-rated line officers. In 1975, pilots made up 37% of the total line officers, and non-rated officers made up 47% of the total line officers. See "Analysis of RIF Board Results," *Air Force Times*, March 12, 1975: 14.

3. In figure 9.2, the years FY1957–FY1963 do not include general officers, and FY1976–FY2003 excludes general officers, colonels, and UPT students.

4. "All about Money—IV: Hazardous Duty Pay Goes to 100,000-Plus," *Air Force Times*, September 28, 1966: 13. The pay itself, whether loosely labeled flight pay, proficiency pay, or incentive pay, was paid before 1974 on the basis of whether the flier logged the requisite four hours a month. Congress changed the flight pay system in 1974 and gave the services the period through May 1977 to transition to the new system. After 1977, the pay was based on the officer maintaining flying status (which means primarily being medically qualified to fly and having no disciplinary problems—not actually flying) and meeting the flying time gates. In neither case did/does flight pay equate to being qualified (e.g., as a co-pilot) or current (e.g., having so many night hours or landings within the last six-month window). Although navigators needed a navigator station on the aircraft to count the time, students and fliers that were not "current" could still count flying time under an instructor or first pilot's supervision toward flight pay.

5. Bruce Callander, "'Excused' Fliers Pass Screening," *Air Force Times*, November 11, 1970: 8.

6. Bruce Callander, "Flight Board Will Weigh 5000 Rated," *Air Force Times*, May 13, 1970: 8.

7. Callander, "Flight Board Will Weigh 5000 Rated," 8.

8. Callander, "Flight Board Will Weigh 5000 Rated," 8.

9. "Hubbell Group to Look Hard at Flight Pay," *Air Force Times*, May 11, 1966: 1.

10. Ed Gates, "Officers Exits Probed," *Air Force Times*, May 10, 1967: 10.

11. "Hubbell Group to Look Hard at Flight Pay," 1. In addition, rated officers dropped from 50% to 48% of the total Air Force officer corps from the end of FY1965 to the end of FY1966. At the end of FY1966, pilots made up only 34% of the total Air Force officer corps. The general officer ranks were 85% pilots on flying status at the end of FY1966. A year later, the *Air Force Times*, citing Air Force Headquarters officials, was even more vocal about the pilots taking back control of the Air Force. "After nearly a year of whittling away at the rated force and preparing for the predominance of the missile, AF has done alomst [*sic*] a 180 degree turn. For the foreseeable future, it again sees itself as a 'pilot's air force.' Aeronautical ratings which have been losing career value in recent years now promise to be worth more in the assignment and promotion market, Hq USAF officials said here last week." See "AF Restores 'Pilot' Image," *Air Force Times*, May 24, 1967: 4.

12. The flight pay scale is somewhat diamond shaped. It starts out low but increases quickly in the early years, maximizing pay in the middle years, then decreasing at the end, effectively eliminating the economic incentive for colonels and general officers. The officer also has to remain on flight status, which means primarily passing an annual flight physical when not actively flying.

13. This has been a problem in AWACS (and JSTARS) squadrons, for example, where the crew positions actually require field grade officers to head the mission crews, since an AWACS could end up running an air defense sector or an entire operation if ground sites go down or lose communications links to the aircraft. However, promotion boards do not understand the large number of field grade officers who are not squadron commanders or operations officers but are instead just line fliers, presumably doing nothing more than captains, lieutenants, and non-commissioned officers.

14. The Goldwater-Nichols requirements push the services to maintain an average three-year joint tour length, which can then lead to non-rated officers serving longer joint tours to keep the average up as pilots are pulled out of the joint tours earlier.

15. Furthermore, an officer that cross-trains into pilot training after beginning on another career track cannot typically be used in a dual-track status, rotating between tours as a pilot and in his previous career field. Officers who switch to the pilot (or navigator or air battle manager) career field technically start their clock for their flying gates later and have the same amount of time to meet their gates for flight pay purposes. However, in order to remain competitive for field grade promotions and command opportunities, such officers must make up the lost flying time. The newer pilots are expected to reasonably match their on-time peers in terms of flying hours and job progression within a flying squadron. In effect, starting later means that they have less time.

16. Of course, the fliers must continue to serve and be promoted in order to reap the benefits of the gated flight pay system.

17. It is possible for a non-rated officer to apply to periodic boards for selection to pilot, navigator, or now ABM training. The officer must meet the qualifications for flight training, which include medical as well as age restrictions. The age/rank restrictions are in place partly because a flier's life begins with undergraduate pilot, navigator, or ABM training. A captain navigator selected for UPT starts at the same place as a 2nd lieutenant fresh from the Academy, and the navigator hours are largely meaningless in terms of progression through the pilot phases to, for example, co-pilot then pilot then instructor pilot. A rather limited number of officers is selected, with the

total determined by Air Force needs and previously screened pilot candidates coming directly from the Academy, AFROTC, and OTS.

18. The bonuses are typically not offered until a flier nears his initial service obligation or is still in service past that point. The bonus programs are not one-time deals but multiyear contracts, and pilots have frequently been able to move from one bonus plan to another as they gain seniority until they hit the 25 years of aviation service point. The bonuses amplify the effect of the longer initial service commitments. Fliers are offered large sums of money to stay in the Air Force but not necessarily to fly anymore. Paying pilot colonels $25,000 annual bonuses on top of flight pay to stay in and then giving them promotable staff positions that do not require rated experience is frequently interpreted as evidence of a lingering high-level bias against non-rated officers. The Air Force has also at times threatened to ground pilots who did not take the bonuses, arguing that they were indicating an intention to resign as soon as possible and that they were therefore not worthy of further flying time.

Navigators and ABMs were offered retention bonuses for the first time in FY2003. At that time, navigators had to have at least a senior navigator rating, 15 years of aviation service, and 18 years of service. ABMs had to be past their initial service obligation. Navigators and ABMs could sign up for a three-year commitment and receive $10,000 per year or sign up for five years at $15,000 per year. Pilots were offered $15,000 and $25,000. The Air Force was offering the bonuses to old navigators specifically so that they would stay and fill rated staff jobs so that pilots, presumably on bonuses, could return to flying. See Gordon Trowbridge, "New Retention Bonus Brings Navigators, ABMs Out in Droves," *Air Force Times*, November 18, 2002: 22.

19. The USAF *Statistical Digest's* use of the *operations/combat* category between FY1954 and FY1960 clouds the issue somewhat, since the category included non-rated operations-type officer billets that could have been filled by rated or non-rated officers, so I counted them all as rated billets, which downplays the numbers of rated officers serving in non-rated billets.

20. In figures 9.4 and 9.5, the years from FY1957 through FY1963 do not include general officers, and the years from FY1976 through FY2003 exclude general officers, colonels, and UPT or UNT students.

21. For 1954–1960, the *Statistical Digest* series did not break out pilots and navigators in pilot and navigator billets or non-rated officers in operations. Instead, these officers were lumped together under the term *operations*. In order to show some continuity with the curves, I subtracted the total pilots and navigators on flying status from the operations category to get an estimate of the non-rated operators. However, this results in all of the pilots and navigators on flying status being counted as if they were in pilot and navigator billets within operations, which was not the case. Judging by the jumps both in pilots-and-navigators-on-flying-status-but-not-in-pilot/navigator-billets and in C4ISR in 1960, when the *Statistical Digest* reverted to the old categories, it is possible that in 1960, for example, figure 9.5 underestimated the total of the number of C4ISR (non-rated operators) and the number of pilots-and-navigators-on-flying-status-but-not-in-pilot/navigator-billets by around 7,000.

22. By comparison, using the 3.5:1 and 1.2:1 ratios, the Air Force was 6% short (864 pilots) of pilots and essentially even with regard to navigators.

23. This correlates loosely with the FY1966–FY1967 data gained by subtracting the general officers and colonels on excused status from the total on flying status, which yielded 36% and 32% respectively. The data on excused general officer and colonels for FY1966 and FY1967 are from the *Air Force Times*. See "Commercial Aviation Jobs Draw

60 Percent of Pilot Resignees," *Air Force Times*, August 24, 1966: 10. The 2003 spike in pilot general officers and colonels actually flying may be a coding error, since there is no apparent basis for the dramatic change.

24. The picture is different for fliers in the rank of lieutenant colonel and below. Whereas 90% or more of the total pilots and 85% or more of the total navigators in these ranks were traditionally on flight status, most were not in excused status. In fact, the FY1966–FY1967 data points on excused fliers show that 91% and 90% respectively of pilots and navigators on flying status were actually flying in some capacity, either in front-line units or in the four-for-pay club. In the gated system, the percentage of pilots at lieutenant colonel and below serving in flying units has ranged between 71% and 86%. Navigators, however, continued to be in flying billets at much lower rates, dropping as low as 52% at times. This was at least partly the result of a general decrease in navigator requirements in flying units combined with a surplus of navigators in field grade ranks, the so-called "graying" of the navigator force. The data from 1949 to 1966 indicate the percentages of the total pilots and navigators on flying status, which included at various times and in various numbers officers serving in front-line flying units flying routinely, officers flying four-hours-a-month-for-proficiency-pay, and officers on excused status receiving flight pay without flying. The data from 1966 indicate that almost two-thirds of these officers were not actually flying in any capacity. The data on excused general officer and colonels for 1966 and 1967 are from the *Air Force Times*. The USAF *Statistical Digest* series provides data on general officer and colonel pilots and navigators on flying status from FY1949 through FY1966. See "Commercial Aviation Jobs Draw 60 Percent of Pilot Resignees," 10.

25. For example, Maxwell Air Force Base kept 54 aircraft and about 255 maintainers and spent about $2 million per year just for student proficiency pay so that students would not loose flight pay while attending Squadron Officers School, Air Command and Staff College, Air War College, or other, longer courses offered at Maxwell. These aircraft, maintainers, and money were in addition to those needed to support fliers serving as instructors, staff, and permanent party at Maxwell AFB. See Bruce Callander, "Rated Force Freed from Four-for-Pay," *Air Force Times*, August 17, 1966: 43.

26. "Proficiency Flying in Jeopardy," *Air Force Times*, December 3, 1975: 10. The German Luftwaffe continues to use a proficiency flying system; so fliers must periodically disappear from staff jobs at all levels to get their required flight time. The German fliers maintain their proficiency with their previous unit and stay current in the aircraft, which requires much more involvement than the Air Force's four-for-pay in simple, non-combat aircraft. Nevertheless, non-rated officers serving on the same staffs are invariably suspicious when fliers coincidentally need to go fly for proficiency when major projects require lots of overtime.

27. "Pilot Manning Problems: Other Areas Affected," *Air Force Times*, April 9, 1969: 5. In May 1967, the *Air Force Times* staunchly defended the Air Force's flier "reserve": "For the first time in history, it was able to meet a shooting war emergency without calling up Reserves, holding fliers involuntarily or lowering standards to expand pilot production in a hurry." See "AF Restores 'Pilot' Image," 4. Reserve pilots were later called up and the Air Force did institute a stop-loss for pilots. See Ed Gates, "Pilot Losses Drop Sharply," *Air Force Times*, May 22, 1968: 1.

28. In the post-Vietnam drawdown in the mid-1970s, the Air Force dumped over 10% of its pilots on flying status into the Rated Supplement program, putting the excess pilots in non-rated jobs. The Air Force planned on using Reserve Supplement

Officers (RSOs) to back-fill the billets if the pilots returned to combat cockpits in time of war. However, the Air Force Reserve reported resistance to training the RSOs. Perhaps there was no point in training RSOs if the Rated Supplement pilots they were to replace were not particularly well trained. See "Systems Command Draws Top Number: Rated Supplement Quotas Listed," *Air Force Times*, August 6, 1975: 21.

29. The mixing of crews and aircraft between active and reserve forces as is done with cargo aircraft, AWACS, and JSTARS, for example, reinforces the point that the Air Force Reserve and Air National Guard are the Air Force's reserves. The reserve is not supposed to be an amorphous group of pilots serving in non-rated billets in the active forces.

CONCLUSIONS AND IMPLICATIONS

1. Ben Pearse, "It's Still His Air Force," *Air Force Magazine*, August 1956: 261.

APPENDIX

1. The USAF *Statistical Digest* series stopped providing data on line versus non-line general officers after FY1980. I do not have any reason to believe that the trends shown on the graphs would change if line general officer data were found and added to the charts for the 1983 through 2002 samples. Non-line officers continue to be over-represented at Air Force Headquarters.

Bibliography

Abbott, Andrew. *The System of Professions: An Essay on the Division of Expert Labor.* Chicago: University of Chicago Press, 1988.

"AF Restores 'Pilot' Image." *Air Force Times*, May 24, 1967: 4.

"Air Force General Officer Biographies." *US Air Force* http://www.af.mil/bios.

Air Force Magazine (Annual Air Force Almanac Issue). Vol. 55. No. 5. May 1972.

Air Force Magazine (Annual Air Force Almanac Issue). Vol. 56. No. 5. May 1973.

Air Force Magazine (Annual Air Force Almanac Issue). Vol. 57. No. 5. May 1974.

Air Force Magazine (Annual Air Force Almanac Issue). Vol. 58. No. 5. May 1975.

Air Force Magazine (Annual Air Force Almanac Issue). Vol. 59. No. 5. May 1976.

Air Force Magazine (Annual Air Force Almanac Issue). Vol. 60. No. 5. May 1977.

Air Force Magazine (Annual Air Force Almanac Issue). Vol. 65. No. 5. May 1982.

Air Force Magazine (USAF Almanac Issue). Vol. 70. No. 5. May 1987.

Air Force Magazine (USAF Almanac Issue). Vol. 72. No. 5. May 1989.

Air Force Magazine (USAF Almanac Issue). Vol. 73. No. 5. May 1990.

Air Force Magazine (USAF Almanac Issue). Vol. 74. No. 5. May 1991.

Air Force Magazine (USAF Almanac Issue). Vol. 75. No. 5. May 1992.

Air Force Magazine (USAF Almanac Issue). Vol. 77. No. 5. May 1994.

Air Force Magazine (USAF Almanac Issue). Vol. 80. No. 5. May 1997.

Air Force Magazine (USAF Almanac Issue). Vol. 81. No. 5. May 1998.

Air Force Magazine (USAF Almanac Issue). Vol. 82. No. 5. May 1999.

Air Force Magazine (USAF Almanac Issue). Vol. 84. No. 5. May 2001.

Air Force Magazine (USAF Almanac Issue). Vol. 85. No. 5. May 2002.

Air Force Magazine (USAF Almanac Issue). Vol. 86. No. 5. May 2003.

Air Force Magazine (USAF Almanac Issue). Vol. 87. No. 5. May 2004.

"All about Money—IV: Hazardous Duty Pay Goes to 100,000-Plus." *Air Force Times*, September 28, 1966: 13.

Allen, John. "Stake Your Claim: Shavetail Commands F-4." *Air Force Times*, September 11, 1968: 11.

"Analysis of RIF Board Results." *Air Force Times*, March 12, 1975: 14.

Anton, Genevieve. "Cadets Staying at Academy despite Cut in Pilot Slots." *Air Force Times*, September 14, 1992: 24.

Anton, Genevieve. "Who Will Fly? The Air Force Wants More Pilots, but Fewer New Officers Are Qualified ... or Interested." *Air Force Times*, November 24, 1997: 12–13.

Army Air Forces. Army Regulation No. 95–60. "Aeronautical Ratings; Flying Officers; Command of Flying Units." Washington, DC: War Department, August 20, 1942.

Army Air Forces. *Aviation Cadet Training*. [?] Washington DC: U.S. Army Recruiting Publicity Bureau, May 25, 1943.

Assistant Secretary of the Air Force (Financial Management and Comptroller of the Air Force), Deputy Assistant Secretary (Cost and Economics). *United States Air Force Statistical Digest (Abridged) Fiscal Year 1991 Estimate*. Washington, DC: Assistant Secretary of the Air Force (GPO), 1990.

Assistant Secretary of the Air Force (Financial Management and Comptroller of the Air Force), Deputy Assistant Secretary (Cost and Economics). *United States Air Force Statistical Digest Fiscal Year 1991*. Washington, DC: Assistant Secretary of the Air Force (GPO), 1993.

Assistant Secretary of the Air Force (Financial Management and Comptroller of the Air Force), Deputy Assistant Secretary (Cost and Economics). *United States Air Force Statistical Digest Fiscal Year 1992/1993 Estimate*. Washington, DC: Assistant Secretary of the Air Force (GPO), 1991.

Assistant Secretary of the Air Force (Financial Management and Comptroller of the Air Force), Deputy Assistant Secretary (Cost and Economics). *United States Air Force Statistical Digest Fiscal Year 1993*. Washington, DC: Assistant Secretary of the Air Force, 1994.

Assistant Secretary of the Air Force (Financial Management and Comptroller of the Air Force), Deputy Assistant Secretary (Cost and Economics). *United States Air Force Statistical Digest Fiscal Year 1994*. Washington, DC: Assistant Secretary of the Air Force (GPO), 1995.

Assistant Secretary of the Air Force (Financial Management and Comptroller of the Air Force), Deputy Assistant Secretary (Cost and Economics). *United States Air Force Statistical Digest Fiscal Year 1995*. Washington, DC: Assistant Secretary of the Air Force, 1996.

Assistant Secretary of the Air Force (Financial Management and Comptroller of the Air Force), Deputy Assistant Secretary (Cost and Economics). *United States Air Force Statistical Digest Fiscal Year 1996*. Washington, DC: Assistant Secretary of the Air Force (GPO), 1997.

Assistant Secretary of the Air Force (Financial Management and Comptroller of the Air Force), Deputy Assistant Secretary (Cost and Economics). *United States Air Force Statistical Digest Fiscal Year 1997 (50th Anniversary Issue)*. Washington, DC: Assistant Secretary of the Air Force (GPO), 1998.

Assistant Secretary of the Air Force (Financial Management and Comptroller of the Air Force), Deputy Assistant Secretary (Cost and Economics). *United States Air Force Statistical Digest Fiscal Year 1998*. Washington, DC: Assistant Secretary of the Air Force (GPO), 1999.

Assistant Secretary of the Air Force (Financial Management and Comptroller of the Air Force), Deputy Assistant Secretary (Cost and Economics). *United States Air*

Force Statistical Digest Fiscal Year 1999. Washington, DC: Assistant Secretary of the Air Force, 2000.

Assistant Secretary of the Air Force (Financial Management and Comptroller of the Air Force), Deputy Assistant Secretary (Cost and Economics). *United States Air Force Statistical Digest Fiscal Year 2000*. Washington, DC: Assistant Secretary of the Air Force.

Assistant Secretary of the Air Force (Financial Management and Comptroller of the Air Force), Deputy Assistant Secretary (Cost and Economics). *United States Air Force Statistical Digest Fiscal Year 2001*. Washington: Assistant Secretary of the Air Force.

Assistant Secretary of the Air Force (Financial Management and Comptroller of the Air Force), Deputy Assistant Secretary (Cost and Economics). *United States Air Force Statistical Digest Fiscal Year 2002*. Washington: Assistant Secretary of the Air Force.

Assistant Secretary of the Air Force (Financial Management and Comptroller of the Air Force), Deputy Assistant Secretary (Cost and Economics). *United States Air Force Statistical Digest Fiscal Year 2003*. Washington: Assistant Secretary of the Air Force.

Aviation Service Act. Pub. L. 63–143. 63rd Cong. Ch. 186. July 18, 1914. Stat. 38–514.

Berger, Carl, ed. *The United States Air Force in Southeast Asia, 1961–1973*. Washington, DC: Office of Air Force History (GPO), 1977.

Builder, Carl H. *The Icarus Syndrome: The Role of Air Power Theory in the Evolution and Fate of the U.S. Air Force*. 1994. New Brunswick, NJ: Transaction Publishers, 2003.

Builder, Carl H. *The Masks of War: American Military Styles in Strategy and Analysis*. Baltimore: Johns Hopkins University Press, 1989.

Callander, Bruce. "'Excused' Fliers Pass Screening." *Air Force Times*, November 11, 1970: 8.

Callander, Bruce. "Flight Board Will Weigh 5000 Rated," *Air Force Times*, May 13, 1970: 8.

Callander, Bruce. "Rated Force Freed from Four-for-Pay." *Air Force Times*, August 17, 1966: 43.

Command of Flying Units. Pub. L 93–525. December 18, 1974. Stat. 88–3906.

"Commercial Aviation Jobs Draw 60 Percent of Pilot Resignees." *Air Force Times*, August 24, 1966: 10.

Compart, Andrew. "Officer System Will Undergo Major Changes." *Air Force Times*, March 27, 1995: 3.

Comptroller of the Air Force, Deputy Comptroller Cost and Economics, Economics and Field Support Division. *United States Air Force Summary Fiscal Years 1988/1989*. Washington, DC: Comptroller of the Air Force, 1987.

Comptroller of the Air Force, Deputy Comptroller Cost and Economics. *United States Air Force Summary FY 1988/1989 (Amended)*. Washington, DC: Comptroller of the Air Force, 1988.

Comptroller of the Air Force, Directorate of Cost and Management Analysis. *USAF Summary 1981*. Washington, DC: HQ USAF, 1981.

Comptroller of the Air Force, Directorate of Cost and Management Analysis. *USAF Summary 1982*. Washington: HQ USAF, 1982.

De La Cruz, Donna. "Report Blames Pilot in School Strafing." *Air Force Times*, January 3, 2005: 20.

Department of Defense. *Dictionary of Military and Associated Terms*. Joint Publication 1–02, April 12, 2001.

Deptula, David A., Brigadier General, USAF. *Effects-Based Operations: Change in the Nature of War*. Arlington, VA: Aerospace Education Foundation (Air Force Association), 2001.

Douhet, Giulio. *The Command of the Air*. Trans. Dino Ferrari. Washington, DC: Air Force History and Museums Program (GPO), 1998.

Editors of *Air Force Magazine*. *The Almanac of Airpower*. New York: Simon & Schuster, 1989.

Ewing, Lee. "Regulars 'Generally Better': Jones on Records of Officers." *Air Force Times*, March 1, 1976: 3.

Ewing, Lee. "Some Career Ideas OKd, 12 Killed." *Air Force Times*, August 13, 1975: 4.

Fechet, J. E., Major General, USA. *Annual Report, Chief of the Air Corps, Report to the Army Adjutant General*. August 22, 1930.

Fogerty, Robert P. *United States Air Force Historical Study No. 91: Biographical Study of USAF General Officers, 1917–1952*. Maxwell Air Force Base, AL: USAF Historical Division, Air University, 1953.

Foster, George. "6472 New Majors, 5829 Go Up on First Try." *Air Force Times*, June 18, 1969: 4.

Foster, George. "Foes Slow Command Navigator Bill." *Air Force Times*, October 16, 1974: 3.

Foster, George. "Promotion Edge in RegAF Denied." *Air Force Times*, January 21, 1970: 1.

Frank, Richard B. *Downfall: The End of the Imperial Japanese Empire*. New York: Random House, 1999.

Gates, Ed. "2469 Will Receive Selection for RegAF." *Air Force Times*, May 8, 1968: 1.

Gates, Ed. "Officers Exits Probed." *Air Force Times*, May 10, 1967: 10.

Gates, Ed. "Pilot Losses Drop Sharply." *Air Force Times*, May 22, 1968: 1.

Ginsburgh, Robert T., Major General, USAF. Letter to Lt General Charles B. Westover. December 9, 1971. Washington, DC: Office of Air Force History, Anacostia Annex (USN), DC.

Gunston, Bill. ed. *The Encyclopedia of World Air Power*. New York: Crescent Books, 1981.

Hafemeister, Rod. "A New Degree of Anonymity: Civilian Education to Be Hidden from Promotion Boards." *Air Force Times*, February 14, 2005: 13.

Hafemeister, Rod. "Officers: Your Civilian Education Is Showing." *Air Force Times*, May 1, 2006: 10.

Headquarters United States Air Force, Comptroller, Director of Statistical Services, *United States Air Force Statistical Digest 1947*. Washington, DC: HQ USAF, 1948.

Headquarters United States Air Force, Office of the Comptroller, Directorate of Statistical Services. *United States Air Force Statistical Digest 1948 Vol. I*. Washington, DC: HQ US Air Force (GPO), 1949.

Headquarters United States Air Force, Office of the Comptroller, Directorate of Statistical Services. *United States Air Force Statistical Digest 1948 Vol. II*. Washington, DC: HQ US Air Force (GPO), 1949.

Headquarters United States Air Force, DCS Comptroller, D/Statistical Services, Operations Statistics Division. *United States Air Force Statistical Digest JAN 1949–JUN 1950*. Washington, DC: HQ US Air Force (GPO), 1951.

Headquarters United States Air Force, DCS Comptroller, D Statistical Services, Operations Statistics Division. *United States Air Force Statistical Digest Fiscal Year 1951.* Washington, DC: HQ US Air Force (GPO), 1953.

Headquarters United States Air Force, Deputy Chief of Staff Comptroller, Directorate of Statistical Services. *United States Air Force Statistical Digest Fiscal Year 1952.* Washington, DC: HQ US Air Force.

Headquarters United States Air Force, Deputy Chief of Staff Comptroller, Directorate of Statistical Services. *United States Air Force Statistical Digest Fiscal Year 1953.* Washington, DC: HQ US Air Force (GPO), 1954.

Headquarters United States Air Force, Deputy Chief of Staff Comptroller, Directorate of Statistical Services. *United States Air Force Statistical Digest Fiscal Year 1954.* Washington, DC: HQ US Air Force.

Headquarters United States Air Force, Deputy Chief of Staff Comptroller, Directorate of Statistical Services. *United States Air Force Statistical Digest Fiscal Year 1955.* Washington, DC: HQ US Air Force.

Headquarters United States Air Force, Comptroller of the Air Force, Directorate of Statistical Services. *United States Air Force Statistical Digest Fiscal Year 1956.* Washington, DC: HQ US Air Force.

Headquarters United States Air Force, Comptroller of the Air Force, Directorate of Statistical Services. *United States Air Force Statistical Digest Fiscal Year 1957.* Washington, DC: HQ US Air Force.

Headquarters United States Air Force, Comptroller of the Air Force, Directorate of Statistical Services. *United States Air Force Statistical Digest Fiscal Year 1958.* Washington, DC: HQ US Air Force.

Headquarters United States Air Force, Comptroller of the Air Force, Directorate of Statistical Services. *United States Air Force Statistical Digest Fiscal Year 1959.* Washington, DC: HQ US Air Force.

Headquarters United States Air Force, Comptroller of the Air Force, Directorate of Data Systems and Statistics. *United States Air Force Statistical Digest Fiscal Year 1960.* Washington, DC: HQ US Air Force (GPO), 1961.

Headquarters United States Air Force, Comptroller of the Air Force, Directorate of Data Systems and Statistics. *United States Air Force Statistical Digest Fiscal Year 1961.* Washington, DC: HQ US Air Force.

Headquarters United States Air Force, Comptroller of the Air Force, Directorate of Data Automation. *United States Air Force Statistical Digest Fiscal Year 1962.* Washington, DC: HQ US Air Force.

Headquarters United States Air Force, Comptroller of the Air Force, Directorate of Data Automation. *United States Air Force Statistical Digest Fiscal Year 1963.* Washington, DC: HQ US Air Force.

Headquarters United States Air Force, Comptroller of the Air Force, Directorate of Data Automation. *United States Air Force Statistical Digest Fiscal Year 1964.* Washington, DC: HQ US Air Force.

Headquarters United States Air Force, Comptroller of the Air Force, Directorate of Data Automation, Data Services Center. *United States Air Force Statistical Digest Fiscal Year 1965.* Washington, DC: HQ US Air Force.

Headquarters United States Air Force, Comptroller of the Air Force, Directorate of Data Automation, Data Services Center. *United States Air Force Statistical Digest Fiscal Year 1966.* Washington, DC: HQ US Air Force.

Headquarters United States Air Force, Comptroller of the Air Force, Directorate of Data Automation, Data Services Center. *United States Air Force Statistical Digest Fiscal Year 1967.* Washington, DC: HQ US Air Force.

Headquarters United States Air Force, Comptroller of the Air Force, Directorate of Data Automation, Data Services Center. *United States Air Force Statistical Digest Fiscal Year 1968.* Washington, DC: HQ US Air Force.

Headquarters United States Air Force, Comptroller of the Air Force, Directorate of Data Automation, Data Services Center. *United States Air Force Statistical Digest Fiscal Year 1969.* Washington, DC: HQ US Air Force, 1970.

Headquarters United States Air Force, Comptroller of the Air Force, Directorate of Data Automation, Data Services Center. *United States Air Force Statistical Digest Fiscal Year 1970.* Washington, DC: HQ US Air Force, 1971.

Headquarters United States Air Force, Comptroller of the Air Force, Directorate of Data Automation, Data Services Center. *United States Air Force Statistical Digest Fiscal Year 1971.* Washington, DC: HQ US Air Force, 1972.

Headquarters United States Air Force, Comptroller of the Air Force, Directorate of Management Analysis, Management Information Division. *United States Air Force Statistical Digest Fiscal Year 1972.* Washington, DC: HQ USAF, 1973.

Headquarters United States Air Force, Comptroller of the Air Force, Directorate of Management Analysis, Management Information Division. *United States Air Force Statistical Digest Fiscal Year 1973.* Washington, DC: HQ USAF, 1974.

Headquarters United States Air Force, Comptroller of the Air Force, Directorate of Management Analysis, Management Information Division. *United States Air Force Statistical Digest Fiscal Year 1974.* Washington, DC: HQ USAF, 1975.

Headquarters United States Air Force, Comptroller of the Air Force, Directorate of Management Analysis, Management Information Division. *United States Air Force Statistical Digest Fiscal Year 1975.* Washington, DC: HQ USAF, 1976.

Headquarters United States Air Force, Comptroller of the Air Force, Directorate of Management Analysis, Management Information Division. *United States Air Force Statistical Digest Fiscal Year 1976 and Transition Quarter (TQ).* Washington, DC: HQ US Air Force, 1977.

Headquarters United States Air Force, Comptroller of the Air Force, Directorate of Management Analysis, Management Information Division. *United States Air Force Statistical Digest Fiscal Year 1977.* Washington, DC: HQ USAF, 1978.

Headquarters United States Air Force, Comptroller of the Air Force, Directorate of Cost and Management Analysis, Cost Analysis and Management Division. *United States Air Force Statistical Digest Fiscal Year 1978.* Washington, DC: HQ USAF, 1979.

Headquarters United States Air Force, Comptroller of the Air Force, Directorate of Cost and Management Analysis, Management and Economics Division. *United States Air Force Statistical Digest Fiscal Year 1979.* Washington, DC: HQ USAF, 1980.

Headquarters United States Air Force, Comptroller of the Air Force, Directorate of Cost and Management Analysis, Management and Economics Division. *United States Air Force Statistical Digest Fiscal Year 1980.* Washington, DC: HQ USAF, 1981.

Headquarters United States Air Force, Comptroller of the Air Force, Directorate of Cost and Management Analysis, Management and Economics Division. *United*

States Air Force Summary (Consolidation of Statistical Digest and USAF Summary) 1983. Washington, DC: HQ USAF, 1983.

Headquarters United States Air Force, Comptroller of the Air Force, Directorate of Cost and Management Analysis, Policy and Procedures Division. *United States Air Force Summary (Consolidation of Statistical Digest and USAF Summary) 1984.* Washington, DC: HQ USAF, 1984.

Headquarters United States Air Force, Comptroller of the Air Force, Directorate of Cost and Management Analysis, Policy and Procedures Division. *United States Air Force Summary 1985.* Washington, DC: HQ USAF, 1985.

Headquarters United States Air Force, Comptroller of the Air Force, Directorate of Cost, Economics and Field Support Division. *United States Air Force Summary 1986.* Washington, DC: HQ USAF, 1986.

HQ Air Force Personnel Center, Analysis and Reports Branch (HQ AFPC/DPSAR), *Officer Accessions and Remaining Inventory by Source of Commissions and Rating.* 2003.

"Hubbell Group to Look Hard at Flight Pay." *Air Force Times,* May 11, 1966: 1.

Huntington, Samuel P. *The Soldier and the State: The Theory and Politics of Civil-Military Relations.* Cambridge, MA: Belnap Press, 1985.

Janowitz, Morris. *The Professional Soldier: A Social and Political Portrait.* New York: Free Press, 1960.

"Job Specialty Name Tags OK'd … But." *Air Force Times,* January 8, 1969: 3.

Jordan, Bryant. "Air-Battle Managers Will Be Rated: New Status for Career Field May Begin in October." *Air Force Times,* May 25, 1998: 4.

Jordan, Bryant. "Education No Longer Make-or-Break Criterion for Promotion: Ops Tempo Prevented Officers from Getting Degrees and PME." *Air Force Times,* September 6, 1999: 10.

Jordan, Bryant. "Promotion-Folder Change: Advanced Degrees Lose Luster for Captains, Majors." *Air Force Times,* January 15, 1996: 10.

Kenley, William L., Major General, USA. *Annual Report of the Director of Military Aeronautics, U.S. Army to the Secretary of War, 1918.* Washington: GPO, 1918.

Legasey, Ted. "Online News: AOG Board Chair Addresses the Membership," *ZoomiEnews,* September 26, 2005, Association of Graduates US Air Force Academy, July 21, 2006 http://www.usafa.org/zoomienews.

"Legislative Actions: Nav-Command Bill Passes House." *Air Force Times,* December 25, 1974: 2.

Mitchell, Vance O. *Air Force Officers Personnel Policy Development 1944–1974.* Washington, DC: Air Force History and Museums Program (GPO), 1996.

Momyer, William W., General, USAF, Ret. *Air Power in Three Wars (WWII, Korea, Vietnam).* Washington, DC: Department of the Air Force, 1978.

Moseley, T. Michael. "Transforming Air Force Intelligence, Surveillance, Reconnaissance." *CSAF's Vector,* January 29, 2007.

National Defense Act. Pub. L. 64–85. Ch. 134. June 3, 1916. Stat. 39–166.

National Defense Act Amendment. Pub. L. 66–242. Ch. 227. June 4, 1920. Stat. 41–759.

National Defense Act Amendment. [Public—No. 446—69th Cong.] [H.R. 10827]. July 2, 1926. Washington, DC: GPO.

National Defense Act Amendment, Pub. L. 76–795. Ch. 742. October 4, 1940. Stat. 54–963.

"Navigator to Head Combat Flying Unit." *Air Force Times,* February 12, 1975: 2.

"Navigators in Command: Long Road Ahead." *Air Force Times*, January 29, 1975: 5.

"Navigators Near Command Role." *Air Force Times*, September 25, 1974: 4.

"New 'Kill' Policy Set for Pilots." *Air Force Times*, November 30, 1966: 15.

"No Credit Given 'Kills' on Ground." *Air Force Times*, January 4, 1967: 11.

Palmer, Jennifer. "Air-Battle Managers Get Rated Status: Move Means Incentive Pay, Better Career Opportunities." *Air Force Times*, October 18, 1999: 35.

"Part II, Command and Control Report." In *Gulf War Air Power Survey, Volume 1, Planning and Command and Control*. Washington, DC: GPO, 1993.

Pearse, Ben. "It's Still His Air Force." *Air Force Magazine*, August 1956.

"Pilot Manning Problems: Other Areas Affected." *Air Force Times*, April 9, 1969: 5.

"Pilots to Leave F-4 Rear Seats." *Air Force Times*, November 18, 1970: 8.

"Proficiency Flying in Jeopardy." *Air Force Times*, December 3, 1975: 10.

"Razon-Tarzon." Wright-Patterson AFB, Ohio, November 7, 2005 http://www.ascho. wpafb.af.mil/korea/tarzonRazon.htm.

Reorganization of the Army Air Service: Hearing before the Committee on Military Affairs United States Senate, Sixty-ninth Congress, First Session on S. 2614, A Bill to Increase the Efficiency of the Air Service of the United States Army, February 5, 1926. Washington, DC: GPO, 1926.

Rolfsen, Bruce. "C-5 Takes Enemy Fire Leaving Baghdad." *Air Force Times*, January 19, 2004: 10.

Rolfsen, Bruce. "Cyberspace Deemed New Warfare Theater." *Air Force Times*, December 19, 2005: 13.

Rolfsen, Bruce. "Cyberspace: The Next Frontier, Concept of 'Cyber Command' Still in Its Infancy." *Air Force Times*, March 20, 2006: 10.

Rolfsen, Bruce. "Targets in the Sky." *Air Force Times*, January 26, 2004: 14.

"SAC Begins JO Staff Program." *Air Force Times*, May 27, 1970: 2.

Secretary of the Air Force, Office of Information. *Fact Sheet (79–12): F-106 Delta Dart*. Washington, DC: Secretary of the Air Force, 1979.

Secretary of the Air Force, Officer of Information. "First Air Force Ace in Southeast Asia." *Air Force Fact Sheet 73–7, AF Aces/ 1918–1972*. Washington, DC: Secretary of the Air Force, May 1973.

Secretary of the Air Force, Officer of Information. "Tribute to an Ace." *Air Force Fact Sheet 73–7, AF Aces/ 1918–1972*. Washington, DC: Secretary of the Air Force, May 1973.

"745 Named Temporary Colonels." *Air Force Times*, October 7, 1970: 1, 26.

Simpson, Albert, and Robert Futrell. "Interdiction—Razon Attacks." In *United States Air Force Operations in the Korean Conflict, 25 June–November 1950, USAF Historical Study No. 71—USAF Museum*, July 1, 1952, Wright-Patterson AFB, Ohio, November 7, 2005 http://www.wpafb.af.mil/museum/history/korea/no71–55.htm.

Sivulich, Nick. "Forty Colonels, 15 BGs Named for Promotions." *Air Force Times*, August 18, 1966: 1, 10.

Snook, Scott A. *Friendly Fire: The Accidental Shootdown of U.S. Black Hawks over Northern Iraq*. Princeton, NJ: Princeton University Press, 2000.

"Systems Command Draws Top Number: Rated Supplement Quotas Listed." *Air Force Times*, August 6, 1975: 21.

"10 Navs Head Flight Units." *Air Force Times*, September 10, 1975: 24.

Trowbridge, Gordon. "Aviator Bonuses Tell Nonpilots They Count, Too: Officers: First-Time Perk a Big Step toward Recognition." *Air Force Times*, August 19, 2002: 24.

Trowbridge, Gordon. "New Retention Bonus Brings Navigators, ABMs Out in Droves." *Air Force Times*, November 18, 2002: 22.

USAF Personnel Center http://www.afpc.randolph.af.mil/demographics/.

U.S. Senate, Committee on Military Affairs. *The Army Air Service Hearing on H.R. 10827*. 69th Cong., 1st sess, May 10, 1926. Washington, DC: GPO, 1926.

"VB-1 Azon Guided Bomb." *US Air Force Museum Weapons Gallery*, Wright-Patterson AFB, Ohio, November 7, 2005 http://www.wpafb.af.mil/museum/arm/arm34.htm.

"VB-3 Razon Guided Bomb." *US Air Force Museum Weapons Gallery*, Wright-Patterson AFB, Ohio, November 7, 2005 http://www.wpafb.af.mil/museum/arm/arm35.htm.

Von Clausewitz, Carl. *On War*. Ed. and Trans. Michael Howard and Peter Paret. Princeton, NJ: Princeton University Press, 1989.

War Department, Headquarters Army Air Forces. *AAF Regulation No. 35–3*, "Personnel, Military: Eligibility for Appointment as Flight Officers in the Army of the United States." Washington, DC, January 21, 1943.

War Department, Headquarters Army Air Forces. *AAF Regulation No. 35–8*, "Personnel, Military: System for Selecting Flight Officers to Be Commissioned as Second Lieutenants in the Army of the United States." Washington, DC, November 12, 1942.

War Department, Headquarters Army Air Forces. *AAF Regulation No. 35–9*, "Personnel, Military: System for Selecting Aviation Cadets to Be Commissioned as Second Lieutenants in the Army of the United States." Washington, DC, November 12, 1942.

War Department, Headquarters Army Air Forces. *AAF Regulation No. 35–29*, "Personnel, Military: Flying Status of Enlisted Men." Washington, DC, July 20, 1942.

War Department, Headquarters Army Air Forces. *AAF Regulation No. 35–46*, "Personnel, Military: Use of Military Occupational Specialties for AAF Enlisted Personnel." Washington, DC, December 11, 1943.

War Department, Headquarters Army Air Forces. *AAF Regulation No. 55–1*, "Operations, Flying Units—Command." Washington, DC, August 4, 1943.

"Weapons, Tactics and Training." In *Gulf War Air Power Survey Volume IV*. Washington, DC: GPO, 1993.

West, Joe. "Pilot Training Slots Slashed for Academy Grads." *Air Force Times*, August 3, 1992: 3.

Western Electric Company, Inc. *The SAGE Direction Center, SAGE Air Defense System*. [USAF Contract No. AF 33 (600) 29307]. August 15, 1958.

Wilson, George. "Leaders Heed the AWACS Lesson: Ways Are Sought to Avoid an Exodus of Overtaxed Crews." *Air Force Times*, January 26, 1998: 7.

Wolf, Richard I. *The United States Air Force Basic Documents on Roles and Missions*. Washington, DC: Office of Air Force History, 1987.

Wolfe, Tom. *The Right Stuff*. New York: Farrar, Straus, Giroux, 1979.

Index

About the Author

COLONEL BRIAN J. COLLINS, USAF, is currently serving his second tour teaching military strategy and operations at the National War College. Previous assignments include Chief, Policy Branch, NATO Division, Plans Directorate (J-5), Joint Staff; Component Test Director, NATO Airborne Warning and Control System; and Senior Soviet Air Forces Analyst, Supreme Headquarters Allied Powers Europe. He is an Olmsted Scholar and his articles have appeared in *International Defense Review*, *Georgetown Journal of International Affairs*, *Journal of Slavic Military Studies*, *Allgemeine Schweizerisch Militärzeitschrift*, *Air Force* Magazine, and *Joint Force Quarterly*.